Lynn –

Thank you for your
interest. Be Blessed...
with your feng shuiing!
Continue to live and love
with

日
的

Purpose

The
DANCE
of Balance

H 2006

intention,
blessings & grace.

[signature]

8th
ANNIVERSARY
EAST COAST
FENG SHUI
1898   2006

The DANCE *of* Balance

for
Body
Mind
and
Spirit

feng shui

ANNIE PANE

White Dove Publishing
www.DanceofBalance.com

Copyright © 2005 by Annie Pane

ISBN 0–9763830–2–0 (softcover)
ISBN 0–9763830–3–9 (hardcover)

Characters, events and places portrayed in this work are
based on real situations and were developed from years
of the author's experience. Names have been changed and
facts altered and/or combined to best fit the example they
are being used to illustrate.

Cover and Interior Design and Typesetting
by Desktop Miracles, Inc.

Original Artwork & Calligraphy
by Pei-Hua Chiang
www.dynastychineseart.com

Printed in the United States of America

勵

Encouragement

This book is dedicated to
All of the Angels who have helped me
on my journey . . .
You know who you are.
May you all hear the
Chinese Whispers in the silence.

Source

Table of Contents

PART I
UNDERSTANDING THE FOUNDATIONAL CONCEPTS

PART II

MEANING OF THE MAP

PART III

MORE STORIES THAT COULD BE YOU

APPENDICES

Promises

A Message for My Readers

The information in this book does not constitute medical, emotional, or spiritual advice and is one person's opinion. No suggestion made to the characters applies to your particular situation, and you should consult the appropriate professional if questions arise. Neither the author nor publisher take any responsibility for ill effects which may be produced as a result of your following any advice given to the characters in the examples in this book. The reader does so at his or her own risk or reward.

Characters, events and places portrayed in this work are based on real situations and were developed from years of the author's experience. Names have been changed and facts altered and/or combined to best fit the example they are being used to illustrate.

Accountability

Foreword

A World Unified

For the world to be as one . . .
    we would need to be blind to color,
    we could no longer be deaf to poverty and pain,
    we would have to save the forest and seas,
    we would have to feed the hungry and helpless,
    we would have to touch each other's hearts,
For the world to be as one . . .
We will each have to know our God.

—ANNIE PANE 1990

Illumination

An Open Letter
to Readers of Faith

I appreciate and understand your apprehension about Feng Shui. Let me share my viewpoint based on my exposure and experience. Regardless of whether we acknowledge the principles of Feng Shui we all have to admit that we have seen first hand how our surroundings ergonomically affect us.

If you take the definition of ergonomics, it is the same as the resulting and actual function of Feng Shui. According to Webster, Ergonomics is "the designing and arranging of things people use so that the people and things interact more efficiently and safely." That definition also fits the practice of Westernized Feng Shui, which is one of approximately 33 different kinds of Feng Shui. It is based on the form and nature of energy flow plus the literal and metaphorical interpretation of everyday subtleties and symbols covering every aspect of life within our environment.

Our environments are nothing more than the aggregate of social and cultural conditions that influence the life of an individual or community. My goal in Feng Shui is to help people re-create personal spaces that serve them well, and help them be conscious of the everyday nuances of meaning in those spaces. I practice a kind of Feng Shui that is transformational in nature where an individual can intentionally alter environments and influence themselves and others through deliberate ergonomic placement.

Basically I am saying you become your environment, physically, mentally, and spiritually, whether positive or negative. You are constantly absorbing all the negative effects and energy of your clutter, or you're taking on the effects of being in a vulnerable position. Your pile of unread magazines constantly talks to you and tugs at you every time you walk by, as does that pile of unpaid bills or stacks of mail. You also know well, the tightness in your neck at the sense of being stared at.

These tugging or negative thoughts are caused by our personal perceptions of our surroundings and our choices. These thoughts can continuously and subconsciously plague us until we address them. Here is an example: Just because you clean out a closet or the garage doesn't mean the job is done, if you've simply hidden or boxed up the junk or put it in the basement. You still know the junk is there, whether it is out of sight or not, and it's still talking to you like piranhas nibbling away on your sense of self.

Practicing Feng Shui principles is about being aware that you are an integral part of the world. It's about being conscious, and awake, to the outcomes that result from what are seemingly insignificant choices in life, and making them intentional choices. When you become aware of what is good for you in your environment, you make discerning choices consciously, whether that environment is your mind, how you keep your home, your office, what you wear, how you act, what you say, etc. These principles are designed to make you mindful of what you do and with whom you associate. It is those kinds of choices that shape your future.

Our culture is predisposed to be at the mercy of suggestion. We all are bombarded by the suggestive energy in newspaper ads, television ads and programs, teachers, our spouse, preacher, and politicians, whether good or bad. It is our responsibility to monitor our environments consciously in order to allow and attract only the kind of energy or circumstances and situations that would be reflective of our highest and best good. That is what the practice of Feng Shui is about: Empowering people to develop that same kind of thought process in making intentional and environmental decisions that serve them well rather than letting someone else choose for them.

God created a universe of order out of chaos. Feng Shui follows that example; it is a lifestyle process that teaches people how to live better in their own environments and their own skin. Often, the insight it gives people brings them to the core of their being and back to surrender to a higher power. When these principles are practiced, it is quickly discovered and made quite apparent that there is an intelligent design to all that exists.

My purpose and my calling is to wake people up from the semi-sleep state of thinking that they have no input into what happens to them daily. Within these pages, I have a great responsibility to give information in a way it can be rightfully received. It is my responsibility to convey the message so that it is understood and its intention clear. I hope that I have done that for you here.

Respectfully,

Annie

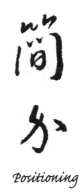

Positioning

Introduction

This book had to be written because our lives have become like fast food. Predictable. Bland. Unhealthy. We have complicated our lives and, in the process, we have lost touch with who we really are and with a sense of our soul's purpose. In these pages you will see how others have used the practice of Feng Shui techniques to regain a sense of balance and ultimately live better in their own skin.

We have all, as a society, as a culture and as individuals, gotten far, far away from the basics that allow us to live meaningful, satisfying lives. We have become wrapped up in the dynamics of commerce, and become both consumer and product. Our search for comfort has driven us away from creativity and challenge and toward the overwhelmingly numbing powers in our lives: television, shopping, alcohol, drugs, and shallow relationships.

What can we do to break free of the limitations that leave us living superficial, unhappy and unsatisfying lives? For starters, we have to get back to basics, the real meaning of living. We have to be willing to look deeply at the world and ourselves, not for whatever is "new" or "in," but for what has always been true and real. The vision and truths presented here are consistent with creeds and faith principles throughout history. Although first articulated in the East, they are now true companions to every teaching from East to West.

Meaning exists, but in our modern world we have masked it. Our task is to unmask and reveal what is, and what always has been. We have blocked this meaning behind the obstacles of our day-to-day experience, and we have hidden from ourselves just how divine we really are. This unmasking does not necessarily demand sacrifice, but it does demand personal honesty. We might finally have to give up things we have held onto unrealistically. It is those very things that hold us back, and contribute tension and pain in our lives. This book celebrates letting go at every level. It celebrates success. It empowers us with happiness and balance.

Our society is so engrossed with the trappings of physical comfort that it has lost the genuine psychological and spiritual values that contribute to real comfort. But we don't have to make a choice between one or the other. There are some who say that physical and spiritual comforts are not compatible, that it is impossible to have both. They are wrong. In fact, the physical and the spiritual are intimately related. It is only by appreciating there is a thread that runs through all three planes of existence—the physical, the psychological, (which is composed of mental and emotional parts) and the spiritual—any of us can experience true mastery and balance in life.

The real key to such happiness is an understanding that it is the spiritual aspect of life that ties all three together. Our spirituality is the thread that connects everything. The physical cannot reach the spiritual; but they are connected because the physical can be infused or enriched by the spiritual. The same is true of the psychological. We cannot psychologically reach spirituality but we can infuse our psychological lives with spirituality.

Without the spiritual, the psychological is only meandering emotion and thought.

Without the spiritual, the physical is only motion.

But with the spiritual, all aspects of our lives are knitted together with energy, life and power.

Feng Shui is the art and science by which the spiritual energy of life is allowed to move freely through all aspects of our lives in order to bring all those aspects into balance. That is what Feng Shui is about: the free flow of chi, or life energy.

We know from physics that all things flow. Light waves. Electricity. Water. Even things that never seem to change are in a state of flux and flow. Even rocks flow when they tumble on the surface of the earth. Internally their unseen atoms and molecules inside are in constant motion. It is easy for us to comprehend that the physical world is in constant motion. What is not so obvious is that the psychological and spiritual worlds flow too, and that flowing unseen chi is our divine essence.

The real meaning of this spiritual communication is intention. It is this clear line of communication between the spiritual, the mental (or psychological), and the physical levels in life that allows us to begin achieving balance and connection. However, too often in life, we inhibit this communication, this flow of energy. Upsetting that line of communication blurs our intentions and throws our lives out of balance because the connection is broken. Feng Shui helps us clarify our intentions through the flow of energy on all three levels of existence—physical, mental (psychological), and spiritual—and in every area of our lives from finances to love. It also teaches us a method that removes the obstacles to the free flow of energy which helps clarify our intent on all three levels.

It is a technique, not a dogma.

It is a method, not a teaching.

It is form, not content.

Because of these truths, Feng Shui does not contradict but is consistent with true faith and belief. The fundamental truth of Feng Shui is the same fundamental truth found in spiritual teaching, that Spirit is life affirming energy and it flows through time, space and physical reality. Feng Shui is a physical process that allows us to release the life energy all around us, to amazing rewards and results! It begins to bring our world into balance.

While removing obstacles is clearly understandable in the physical world, it is not always so evident in the spiritual and mental world. Often, people misunderstand Feng Shui and reduce it to little more than glorified interior decorating. Others appreciate the symbolic associations so important in Feng Shui, but even that appreciation only takes us to a mental plane. It is spirituality born of intent, made of decision and resolve that completes the picture.

Feng Shui takes all of these elements and melds them into a single whole.

Making love could be used as an analogy to what Feng Shui is. When we make love, we are physically engaged in the act of lovemaking. At the same time, we are mentally connected to our partner, anticipating needs and desires while engaging in the fulfillment of our own desires. Finally, we are spiritually engaged because our lovemaking causes us to experience profound intimacy with our partner and ourselves.

Remove any of these three aspects of lovemaking and we diminish it. Remove the spiritual and we are mentally engaged in a physical act of gratification. Remove the physical and we are lost in fantasy. Remove the mental and we are floundering, without the intelligence to fully enjoy or create enjoyment.

So it is with how we live our lives. We should all be making love in all areas of life, striving for the balance and oneness of body, mind, and spirit. Feng Shui is a wonderful tool to help us learn this dance of balance.

Now About You—The Next Step in the Dance.

The Healing Place

We all have need of a special place
    our place,
    no one else's.
A place to think,
    and wonder and dream.
A place to rest,
    to get away from all
    that stuff invading our space.
A place to shake off demons
    and regain control.
A place to begin again
    each day.
A place protected and
    guarded.

A place cherished for its nurturing
    affect on our lives,
    important only to us
    but needed by all.
A place to renew the soul.

        —ANNIE PANE 1990

PART I

Understanding the Foundational Concepts

喻

Metaphor

CHAPTER 1

It's About Life, Not Furniture

I HAVE TO ADMIT I was once skeptical about Feng Shui. Years ago when I owned a real estate company, many of my Asian real estate clients brought that philosophy into their home buying process. But I didn't really get it in the beginning. Years later, I now marvel that my profession is not only based on the concepts of Feng Shui, but I constantly apply the principles in my own life and teach them to others.

When people ask me what I do on a consultation, I have to admit it is a little like being on the television shows *Clean Sweep, Trading Spaces, Merge,* and *While You Were Out* all at one time. Combine the premises of all those shows and you would have an idea of what a consultation is like for my clients and me. Imagine yourself as my client. First we clear out the clutter blocking the free flow of energy. Then we take the possessions you already have and make your space beautiful without buying anything. Most of the time everyone has exactly what they need, it's just in the wrong room! We also bring together your vision for yourself and your family, and make the space support all of you. Sometimes the new arrangement is even a big surprise when someone gets home!

Since this art is such an individual event for each person, I want to share the principles in a way that will make it easy for you to take the information and relate it to your own life. Not every circumstance will be exactly the same, but they will be similar, and by seeing how the situation was handled for another, you may gain insight into your own circumstances. Feng Shui is not only about space and placement and furniture and décor. It's about you. In fact it's all about you. Now it's your turn to be like a fly on the wall and learn.

A few years ago, a young woman I'll call Debbie stopped me on the sidewalk outside my studio to talk, sharing with me some things weighing heavily on her mind.

Her relationship with her husband was going through some "very difficult times." Debbie also was physically uncomfortable. Not only was her body still adjusting to recently having had a baby, but she also had a nervous skin rash that she said felt as bad as it looked. Worse, her baby daughter was colicky and up all night long.

"I keep moving the furniture around and all that stuff, but nothing seems to help," she said to me, close to tears.

I asked her what she meant.

"Well, you know, Feng Shui," she said. "To make the baby calmer. I tried the crib next to our bed. In another room. Near the door. By the window. Nothing seems to work," she added in frustration. She began to cry softly. "I don't know what to try anymore."

The first thing I did was to reassure her that everything would be alright. And then I put my arms out and hugged her. Before I could even begin to teach her about Feng Shui, I needed to help her get rid of some of the negative energy that had overwhelmed her. All the things she was experiencing, from the baby to the rash, were normal occurrences, but when you're overloaded they become like mountains to surmount.

"Come inside and sit down," I offered, opening the door that led into my studio. We walked from the sun's glare and the traffic noise on the street into a quiet, calm place. She sat in a comfortable chair alongside a small table holding a vase of fresh flowers. A gentle wind chime was hanging by the window. In the background, the faint gurgling of a fountain whispered notes of calmness throughout the room.

Debbie closed her eyes and seemed to melt into the chair. "Now this is nice," she said. She opened her eyes, and I could see her making mental notes about the layout of my studio and thinking about rearranging her home so that it would closely mimic the space she was in now.

"I feel so relaxed here," she sighed. "No, relaxed isn't the right word. I feel safe here. I feel protected here. I feel okay, I feel more healthy."

I smiled. I knew exactly what she was experiencing. A number of times in my life I've experienced the same sort of feeling. Not only in my own studio, which inhabits me as much as I have come to inhabit it, but other places I have visited. Most people believe that they must visit a holy place to find the kind of peace and sanctuary Debbie was experiencing. Certainly, a holy place, like a church, a synagogue, or a mosque, grants its visitors the same kind of sanctuary Debbie was feeling in my studio, but the reality is there are a great many places where the one can feel the same thing. That's because peace and sanctuary are not strictly about place. In fact, they're not about geography at all.

When I was teenager, I visited my best friend who had moved to the big city because her father had been assigned to minister in a new church. Charlotte played the guitar. I loved to listen to her practice and play. On one of my visits, she broke a string and asked if I'd go with her to the store to get her guitar fixed. It sounded like another city adventure, so I agreed to go.

We took a bus into the downtown area. The bus was hot and crowded. There was a lot of traffic that day, so the ride took about forty minutes. By the time we arrived, I was hot and bothered from the lurching, uncomfortable ride. I'd been so banged about by strangers and my friend's guitar case that I was sure I'd have bruises all over my body. When we stepped off the bus, the sidewalks were so hot that they made the bus seem as if it had been air-conditioned.

"How far is it?" I asked, my voice echoing my annoyance as only a teenager can.

"Only a couple of blocks," she said.

A couple of blocks? How I wished we'd never decided to go!

Those were the longest blocks I'd ever walked. I trudged along, my mood growing more and more sour with each hot step that seemed to melt into the blistering sidewalk. We slouched past novelty shops and cheap five-and-dimes. The entire neighborhood seemed so oppressive to me. Strange people occupied the nooks and crannies of the block, eying us as we went by. I felt sick as we passed an old fashioned butcher shop with its wares displayed in the window.

"Are we there yet?" I asked, sounding, I'm sure, like a three-year-old in her parents' car.

"Almost," Charlotte said, marching forward. "Yes, here we are!"

She pushed open the door of a nondescript shop. The sign in the window stated simply, "A. Woodhouse and Sons." I remember a little bell announcing our entrance. And then

I remember calmness. Simple calmness. It was as if all the irritation and discomfort of the journey was simply being washed away from me. I'm sure there was no air conditioner there, but the air felt cool and dry. When I looked up all I could see were shelves nearly two times my height filled with old books and musical instrument cases, with an occasional instrument peeking out here and there. The atmosphere was much darker than the bright sunlight outside, but that darkness made the walls feel solid and safe. It was like that safe feeling you experience when you're being wrapped in the nurturing arms of your grandmother.

That shop, along that block, in that city, on that hot and uncomfortable day, had what every holy place has: sanctuary. The shop of A. Woodhouse and Sons shared nothing in the way of interior design with my studio, just as my studio shares nothing in layout or design with the interior of a holy place. The sanctuary I'm talking about is a feeling in your body that quiets your mind. You can feel the calmness in your shoulders and your neck. Your brow line loosens and you breathe deeper. Your shoulders go back and you become physically as well as mentally more open. That store, my studio, and holy places, all offer sanctuary in this palpable way. You can feel it.

I had another sanctuary experience with Charlotte on that same visit. It happened while we were exploring the Cathedral where her father preached. When you're very young and have never seen a cathedral, you are curious about all kinds of things. One day her father asked if I'd ever seen a Cathedral and would we like to go because he had some last minute work to do before Sunday.

Another adventure! "Of course I'll go," I told him.

When we entered the Cathedral I had exactly the same reaction as I'd had at the Music shop. It was cool, quiet, and peaceful, as well as quite deserted. Charlotte's father left us in the church's sanctuary alone and told us not to touch anything. I think I was in too much amazement to think about doing something wrong in there. The floor was marble and there were huge columns reaching I don't know how many stories. The pews were like rows and rows of long wooden boats. It seemed as if everything was huge, bigger than life itself, like I imagined God. The altar was adorned with beautiful stained glass that looked like jewels reflecting the sunlight shining behind them. I was in awe. I felt all the same feelings I had felt in A. Woodhouse's music shop. Calm. Relaxed. Quiet. And safe. The cathedral, I would come to know, was another example of a more common kind of sanctuary.

Again, the reason is not due simply to geography. The mantra of commercial interests—location, location, location—does not have the same significance in the spiritual world as it does in the world of commerce (although, as you will learn, there is a connection). And the reason is not interior decorating (although, as you will learn, there are things that you can and must do to your interior spaces to maximize your sense of well-being and sanctuary).

The reason that A. Woodhouse and Sons, the Cathedral, and my studio share the same feeling of sanctuary is because of the positive energy harnessed in each place. Harnessing, or using, this energy is not about direction in westernized Feng Shui. It is not about north, south, east, or west. No ship's captain could navigate his way toward it. Rather, harnessing this energy is all about orientation or a point of reference.

Rather than thinking about a static place, conjure up in your mind the workings of the tumblers inside a door lock. The tumblers in a lock must work together in relation to one another. When all the tumblers turn the right way so that they are in line relative to one another, the lock opens.

That is the goal of Feng Shui: to align all the tumblers in a space so that you can unlock the positive energy in your life. Location and direction are part of this dynamic; they are not the only aspects of it. That is why I believe there is no simple blueprint that works for everyone in Feng Shui, no hard and fast rules that never vary. There are general guidelines that apply to every situation, but like everything else of worth, it is a lot more subtle than that.

Feng Shui is not only about moving furniture (although it often does mean moving and rearranging furniture). It is not only about light and sound (although it often means adjusting the way light and sound play in the spaces you occupy). It is not simply about any one thing or another. Remember the image of the tumblers in a lock. It is about reorienting and readjusting your life, and the things in it, to take advantage of the positive energy all around you.

Feng Shui is about finding the balance of positive energies and freeing them to move unencumbered. It is like a dance that changes in energy and feeling each time it is performed, even when the steps are the same—a dance of balance. And, like a beautiful ballet or an inspiring flamenco, it must be danced with the whole being—physical, mental (psychological), and spiritual.

You'll soon see what I mean through the experiences of Debbie and others.

Now About You—The Next Step in the Dance

Let your body begin to acknowledge how it feels in different environments.

Recognize sanctuary by recalling a time your body felt totally connected to a space: a special room, a beach, a holy place, a spa, a vacation spot, etc.

Ask yourself specifically what it was about that space that intrigued you and made you feel that sense of sanctuary.

Remember what that place felt like. Once you remember the feeling it will be easier to re-create it again using symbols from those sanctuaries like music, colors, fragrances, etc.

Fear

CHAPTER 2

The Masks We Wear

$\int$ AMMY IS LIKE MOST of us, typical in many ways, but special in others. He grew up in a working-class home with the common tensions and strains of a family on a tight budget. His father was a shopkeeper, and the pressure on his father to make sales was a constant reality in Sammy's home life. Although Sammy swore to himself that he would never be a shopkeeper, the trajectory of his life took him exactly there. It wasn't a direct path. Unlike his father, he went to college and to graduate school to became a pharmacist. Then he opened his own pharmacy.

Knowing what he did about traditional Western medicine, Sammy became interested in alternative medicine and homeopathy. With training, he became a knowledgeable homoeopath and enlarged his inventory to include homeo-pathic medicines. He purchased additional shop space to sell health foods. Spurred by the changes in medical insurance, the pharmacy part of his business became a smaller and smaller part of his commercial life. Which was fine with him. He cared deeply about homeopathy, and he believed that his customers also benefited from the health foods he sold. The only problem was, he was losing money and, as a result, feeling the same pressures his father had felt.

"I've become my father," he complained bitterly to me, his eyes moist with emotion. "My whole life, I've consciously wanted only one thing, to not be like my father. And now, that's exactly what I am."

He was feeling the strain in his store. He was feeling the strain at home. And he was feeling the strain with his children.

"What am I going to do?" he asked.

With Sammy, as with Debbie, the answer was to begin at the beginning. First, I needed to explain the Feng Shui process and the energy that exists in the world. To understand Feng Shui, one needs to appreciate three basic principles:*

1. Everything is alive with the life force.
2. Everything is connected to everything else.
3. Everything is constantly changing.

These simple principles might seem straightforward and self-evident, but for most people, there is a very real disconnect between knowledge and life, between knowing and living. While most people think they know how to live life well, they don't actually live it well. Ask almost anyone you meet, and they'll tell you how important it is to take time

---

* Adapted from *The Western Guide to Feng Shui: Creating Balance, Harmony and Prosperity in Your Environment.* Terah Kathryn Collins. Hay House, Inc., 1196.

to stop and smell the roses. But how many of us actually do stop and smell the roses? Precious few, I'm afraid. In fact, we are so distanced from the ability to stop and smell the roses (both figuratively and literally) that we have grown confused as to how to do it. Debbie and Sammy both were trying very hard to smell the figurative flowers, but they couldn't. Not without guidance.

Where does one go to get such guidance? While Feng Shui certainly is not the only path to finding answers in our lives, it is one path toward those answers that has a long history, and it can complement the answer search you may be doing in other ways.

Feng Shui also has a number of advantages. Though it is often subtle, at the same time it can be simple and easy to apply. You don't have to "believe in it" for it to work, and it does not contradict any religious beliefs of which I'm aware. It simply *is*. Like the weather. Like air. Like flowers. All you have to do is engage in the process. All you have to do is follow the map. The process guides you in terms of where to look and for what. It's a way to live in alignment with the highest version of yourself.

In our society, many of us have little if any direct contact with death. Through Feng Shui, we may come to realize we have had equally little contact with life. Chi is a Chinese word that describes the life force. Chi inhabits everything that exists in the world. It is chi's reality upon which the first principle of Feng Shui is established: Everything has the life force. People have chi. Animals have chi. Plants have chi. Places have chi. Everything is alive.

Chi is an elemental reality of the world. It is energy. It is the life force.

Curiously, Feng Shui developed from a place where you would not expect to find the life force, the burial of the dead. In the ancient Orient, Feng Shui began as people sought the most auspicious place to bury their dead. They needed a place where the dead's energy could continue unabated, showering their living relations with abundance, protection and good lives. The discipline of Feng Shui grew from this straightforward desire to find a place protected from the harshness of the elements, where there was not too much of any one thing.

What those ancient Asians understood, and what we need to understand, is how to unencumber the flow of chi. In other words, our task is less about increasing the life force than it is about not inhibiting it. This was the subject of a lesson I shared with Debbie when I visited her in her home. What I found there was a space cluttered with things, things that occupied the space for no apparent reason. There were partitions in the middle of rooms, for example, which Debbie called screens.

"I thought they created intimate, private spaces," she explained.

Right inside the bedroom door, she had a clothes-drying rack. Several of the windows in the house could not be opened. There were three artificial flower arrangements.

"Debbie," I said solemnly when we went back outside. "We've got some work to do."

Most of us devote a great deal of energy to how we present ourselves to the world. We spend time on our physical presentation—our makeup, our hair, our clothes—in order to hide our imperfections and emphasize what we believe are our good points. If you doubt what I'm saying, take a stroll through the cosmetics department in any drugstore or department store in the country. You'll see row after row of hair color, lipstick, eyeliner, etc. We do the same thing with our cars and our houses. The saddest part of all this is that it is all such a waste of energy. We cannot be anything or anyone other than who we are. Let me repeat that: We cannot be anything or anyone other than who we are.

No amount of makeup will really change how we look. No push-up bra or expensive suit will change who we are. No fancy car will make us something other than ourselves. We are who we are, and we occupy the space we occupy. The irony is that each and every one of us is much better than we give ourselves credit for. That was certainly the case with Debbie. She has great energy, but she was blocking it.

Approaching her home through Feng Shui allowed her to unblock her energy by a simple equation: Our lives are mirrored in the spaces we occupy and vice versa. That is, the energy of the space that we occupy is mirrored in the way we live our lives. The significance of this equation is exhilarating. What this teaches us is that not only can we change our lives and our space by changing our energy but we also can change our lives and energy by changing our space. We can free our chi and, in the process, make our lives better.

Everything about Debbie's space conspired to block her chi. The first thing we did was to unclutter her house. Together, we removed knickknacks that took up space but didn't really occupy it, in the sense of promoting the flow of chi. We tossed the pile of unread magazines and old newspapers. We brought some living plants into the house. Using a little muscle and determination, we managed to open those stuck windows.

The change in Debbie was almost immediate. In the same way that her house was opened up, she seemed to open up, too, to new ideas and possibilities. Energy shifts are fast.

In her relationships with her husband, her baby, and herself, Debbie had blocked essential energy, making it impossible for the wonderful to happen. Once she changed her space to allow her chi to flow freely, other things changed as well. Her skin began to clear up. She was more open to a deeper and more nuanced relationship with her husband. And though her baby was still colicky, Debby no longer took the baby's crying personally and was able to enjoy the baby more. She began to see that the life force that moves through everything was moving through her as well. And that enabled her to feel better about herself and her relationships.

This is typical of my clients, as you will see.

Now About You—The Next Step in the Dance

Assure the energy flows through your space freely.

Test rooms to see if they, and you, can breathe. Close your eyes and stand in the doorway of the room. Imagine the energy flow behind you about waist high and colored green, building up pressure.

Step aside, open your eyes and release the imagined green energy flow into, around, and then watch it go out of the room. It will move in a large flowing often circular path.

Wherever the energy stops, the flow is blocked: in a corner, between the furniture, or even as it goes in or out of the room. One quick fix to re-direct stuck energy is to move the furniture away from the walls and set it on a slight angle.

Sage

CHAPTER 3

Remembering Who You Are

*I*N THE PREVIOUS CHAPTER, you saw how Debbie unlocked her chi by a few simple changes to her room arrangement. Something similar happened with Sammy, the pharmacist and homeopath. Although he had lots of good intentions, my visit to his store showed me clearly that he had put up barriers to the free flow of chi. Tall displays, filled with items of varying shape and color, competed for floor space with cluttered aisles. Homeopathic remedies were displayed alongside cosmetics. It was almost as if he had made a conscious effort to thwart his customers' search for items in which they might have been interested.

We began our work right at the entrance to the store. We replaced the harsh buzzer that announced each customer's entrance with chimes that rang out gently every time the door was opened.

"I like that," Sammy said with a sincere smile the first time he heard the chimes. "I don't know what it reminds me of, but it makes me feel good."

We removed much of the clutter from the aisles. We even took out some of the inventory. At first Sammy protested, but I assured him that he would more than make up for the loss of display space with increased sales. We put rugs down to soften the harsh linoleum floors. We unblocked a window that had been partially hidden by a cardboard display for suntan lotion, so it could let in a gauzy, afternoon light. It became the perfect spot for a couple of chairs and a display of the health books. The cosmetics were confined to one corner of the store. Homeopathic medications were placed in an aisle by the pharmacy counter.

"I bet you'll want me to play New Age music over the speakers, too," Sammy said.

"No, not necessarily." I took his hand and led him to the reading chairs. I sat him down and asked him to close his eyes.

"What music do you hear?"

He was quiet for a moment. When he opened his eyes, he looked at me and said, "The Shirelles."

I smiled. "Then that's what it should be."

It was only then, when he began playing oldies music that everything fell into place for him. He needed to create a space that was comfortable to the person he'd been when he was young and happy. The music, the openness, the arrangement of the store, even the chimes all worked together to create a space where Sammy felt at ease. And so did his customers.

About a month after my visit to his store, Sammy called to thank me. "Not even for the increase in profits," he said, his voice filled with sincerity, "but for making me like who I am and what I'm doing."

"I didn't do that, Sammy," I told him. "You did."

"Well, you helped an incredible amount."

Who would have thought that, in reality, what Sammy wanted and needed to do was to become the shopkeeper his father had not been, a successful shopkeeper who loved what he was doing? All he had to do was to release the chi in the store, through several simple steps, and that reality became obvious.

In order to understand how powerful Feng Shui is, you must not only understand that everything that exists has life force, but you also must appreciate what that means.

In thinking about it, you may agree that of course everything has life force. You may even feel the truth of it as well. But even more important than knowing and feeling that everything shares in the life force, is being alive yourself.

"Of course, I'm alive," you may answer. But are you answering from your intellect, or from the place where you feel the reality of being alive? Watch a kitten as it stalks an insect along a garden path, moving stealthily across the gravel. See how it is completely engaged in what it is doing, body and mind. Look at the concentration in its eyes. That kitten is completely in the moment, fully focused on what it is doing. It is alive! Fully alive! Fully in harmony with its life force. You are not a cat, of course, but you carry that same life force. You have that same ability to be completely connected with that energy, fully alive and aware in a way that goes well beyond intellectual awareness.

Have you ever gone to a dance and felt as if everyone were watching you dance? How did that make you feel? Awkward? Self-conscious? Self-aware? Now, close your eyes and picture yourself alone in your own home. No one is watching. No one is listening. You put some music on your stereo. The music begins. You love this song! You start to dance. Your body moves without awkwardness, without self-consciousness, without self-awareness. Your body moves, carried along by the energy conveyed to you through the music. It's as if you become part of the music and the music becomes part of you. You are fully focused, completely in that moment. Fully in harmony with the music and your life force.

That's what I'm getting at!

A friend of mine is an actress. Not long ago, we were walking along the lake together, and she was talking about what it felt like for her to be on stage.

"I forget everything," she said. "I just am. It is the most wonderful feeling in the world."

"What about the audience? Aren't you conscious of them?" I asked her.

"Not at all. I am so caught up in the moment that I am not even aware of anyone being there."

On the stage, she is fully alive. She is not even aware of being alive. She simply is. The cat, as it tracks an insect, is not self-aware of being alive. It simply is. The dancer dancing is not consciously aware of dancing. She is the dance.

For so many of us, self-awareness is not a help so much as a hindrance. We have "self-awared" ourselves to distraction! We know the words of self-help, but we are unable to speak the language. We have actually come to use our awareness to build walls rather than to bring them down, and we feel guilty that our self-help is not helping as we'd hoped.

A flower opening to greet the morning sun does not consider itself. Take some time one early morning to imagine a morning glory unfolding before you. Remain very still. Wait. Wait. What you will find is that, for those moments, you not only observe a magnificent moment of beauty, but you also are drawn into the life energy of the event, in the same way you are drawn to a dancer dancing, or a great moment of acting will astound you. At that moment, you will experience being alive.

That's chi! When the flow of chi in your life is unimpeded, you become the dance, the dance of balance and of life.

Now About You—The Next Step in the Dance

Allowing your passion to show through to others will change your personal energy and you will begin to reveal the real you.

Make sure your work and living space has something in it that is meaningful to you: special music, meaningful art, cherished photos or treasured toys, and at least one private area where you can be alone.

Think about how you can define yourself in ways you'd more like to be, rather than what you think you should be for others: dress differently, play different music, become a vegetarian, or exercise even if they don't.

Mysticism

CHAPTER 4

Everything is Connected

Y OU DON'T REALLY EXPECT me to believe that changing things in my house could make a difference in my success at work, do you? What's one thing got to do with the other?"

Frank, as usual, was direct and to the point. A tall, bullish man, he was more than a little offended when he learned that his wife, Margery, had asked for my assistance. And predictably, he was resistant.

"I don't care if she brings in a decorator or a house painter or a plumber," he went on emphatically. "But I don't feel like I want to bring in some hocus-pocus stuff."

"Frank!" Margery said, shocked by his vehemence.

"It's all right," I said, refusing to be insulted, because I'd heard this all before. The fact is, I am used to people not appreciating how interconnected everything is. It is one of the things that trips people up the most in appreciating the beauty of life. Life is complex, intricate, magnificent, and beautiful, and everything in it is connected to everything else.

"Well, look at it this way," I said to Frank. "Everything's interrelated."

He waved me off. "Come on. That's so general as to be meaningless."

"But it's absolutely true," I continued. "All you have to do is track a particular situation backward and you can see how many factors had to interrelate for it to have come about. Look at Al and June," I said, referring to an older couple that all three of us knew.

"What about them?"

Al was a high school student in Nebraska during the Great Depression. His family, unable to make ends meet on their farm, moved to New York City. They ended up living on the Lower East Side. It was there, among his new friends, where Al first heard about the man who was moving Germany and the world toward war. When his friends enlisted in the army, he enlisted in the Air Force. Shortly after the Japanese attack on Pearl Harbor, Al found himself flying over Europe. He was shot down in western France. For three days, he dragged his broken leg and other injuries through the shadows of night as he headed north. Members of the French Underground eventually found him and helped him get to England, where he was taken to an allied military hospital. One of the nurses' aides there was a young woman named June.

"Your point?" Frank asked.

I smiled. "Come on, Frank. Look what had to happen for Al and June to meet and fall in love. Not only did there have to be a depression, which drove his family from Nebraska, but there had to be a war to get him to Europe. He had to be shot down over France, and then the members of the underground had to find him and take him to England. And then he had to be sent to the military hospital where June was volunteering as an aide."

"I love that story," Margery said, her eyes welling with emotion.

"My point is that everything had to happen exactly as it did or else no Al and June," I said. "Look at the interconnections: The Depression. The War. The Lower East Side. Hitler. The Air Force. The French Underground. The English hospital. They were all players in this drama of June and Al's life."

"But if it wasn't that, it would have been something else," Frank argued.

"Of course it would have," I said. "I'm not saying things are preordained, only that they are interconnected. Everything impacts on everything else. You know, no man is an island?"

"Yes, I've heard that before. But all that has to do with people, not things."

"Well, not exactly. Events like the Depression and the Second World War aren't people."

"No, but they're caused by people. They're not inanimate objects."

"That's true," I agreed. "They're not. But surely you can appreciate how an inanimate object could impact your life."

Frank looked at me as if he didn't know what I was talking about.

"Imagine this," I said. "It's a stormy night. There are very high winds. Suddenly, a fire breaks out down the block. You call the fire department, which immediately responds to the fire. But, as it happens, a tree has been knocked down on the road they must take to the fire. Before they can get to the fire, they must move the tree. They lose valuable time. A house is lost. Maybe someone is hurt."

"Okay, okay, the tree," he grumbled. "I see your point. But what does all that have to do with what you're talking about now?"

"Feng Shui?"

"Yes."

"I guess the tree across the road is a good analogy. Just as that tree blocked the fire department from coming to the fire, objects misplaced can block or inhibit the flow of life energy. That blockage can result in any number of negative outcomes, some relatively minor, others very significant."

Margery initially had asked me to come to the house because she was suffering from exhaustion. She went to the doctor when she couldn't shake her tiredness, but her doctor found nothing wrong with her, medically speaking.

"Are you under any particular stress at this time?" he asked.

She nodded. The truth of the matter was she was always under a lot of stress. Her job as a district supervisor for special education was extremely demanding. She had three teenaged children. Her mother had fallen and broken her hip. Margery and Frank had brought her to the house to stay with them while she finished her convalescence.

"I set up the back room for her," Margery told me.

"Show me the back room," I said.

I had been in Frank and Margery's house any number of times. It is a pleasant Cape Cod house sitting on a quiet block. They have done some lovely things to make it particularly pleasant. They built a small porch. They have window boxes filled with flowers in the spring and summer. With the birth of their third child, they had added a second floor. Margery is very good in the garden, and there are always blossoms and rich, green vines along the picket fence. All in all, it is a warm and inviting house that is filled with lovely things. However, even before going back to the room they had set up for Margery's mother, I knew something was wrong, something had changed the balance of the house.

The back room, which had always been an open, well-lighted room with books, a few comfortable chairs, wide-open windows, and a fresh breeze blowing through, was now a cold, sterile room dominated by a hospital bed and the equipment necessary for her mother's comfort. The change in décor alone would have been enough to change the energy in the house, but illness and injury also have their own energy that has to be addressed. Even more than all that, however, the placement of her mother's recovery room in that particular room changed the way the energy flowed through the entire house.

"Why have you closed the windows and put those heavy curtains on them?" I asked Margery.

"Mother was not sleeping well during the night. I put the curtains up so that she could doze comfortably during the day."

"And the windows and doors?" I quizzed.

"The breeze gave her a chill. I closed them so she would be more comfortable. I'm sure that having my mother here has added to my feeling tired," she added.

"Of course," I said. "How could it not? But you need to make some changes so that you can have more energy and so your mother can as well."

Margery's intentions were good. She had brought her mother into her house to be able to care for her. The problem wasn't having her mother in the house. The problem was where Margery had put her and the things Margery had done to the room to make it comfortable for her mother. I suggested that she move her mother into the den, which occupied a different spot in the house, one that was not so directly affected by the breezes.

"Put the room back the way it was," I told her. "Actually, you might want to bring more flowers and plants into the room."

Margery shrugged. "We could move Mother to the den, couldn't we, Frank?"

He eyed me and then Margery. "I don't see why not. So long as she's on the ground floor. Actually," he added after a moment, "it might be a better idea. That way, she could have her own bathroom rather than having to use the one out in the hallway here."

"And I could have the back door out to the garden again," Margery noted, almost wistfully.

"I think you'll find that it will help," I told them.

Two weeks later, Margery called to thank me. "It was the most amazing thing," she said. "We'd no sooner put the room back the way it was than I felt as if I had my house back. The problem had nothing to do with having Mother there. After all, she's still recuperating, so she's not moving around the house a lot. But suddenly, there wasn't that sense of burden and obligation."

It was simply a matter of allowing the energy of the space to flow smoothly again.

"Even Frank's more cheerful," Margery said, "although he won't admit it!"

The change also showed them how important that room had always been for them and for the energy and feel of the whole house.

"Frank always dozes off in that chair when he's waiting for the kids to come home from parties or dates," Margery told me. "The garage is right out back there, and he could never settle himself in bed until he knew everyone was home safely."

"I'd fall right asleep on that chair though," Frank added with a chuckle in the background.

I could picture Margery smiling sweetly. "The kids' school books are piled on the table by the back door again."

She sighed deeply. "My son's baseball stuff is standing by the door. It feels right. I can go out into the yard to prune my tomatoes. My tools are right there in the garage. I want to thank you."

"I was happy to help," I told her honestly.

"Oh, wait a second. Frank wants to get on the phone."

"Hello?"

"Hi, Frank," I said, knowing what was coming next.

"Now, explain to me again how this stuff works," he said.

"It's really very simple, Frank," I told him. "Everything has an energy, and that energy interacts with people. You were comfortable in your house because your home's energy could move easily, your house was comfortable with you. When you had to make a change, the energy of your house got blocked. It became ergonomically sick because the interaction between the people and things in the space soured.

"It wasn't making the change that was the problem," I added, "rather the particular change that was made. Bringing Margery's mom to the house was the right thing to do. But you had to make that change in a way that respected the energy of your house."

"Still sounds pretty hocus-pocus to me," Frank said. Still, I could hear a new respect in his voice. "But I guess you can't argue with success. And it's true. I'm more comfortable having the house back the way it was. But tell me, why couldn't I do everything I had to do from the living room? Why couldn't I relax and fall asleep waiting for the kids when I was in there?"

"It's exactly because of what I've been telling you, Frank. The space itself has a life energy, too. You couldn't feel the same way in the living room as you did in the back room any more than you could replace a friend on your bowling team with someone else only because he's a good bowler. The balance would be upset."

"Okay, that's just too weird," he said.

"What is?"

"The bowling team thing. Did Margery tell you that my bowling team started losing after Mike had to stop bowling?"

"No," I said honestly.

"Mike was probably our weakest bowler. We always razzed him and told him we should dump him from the team and get a better bowler to take his place. Then, when he left, we found another bowler with a much higher average. We haven't won as a team since."

"That makes sense," I said.

"It does?"

"Of course. All of life is about relationships and about the way people and things mesh together."

"Yeah, yeah. The way everything is connected."

"Exactly." I smiled. "It's a fundamental principle of Feng Shui."

"So, what else should we do to the house?" he asked abruptly.

I was not surprised by his question. Once people get a glimpse of the inner workings of the world of chi, they usually are more than ready to examine ways to further improve those relationships.

"I would suggest you make a change in the kitchen," I told him.

"What kind of change?"

"Change the counter so the sink is facing the entrance to the kitchen. And add a window overlooking the side yard."

"That will mean changing the plumbing," he protested.

"I'm not a contractor," I said gently.

"I'll think about it."

As it turned out, they made the changes I suggested, and they felt they made a positive effect on how they handled everyday challenges. It made a difference. Even though

Margery's responsibilities at work became more demanding, her daughter broke up with her boyfriend, and her mother developed pneumonia and took a turn for the worse, Margery stayed calm and centered.

"I know my stress level is up," she said later when I spoke with her, "but I don't feel tired at all. I feel challenged. And alive."

We risk the quality of our lives by letting a space that doesn't work for us remain the same. Frank and Margery learned how the energy in our lives can be rebalanced by making some simple changes in our environment that will support us better.

Now About You—The Next Step in the Dance

Take care of yourself first, before trying to help someone else.

Make sure that your own needs are met before attempting to help someone else. The oxygen mask rule in airline travel is a good example: put on your mask before helping the person seated next to you.

When spaces must shift for in-home caregiving circumstances, whether permanent or temporary, make sure there is minimal disruption of the original space. Make the home care space nice, but don't give away the best room or completely change your lifestyle.

Your internal strength to care for another person needs to be continually renewed and preserved. The quality of your personal space will sustain your ability to continue to be a caregiver.

Marriage

CHAPTER **5**

When Sharing is Too Much

I HAD A CLIENT NOT too long ago who came to me in tears. I had consulted with her when she moved into a new condo, making sure that it would be perfect for her. Now, she was back, saying she felt like a stranger in her own home.

"What happened, Suzie?" I asked her.

"I guess it changed when Mark moved in," she said, referring to her boyfriend. "I didn't think it was going to be a big deal. I mean, he'd been staying for weekends, even weeks at a time. It seemed silly that we were keeping two homes." She lowered her head. When she looked up, her cheeks were smeared with tears.

"What am I going to do? I really love Mark but now I don't know if we can stay together. We've been fighting. It's horrible."

As we talked, I learned that the big differences between when Mark had stayed over, even for extended periods of time, and when he moved in, were that he had moved a desk into the living room and his toiletries in the bathroom. The desk, a large roll-top, had belonged to his grandfather and had tremendous sentimental value. It was a heavy, mahogany piece of furniture in an apartment dominated by light pine, glass, and aluminum. His toiletries—unlike years ago, when a man's toiletries usually were limited to a hairbrush, a razor, and some cologne—rivaled Suzie's in quantity and variety. She said Mark took over the bathroom countertop with his hair products. He had several colognes and aftershaves. He also took several prescription medications.

"What am I going to do?" Suzie asked again a couple of days later, when I was in her apartment assessing the problem.

Just then, Mark arrived home. Suzie introduced us. Mark brightened in a smile.

"I've heard of Feng Shui," he said, "The mother of one of the law partners in the firm where I work is Asian. She came in and made a few suggestions on how to change the entrance and reception area, and we've had more corporate clients since then."

"Exactly," I said, "We're going to create that kind of positive result for you too."

As we talked, I found him to be a likeable, charming person. He clearly cared very much about Suzie and was, like her, troubled by the change in their relationship. Neither of them knew what was causing the problem.

"We're at each other all the time," Mark admitted.

"We used to be so loving to each other," Suzie said.

"Well, if it helps, I don't think either one of you is the problem," I told them.

"What then?"

"If you were to go away for a vacation, you would find that you got along the same way you used to, but when you came back, you'd fall into the same pattern of bickering," I said.

Unlike many people, they had not waited so long to address the problems in their relationships that they would take their new, troubled energy patterns with them everywhere they went.

"So the problem is here?" Mark asked.

I nodded.

"Where?"

I pointed to the roll-top desk.

"This desk is a problem here."

Then I pointed in the direction of the bathroom.

"And bathrooms are very important spaces. I think your things have become an intrusion on Suzie's space."

"That makes me sound so selfish," Suzie said. "I want to share with Mark."

"I know you do," I said. "But it isn't entirely up to you. Your bathroom, in a sense, has to want to share as well."

When I originally had consulted with Suzie about her apartment, it was clear that her bathroom was very important to her. She had spent a lot of time designing the lighting, deciding on the color, arranging the kind of carved soaps and dishes she liked for the bath. Her bath was one of the luxuries that she genuinely relished. She had told me how she loved to light a scented candle and then relax in a warm, perfume-laden tub for long periods of time.

"Now, it feels as if my bathroom is a shower room," she had said tellingly, when she had called about the problems that had arisen. Although she was happy to share her space, there still needed to be a limit. Yet, she couldn't establish that limit comfortably, so the most comfortable room for her in her apartment had established it for her.

Her bathroom, in a sense, had stated: "This is too much."

"I didn't realize . . . ," Mark said, genuinely upset. "I mean, I know how you like taking your special baths. Remember that time I surprised you with those perfume candles."

"So what should we do?" they asked me.

"Well, it actually isn't that difficult," I said.

The apartment also had a half-bathroom with only a toilet and a sink. With a bit of reconstruction, however, an adjoining closet was transformed into a shower stall and, voila! A bathroom belonging to Mark.

As for the roll-top desk, we rearranged a couple of things and managed to turn the second bedroom into a quasi-office for Mark, complete with his desk. That room became his sanctuary. It was darker than the rest of the apartment, and very masculine. Very much his.

Although solving the problem in Suzie's apartment required a bit of construction (as did the plumbing work in Frank and Margery's kitchen), most of the time a Feng Shui solution can be achieved with minimal effort and expense. And the best part is that any Feng Shui solution has its own reality. As I've said once previously, you do not have to believe in it for it to work. Understanding the reality of the interconnectedness of everything makes the adjustments easier and more comprehensible.

In Suzie's situation, her bathroom mirrored her perfectly. When Mark's presence intruded upon that important part of her, her bathroom rebelled, creating conflict. I came to understand, after Mark's bathroom was completed, they were comfortable in their apartment together. Susie told me that Mark was still infamous for stealing into her bathroom surprising her with all sorts of fancy candles.

It makes perfect sense that everything is interconnected. Everything has chi. It only stands to reason that there would be a constant interplay as that life force moves within and about everything in the world. To presume anything less would be to deny an essential reality of life—that is, everything shares in the life force, and that life force connects everything.

Now About You—The Next Step in the Dance

Merging households means combining energies as well as things.

Keep some mystery and personal privacy for each person. Everyone should have a place of solitude where they can retreat from the ills of the day. A private sacred space can simply be the area surrounding a special chair, a separate office/study, a desk area, a corner of a room, or even a bathroom, etc.

When combining households, it's better to begin developing the "our" mindset over time, than to carry forward the "theirs" and "my" mentality for years. Look around your home and locate something that you definitely identify as "mine" and then, locate something you'd definitely say was "theirs." Even if you have been with someone for some time, His and Hers never become Ours.

Impermanence

CHAPTER 6

Nothing Stays the Same Like Change

EVERYTHING IS ALIVE WITH the life force.
Everything is connected to everything else.

Everything is constantly changing.

There is, perhaps, no greater cause for anxiety and fear for many of us than this simple statement: Everything changes. All the time. Everything in the world around us, and we change all the time.

There is a saying that captures exactly the power that grips us when we are confronted with change: "Better the devil you know than the one you don't." What this little phrase means is that it is better to suffer with something you know than to risk change. After all, things could be worse!

Unfortunately, what often gets lost in our fear is the reality that things could get better!

Change, in itself, is not a bad thing, and the very fact that we are alive means that we change. And really, who would want to remain the same always? Not me! I might glance back at my life longingly and wish I were twenty again. Or thirty-five. Or forty. But you know what? When I was twenty, I couldn't wait to be twenty-one! When I was thirty-five, I couldn't wait for some other change to happen in my life. Sure, I'd want to be forty again if I could be everything I loved about being forty and everything I love about being me now.

What we need to remember is that change brings opportunity. Too many people remain closed to change (as if being closed to change will make it any less likely to happen!) because they cannot conceive of the possibility of things getting better! They face the future, and its inevitable change, with trepidation. They hold to Murphy's Law: What can go wrong, will go wrong. But who says this Murphy guy knew what he was talking about anyway?

If we embrace the first two tenets of Feng Shui, the third is not a fearful reality but a cause for excitement and positive thoughts. Change means life may be bringing you something wonderful, challenging, exciting, uplifting, or the opportunity to move in that direction. Don't be scared; be excited! After all, the two are very similar. They both make our hearts pound and our palms sweaty. They both make us shake. The difference is perspective.

Alice came to me, fearful of almost everything in her life. To meet her, you wouldn't necessarily see her that way. When I first met her, she still had the bouncy cheeriness of her high school cheerleading days. She often spoke in what I call "Hallmark card phrases," quaint little sayings that represent modern philosophy to many people. Cute, sweet phrases that give the impression of cheerfulness. The problem was, it was all a mask. Inside, Alice was a bundle of fear.

If one of her kids had a fever, she was immediately on the phone to the pediatrician. If her husband was a few minutes late from work, she worried that he'd been in an accident or was having an affair. When she looked at her new car, she saw the potential for an accident or of being stranded on a dark, stormy night. She saw every countertop in her house as a breeding ground for bacteria. Bathrooms were war zones. The dishwasher boiled her dishes. Her washer and dryer disinfected her clothes. Her children were slathered in suntan lotion, when they were allowed to play outside at all.

Alice looked at the world around her, and she saw danger. And at the root of that sense of danger was the reality of impermanence. If she could only "hold onto" everything exactly as it was "right now," she believed, she would feel safe. But of course, she couldn't. None of us can. Alice was standing in opposition to the reality of life. She was the largest obstacle to the unobstructed flow of chi in her life. Alice smiled all the time. But she was not happy. She was miserable.

"Oh, it's not that bad," she protested when I spoke with her. "I'm a little cautious, sure, but . . . "

The hardest part of my consultation with Alice was convincing her that she would actually feel safer and happier by embracing life rather than fearing it. When I suggested plants and flowers in her house, for example, her first comment had to do with bugs. She didn't want her kids to have pets because they might be allergic to the pet dander. Doors and windows were never opened for fear of intruders. Even so, Alice was troubled by the central air conditioner in the summer. It wasn't global warming that she feared; it was mold. And although Edwin, Alice's husband, had pretty much accepted Alice's "little silliness," he didn't care for the fact that he was expected to wash his hands more than he might otherwise or that she absolutely forbade him to work on his car himself (it might roll off the stand and crush him).

"I do worry about the message she's giving the kids," Edwin admitted. "I hope this consultation will enable her to relax a little about the house."

The only way to get Alice to appreciate and embrace life was to get her out of her environment and get her to experience life. To that end, I convinced her to take a little trip with me. We went to a small garden near a creek in the park. She looked around us and took a deep breath.

"This is lovely," she said.

I looked at her. "Yes, it is nice, isn't it? Why do you think it's so nice?"

"I don't know. The sound of the water. The flowers."

As we walked and talked, it turned out that the thing that really made her feel comfortable was the very last thing one might have expected. She felt safe because she wasn't in control, couldn't be, didn't have to be, and yet nothing was going wrong. The energy in the garden was so peaceful and uplifting that she was able to relinquish that white-knuckled grip she kept on her life long enough to exhale and relax.

"Wouldn't you like to feel like this in your own home?" I asked her.

"Of course I would. But how?"

"Look at the water," I instructed her. "Pick a spot. Got it? Now, what just happened to it?"

She pointed to the spot as it was carried along the creek bed.

"It's changed, hasn't it? But it wasn't a bad thing."

On the walk back to her house, we talked about the wonderful things that have happened in her life, all of them the result of change. And then we talked about how we could change her living space to make it a place more conducive to

66

positive energy. So much of it, I told her, is about perspective and our personal perceptions. It's when we get stuck in our perceptions that we throw our lives out of balance. Being stuck there keeps us from living fully and enjoying the flow, the change, that is the true source of balance.

Like the creek. If it didn't flow and change, it wouldn't be a creek. It would be a stagnant pond. And a life out of balance, because you get attached to certain perceptions, only draws you into more imbalance. Until your life doesn't represent what you wanted at all.

"Do you mean," Alice asked, "that if I loosened up a bit on the house and let it not be so perfect, I'd be happier?"

"It's a thought," I answered. "It won't be any less nice a home. You know that, and you'll be happier once you can see things from a different perspective. Say a perspective with fresh flowers and a few plants? Living things."

Then we talked about how she could look at her living space in a new way, to make it a place more conducive to positive energy. It would be a different perspective, but that didn't mean it would be bad or wrong.

"For example," I said, "adding representations of strength always helps."

Alice went to the storage area and pulled out a lovely framed oil painting of mountains rising in the distance, over a peaceful lake that was shrouded in green foliage.

"Something like this?" she asked.

"Absolutely," I told her. "Hang it where you can see it often."

Anything that makes you feel a sense of protection, support, or strength will work. I've seen clients use angel collections to represent their belief in God's purpose for their lives. I've seen a career woman use a rooster in the kitchen, depicting cockiness and self-confidence. For someone else, a copy of the Prayer of Jabez on a mirror will work, or even a statue of an elephant reminding them of strength.

Look inside yourself for the feeling you are trying to create in your space. Then bring that feeling into your space in an object, painting, photograph, or affirmation. Let those preconceived notions of the way things "should be" go away.

"This will take some time," Alice said, sighing.

"It will," I agreed, "but take the time and listen to your home. It will help teach you what it needs, if you let it."

Now About You—The Next Step in the Dance

Appreciate that, right now, everything is the way it should be and things will work out all right.

Realize that every choice you make, no matter how small, has its compliment outcome. No choice is ever wrong, it is only a different path in time leading you to a different place.

Understand there is a divine order to the universe. What appears on the surface to be bad may just as easily appear good if you change your position to see it from a different perspective.

In Chinese lore there is a red thread that connects everything in the universe with everything else. Here in the west we might say that the divine tapestry being woven with that red thread has yet to be revealed to you.

流

Flow

CHAPTER 7

The Workings of Feng Shui

I WANT YOU TO BE happy living in your own chi. But, as we all know, living comfortably, with peacefulness and joy, is not always an easy task. Sometimes it seems as if it is the most difficult thing in the world to do.

As we travel along life's path, we very often lose our way. What looked to be the broad, straight path often turns out to have unseen obstacles and dangers. The brief side trip in search of flowers leads us far from our goals and hopes. We find ourselves at too many dead ends. There is nothing bad about finding yourself in the wrong place, unpleasant perhaps, but not bad. After all, the experiences we have often carry us to places we cannot always predict or control. The problem is figuring out how to get from wherever that not-right place is to someplace that is more beneficial and uplifting.

We are all prodigals in one way or another. We are seeking a path that will take us from the place we are to a better place, a path that will lead us back to a state of grace and innocence, to a place where life is beautiful again. Too often, the roadways we encounter that might lead us back are overwhelming or difficult to travel. Even more often, it is unclear exactly where a given road will lead.

Life is a journey, and the trouble with journeys is that the destination is never fully known, even when we think it is. When we set out on a journey, there is no telling when, or if, we will be returning to the place from which we left. There is no telling what adventures we will encounter along the way. And that's scary. It is. I know. But it is the first step that is the most frightening. After that, the fresh breeze in the air, the sun on our faces, the scent of fresh flowers, and the sound of flowing streams are our reward. The first step is always the hardest. To gain the courage to take that step is a blessing. But no path is completely straight or easy. Even those paths that lead us toward a space where life is beautiful again often lead us first to a difficult place, where our lives turn sour.

How often have you said to yourself, "I'm going to turn my life around. I'm going to be a better me. I will be more introspective. I will care about things that are important and stop wasting my time on trivialities." And then, when you moved in the direction of such a life goal, you discovered that you became depressed, angry, or unhappy?

How many times have you needed money but your pride kept you from accepting help or from taking advantage of opportunity? How many times have you told yourself that you would no longer be selfish in your relationships, only to discover that becoming totally absorbed in another is equally dissatisfying?

"Too often," will be your answer if you've lived long enough. Much too often.

The problem is, how do you keep going? How do you muster the energy to keep facing those times of unhappy change and keep taking those first steps?

Feng Shui gives us some important tools to help solve our modern problems. Although rooted in ancient practice and tradition, it is as efficient and true now as it ever was. The timeless principles of Feng Shui are ancient in origin and its applications are priceless in value. For those who balk at taking advantage of something that has been around for so many centuries, I have only this advice: If it isn't broke, don't fix it. By which I mean, these principles have been around for centuries, improving millions of lives. There's no need to reinvent the wheel. Often it's best to keep things simple.

Feng Shui is not hocus-pocus. It isn't mystical in that '60s sort of way. In fact, it's very concrete and literal. No sleight of hand. So don't look for hidden meanings. It is what it is. There are no secrets.

Feng Shui means, literally, wind and water. In order to understand Feng Shui, it is important not to lose sight of what is right in front of you, that is, the literalness of it. Think of water and wind literally. Think of their attributes and their strengths.

Water is, first and foremost, malleable. Into whatever container you pour water, it will conform to fit that shape perfectly. It can take any shape. It also is readily changed from any one its three states of physical matter, gas, liquid, solid, to another. Water is accepting of whatever path is presented before it, whatever change it is asked to make. Although, over time, water can wear down anything in its path, it does not do so by fighting whatever is in its way. If it cannot go through an obstacle, it will go around, finding the path of least resistance. Water finds its own level. In short, water lives easy. That is its nature.

The same qualities exist in wind. Wind forms an invisible shield or force around everything it touches. You are always aware of the wind, but you cannot capture it. You cannot contain it. You cannot put your hands around it or hold it.

As with water and wind, so with Feng Shui. The application of Feng Shui principles in our lives mirrors the attributes of water. The principles do not demand that we live as people lived centuries ago. Feng Shui is perfectly adaptable to our time and our place. It always fits perfectly, in any time and place it is applied. Its results are very much like the wind. We cannot quantify or capture them, but they are very real and very readily noticed.

Feng Shui, like the wind and the water, represents a physical reality. If there is a mystery in it, it is that its logic is so apparent. For those who are determined to understand every detail of the origins and history of Feng Shui, I invite you to delve into the many books dedicated to the near-academic study of it. Meteorologists may wish to study every detail of the weather and how it forms. I, however, am happy to stretch my hand out the door to find out if it is raining or which way the wind blows.

Feng Shui simply is.

Wind and water share another very important attribute that is reflected in Feng Shui: They possess a remarkable store of energy. Energy can be potential, quiet (energy waiting to happen), or it can be kinetic, active (energy that is happening now).

To appreciate the two types of energy, imagine it is a lazy summer day, and you are dozing quietly by the banks of a slow river. The water laps gently along the banks, kissing rocks lightly, singing softly and gently. A gentle breeze blows through your hair. It tickles the hairs on your arms and delights your senses with its touch on your skin. Further downstream, however, that same river might pick up speed and go crashing over rocks and against tall, craggy banks. It might flood over a waterfall with incredible force and power, so much force and power that it can provide the electricity for cities and towns, for whole sections of the country. Likewise, that gentle breeze can be whipped up into a fierce storm that bends trees and lifts rooftops off homes. The wind and water can be riled into absolute chaos so powerful and destructive that anything and everything in their path will be destroyed.

These opposing attributes or qualities are similar to other opposites that we know from our real-life experiences. Life often presents itself as a series of "either-ors." Feast or famine. Peace or war. Happy or sad. Good or bad. Feminine or masculine. Yin or yang.

For much of our lives, we feel that we are at the mercy of these forces, victimized by these opposites. We tremble with the fear that we have no more control over the forces that make us happy than the forces that make us sad, or that we have no control over our feasts or our famines. No wonder we fear change.

Feng Shui teaches us differently. It teaches us that we can learn to create whatever we will, that when we harness the power of the elemental life energy, and our own chi, none of us is a victim. None of us need be at the mercy of any other person or entity. Feng Shui empowers us with all this. As I said at the beginning of this book, it is not simply about interior decoration. It is not simply about moving a few things around. It is about aligning ourselves with this fundamental life force and removing any and all obstacles to the free movement of that force.

For our purposes, you really only need to remember that Feng Shui began as a method for determining an auspicious place to bury the dead. From this simple and deep beginning, a number of different interpretations and methodologies have arisen regarding how one should apply Feng

Shui. Over the last 20 years there has been a cumulative body of work to synthesize a form of Feng Shui applicable to the culture of the West. Westernized Feng Shui is ergonomically based in the form and nature of how people, things, and space metaphorically relate to each other.

Predictably, a number of other variations have evolved over the years. Yet, even with all the variations, all schools of Feng Shui hold a number of things in common. Most significant is that the foundation of Feng Shui is intent. Intent, a purposeful decision, a direction, a desiring, a need, is the first step in moving one's surroundings, one's self, one's life, in a more positive direction. A direction in which chi can flow freely (I'll talk more about this in other chapters).

All that we desire—prosperity, love, comfort, health— are mapped in Feng Shui.

How many times have you said to yourself, "All I want is . . . ?"

What? A good life? A bit more money? A partner who loves me? Good health? That's all.

But none of these things exist or come into your life in a vacuum. Remember, everything is connected. Feng Shui incorporates all aspects of life. Everything in life is a part of the life force. It has to be. In Feng Shui, all these aspects are incorporated into a simple map square of nine blocks, something like a tic-tac-toe board, that represents your life. This map is called the bagua, and, using it, you can learn how to align yourself with the life force, with chi.

So, let's take it slowly and deliberately, remembering that change can be good and that the first step is always the hardest. And that it is also the first step toward creating your new life.

Now About You—The Next Step in the Dance

Comprehend the results you achieve with Feng Shui are an expression of your intent.

Your options create choices.

Your choices become decisions.

Your decisions coupled with intent have resolve.

Those intentions empowered by resolve accomplish results.

Your intent can be emboldened by all things a part of Feng Shui. Energy flow, metaphors, and symbols all act as anchors for action leading you to achieve your desired outcomes.

Vantage

CHAPTER 8

A Different Perspective

I HAVE ALREADY POINTED OUT that Feng Shui is
not hocus-pocus. Still, there are many people who are
confused about how Feng Shui works. A great deal of this
confusion comes from the way we tend to see things in the
West. Too often, we objectify everything in our lives. We set
up competing dichotomies: Us vs. them. Me vs. you. The
good guys vs. the bad guys.

We are always competing. Even when we aren't, we feel
as if we are. Any time we set ourselves apart from something
or someone else, we are competing. I remember having an
interesting discussion with a college professor. During our
conversation, the professor spoke about relationships.

"There is no such thing as equality in a relationship," she announced. "There is always a subtle sadomasochism."

I was a bit taken aback by the perspective she was describing, not to mention the terminology she was using.

"What I mean by that," she said, recognizing my reaction, "is that the inequality always results in one person in a relationship being dominant and the other being submissive. This can be in anything from determining the kind of car a couple buys to the color of toilet paper they use. A so-called "good relationship" is one in which the dominant-submissive quality is dynamic and fluid, in which each partner is sometimes in charge and the other is not. It's balance on a sliding scale between the two, depending on the situation and the strengths of each individual."

I remembered that conversation for some years after we had it because it bothered me, really bothered me. But it was a long time before I could put my finger on what exactly what it was that bothered me. For a long time, I thought it was because I saw too much of my own relationship dynamics in the professor's observations. However, as much as I was troubled by that reality, that wasn't what troubled me the most over all those years. Finally, I came to realize that the dynamic the professor described is the dynamic of most relationships. Not because it has to be, but because our insistence on objectifying or externalizing things extends to how we relate to other people as well. We objectify things and people, by thinking we are not part of the solution or the problem, that we are not divine in nature. As long as we are in a fundamental competition with things or people, we see ourselves as either a victor or the vanquished, as if in a contest.

The religious tradition of the Western world teaches us that human beings have dominion over creation. Indeed, we are taught that the rest of the universe was created for our benefit. While it is true that there are a great number of responsibilities that come with such authority, there is no question that such authority necessarily defines the rest of creation as apart from us and as less than us.

In Feng Shui, the opposite is true. We must come to realize that we are not apart from all that is around us but that we are intimately related to everything around us. It takes an awful lot of energy to dominate anything. When we waste our energy having dominion, we often fail to recognize that we are the beneficiaries of the same life force that flows through everything that exists. The very same energy that flows through everything else flows through us as well. We are not lords over creation; we are a part of creation.

This is the underlying reality that explains how Feng Shui works. Just as a change in your eating habits will affect the energy levels in your body, a change in your environment will change the energy levels around you. Why does a change in eating habits affect energy? Because what we eat becomes a fundamental part of who we are and what our bodies can do. Likewise, a change in our physical environment (and, of course, our spiritual and psychological environments) affects our energy for the same reason. The energy of the space is absorbed into our bodies, and it also becomes a fundamental part of who and what we are. This explains how our bodies subconsciously react to the space we inhabit. Despite our seeming determination to objectify ourselves and the world as separate and unconnected, our bodies know otherwise. It understands that we are a part of everything, where the world is personal and subjective, not external and objective. Rather than build houses and decorate rooms to hide ourselves, we need to understand how to arrange rooms to maximize ourselves. Our bodies never lie, especially about energy.

It isn't our responsibility to impose order on a physical space; that is the beauty of Feng Shui's reality. A physical space is capable of accomplishing order in us because of the subjectivity of our own perceptions. It is through this constant influence of life energy that we become an interactive part of the room, of the space, and of the world.

We do not dominate. We occupy. We do not control. We assume responsibility. We do not own. We share.

Similarly, with the physical world, it does not dominate us. It surrounds us. It does not control. It accepts. It does not own. It provides.

Our relationship with and in the world is not fixed. It is fluid. It is dynamic. It is ever changing. As we change our physical surroundings to support who we want to become, we automatically and subconsciously adapt our personal energy patterns to be more in line with the energy of our surroundings. Subjectively and unconsciously, we begin to become the person our surroundings supports us in being. We create new energy patterns to help us react to situations, people, and events differently than we did in the past. And, as a result, this new energy draws us into the life that we desire. When we design our space to support us on the worst of days, the best of days get even better.

Feng Shui provides a map or a guide that helps us participate in these changes. It is neither magic, sorcery, nor divination. It is simply the understanding of the way the life energy moves through space and through us. By following the map, we can create a balanced life. By applying the principles of Feng Shui correctly, we can create and maintain the kind of environment necessary to support dramatic and positive life changes, life changes that inevitably affect not only our physical selves but our psychological and spiritual selves as well.

An accountant friend of mine was somewhat reluctant to accept what I was teaching him. He is, consistent with his profession, the kind of person who likes to see things in black and white. Or, as he is fond of saying, "I like all the columns to add up."

"This Feng Shui stuff all sounds so . . . New Age," he said, as if being of a new age was somehow a bad thing.

"Tom," I said patiently, "let me give you an example of what I'm talking about."

Now, I am not a mathematician. Anything but! However, I do remember a thing or two from having taken math all those years ago, and I thought I might be able to use that knowledge to help Tom understand something important about Feng Shui. I set up a simple math equation.

"Tom, here's a problem. Tell me what you think." I proceeded to work out the problem with a solution in which I complicated everything. Threes became the product of three and one. Or the sum of two and one. Or zero and three. Rather than add, I subtracted the negative. Where I could have multiplied, I divided by fractions. When I showed it to Tom, he made a face. Not a very pleasant face, I might add.

"What is all this?" he asked.

"A math problem," I replied.

"But . . . but . . . ,"

I explained to him that I knew that I had come to the correction conclusion because I knew that I had followed the rules of math and, as I proudly recalled, so long as the rules of math are followed, one will arrive at the correct solution.

"But it's so . . . so . . ."

"What?" I asked him.

"Inelegant!" he blurted out. "Do you see? Rather than doing this, you could have done this." He took his pencil and proceeded to condense my half-page of math work to two simple lines. "There," he proclaimed, clearly pleased with the result.

I smiled. "I know," I told him.

"You knew?"

"Of course. I wanted to make a point. You see, when you were looking at the problem that I had solved, you were uncomfortable, anxious, even annoyed. And for no good reason. After all, my answer is exactly the same as the one you've gotten. Yet, when you worked the problem, you were clearly pleased, and not because you'd gotten the right answer. Why?"

He stared at me for a second. "I don't know," he admitted softly.

I explained to him that, although both solutions were technically correct, the more elegant and efficient solution, his, was more conducive to the free flow of his mental energy. The method of solution actually made him feel less anxious in his body.

"Why should it surprise you that a physical environment could do the same thing?"

"Good point," he conceded. "When my surroundings become elegant and efficient, my life works better, and I will feel better."

What better point could there be? Your energy will shift with even one change in your behavior. Start experimenting with consciously directing your energy through your actions.

I went on to explain to Tom that these kinds of elegant examples play themselves out even in every day life where you wouldn't normally think to look, as in a mother's relationship with her teenage daughter.

Jody's husband had me Feng Shui his office after hearing a friend from their health club talked about his experience with the process. Steve was a physician and wanted to improve the feel of the office not only for his patients but also for himself and his staff. After a successful consultation on the weekend, he asked if I would go to his home for a consultation.

It seemed that his teenage daughter was at odds with everything and everyone in the house. I knew what he meant. Even though it's been a while, I do remember those years when my head and heart always seemed at odds with someone. He went on to explain that the problem was greatly upsetting his wife and the rest of the family and he wondered if I could help. I agreed to go and we made arrangements for the following week.

When I arrived at the house, Steve's wife Jody welcomed me and showed me through their lovely home. She eventually got around to explaining the situation with her daughter to me, but that didn't seem to be her focus for the consultation. We talked about how she wanted things to be and decided to emphasize the wealth and love areas of the house. To accentuate the love area of the home I had her install mirrors on the back wall of the dining room to extend the feel of the room another 10 feet. The dining room was at the far right corner of the home, and it was crucial to make the home appear to be more of a rectangle, even if this was done by illusion with mirrors.

The master bedroom, which was also in the love position in the home, got some furniture rearrangement for better flow. I knew that those two changes would make both Jody and Steve happier with each other. That kind of happiness always rubs off on the other members of the home, especially if there is any dissension going on.

Finally Jody asked what she could do about her daughter LeAnne's attitude and blatant disrespect. No sooner had she mentioned her daughter than in through the door she came. LeAnne took one look at me and said, "Keep that stuff, whatever it is, out of my room." I told her not to worry, that I'd address her room only if she asked me.

As her mother and I again walked around the home, I mentioned she should probably take down all the 10" x 12" portraits of her girls. There were quite a few, all taken when the girls were at least five years younger. Jody resisted, but I went on to explain that even though they were beautiful to her and her husband, the girls might feel differently. Besides, the maturity level that LeAnne was displaying was something like the age she was in the most recent picture of her, which hung near the kitchen. Unfortunately in that picture, LeAnne was six years younger than now.

Then we went into the Helpful People area of the house, to the right of the front door. There hung a snowy winter scene with no people in it. I suggested switching that picture with one I'd seen in their basement, of a mother and two girls picking flowers, which Jody did.

Upstairs, Jody's youngest daughter was ready to have her room Feng Shui'd and we did so in record time, moving her bed to the best position and changing the position of her dresser. As we finished Jody asked me about LeAnne's room. I said I wouldn't do it without the girl's permission. But Jody wanted to know what to do, so if LeAnne changed her mind later the two of them could do it themselves.

I explained that I'd move the bed and the desk to power positions so LeAnne would easily be able to see out the door without turning around. Then I'd remove all the posters and leave only a couple on the wall away from her line of sight when she was in the bed. This was to keep the eyes of persons in the posters from staring at LeAnne all night. I'd also rearrange the makeup and dressing table area, and get new linens. Jody thanked me as we stepped over clothes and teen things all over the floor, and said she'd fill in LeAnne when her daughter got home.

This consultation was on a Wednesday. The family went on a mini-vacation from Friday to Sunday. I got the call on Saturday the following week from an ecstatic Jody. It seems she did exactly what I told her I would not do. Without getting LeAnne's permission, Jody stripped her daughter's room on Monday, after the girls left for school. She rearranged everything the way I had told her, quickly bought new linens, and fixed the room up beautifully. She was standing at the top of the stairs when LeAnne arrived home from school, and watched with bated breath as LeAnne bounded up the stairs.

Just as LeAnne neared the top step she stopped, seeing her room in the distance. She slowed to a snail's pace, Jody said, and stood in the door of her room, taking in all the changes. Then she quickly turned to Jody and said, "I didn't know you loved me so much," with tears in her eyes. Now we were all crying as she was telling me this that Saturday on the phone. Jody went on to say that was the best week they'd had as a family in months. Subsequent reports for Jody indicated that LeAnne's grades have improved substantially, she's become a participating part of the family again, and the bickering level has dulled compared to where it had been.

Energy doesn't have personal names or boundaries around it. It affects people where it is, adult, child, or teen in whatever manner it is displayed.

Feng Shui is an ergonomic process that positions us to live a more elegant life. It creates and transforms environments by infusing them with the positive emotions and desires of its inhabitants. These environments then interact more efficiently and safely with people, influencing their lives and ultimately influencing their entire social and cultural community.

Now About You—The Next Step in the Dance

Wake up and notice the unobvious energy you are allowing to be absorbed into your body from your surroundings.

Examine your surroundings at home and the office to see if they are congruent with your highest and best vision of yourself. Make sure your spaces represent the kind of life (home, job, relationship) you would want to attract into your life. Make sure your environment mirrors back to you the person you'd like to be.

Start simply by changing even one thing in your individual circumstances. Make your bed. Pick up your clothes. Clear up the paper clutter. Don't call that negative friend, or don't answer the phone. Don't eat that bag of cookies. Don't have "just one more drink" or that next cigarette. Quit cussing, etc.

Changing one thing a day will change your life. Only do what you imagine the person you want to become would do. Make the reflection of yourself you see today in your environment the best you can be.

Resolve

CHAPTER 9

Being in the Present

*I*T OFTEN AMAZES ME that people seem so determined to make their lives more difficult than they need to. Too often, they fight the very things that could make life more balanced and meaningful. Feng Shui is certainly an example. I have often spoken to people who make such a big deal about what it is, how it works, why it works, etc. The simple fact is, it does work. But that's not the only important thing about Feng Shui. Also important is that it works so fast and easily! It doesn't matter if you're a right-brained artistic type or a left-brained analytic type. Either way, Feng Shui works. Engineers and accountants can appreciate Feng Shui because it uses a very logical mapping system. At the same time, it is subtle enough to appeal to the most intuitive soul in search of meaning and balance in life.

Although Feng Shui works by virtue of our connection to the life energy shared by all things, there is another other aspect of Feng Shui that has an undeniable benefit to you as you try to find balance and meaning in your life.

A number of years ago, I met Vicky, an older woman, at a conference. She was clearly articulate and interested in many things. However, as I got to know her, she became more open in expressing a sense of being overwhelmed by life.

"The good news," she told me, with characteristic cheer, "is that I'm somewhat comfortable with this feeling. I've had it my entire life. The bad news is, who wants to be comfortable with feeling overwhelmed?"

The answer to that question is, no one! But the truth is, most of us feel overwhelmed much of the time, and with good reason. Life can be overwhelming. We are bombarded by stimuli: Noises. Colors. Smells. Phones ringing. The neighbor's dog barking and running through our flowers. Just when we think that we have a moment to take a deep breath, the water pipes freeze, or the cable TV goes out, or the job we thought was completed has to be redone, or . . . well, any one of a hundred other things. The world seems to bear down on us, and finding a small space to relax is no easy task.

"The worst part about the way I feel," Vicky said, "is the feeling of being a helpless victim, of being out of control."

The world is a difficult and complex place. We often feel as though it is reeling out of our control. Taking control is not an easy thing to do. Feng Shui makes it easier. The old complaint that life didn't come with instructions is not exactly true. There are instructions, and there is a map to help you make your way. However, before learning to use that map, it is important to know that you can take charge of your own life. You are the captain of your fate! When I told Vicky this, she looked at me as if I were crazy.

"Annie," she said with a laugh. "You're a walleyed optimist is what you are. A hopeless romantic."

I shrugged my shoulders. "Guilty as charged," I told her. "But, Vicky, on this point I'm on the money."

For most of our lives, we have been able to look backward with some degree of clarity. We see our history and our past in apparently perfect detail. We may have regrets. We may feel nostalgia. But we can see it. And, with a little inspiration, most of us can visualize the future. It might not always be realistic. It might be based on hopes and dreams. But it is the future, and it is ours.

"The trick is, Vicky," I said, "you have to learn to take small steps and create small wins, stacked one on top of another. That focuses your attention to the project at hand and gives you a better foundation to tackle the next task."

"But what does that do for me, except make me pay attention?" she asked.

"That's just it, Vicky," I said. "It brings you back to the here and now and makes you conscious of the decisions you are making in the present moment."

"Sounds reasonable," she said. "I'll think about that."

Our problem is that, despite our ability to see our past and our future, we are almost incapable of seeing where we are in the present! The worst part of this inability is that, until we are able to see where we are right now, we cannot really build the future we want. All our hopes and dreams might be achievable, but not unless we can reach them from the here and now.

So many of us live in the world of should or if only. You know what I mean. Our lives should be this way instead of that way. If only we had been born into a wealthy family, everything would be perfect. The trouble is, no one ever exerted control over their life by building on a foundation of "should" and "if only." That foundation is shifting sand indeed. The future, like all structures that can stand the test of time, demands a solid foundation, one that is as strong as a rock. The future demands a foundation on "what is." Feng Shui has the method to lay that foundation. You are not lost on the road of life. You simply haven't looked at the map yet!

Susan, another friend of mine, was a bit doubtful about the map at first. "Come on, Annie, I know that this stuff is helpful and all, but a map?"

The idea of an actual map that allows you to maximize the energy of the spaces you occupy should not be particularly surprising if you've understood all the things I've been saying about Feng Shui. Everything possesses energy, and the way in which that energy flows has a very real impact on our lives. The space we occupy is very important in how we interact with the energy around us. When we were children, no one gave us a map that would lead to a great life. We were all given messages, of course, the things we had to do in order to have a good life: Marry money. Go to college. Invest in computers. The trouble with all that advice was that it inevitably concerned itself only with how we were going to succeed in the material world.

Before I could continue, Susan interrupted me. "Annie, now don't start up with all that Eastern philosophy, that money and things aren't important," she said quite sternly. "I lived through the '60s and, frankly, I am not interested in a life without a certain level of comfort."

"Nor am I," I told her. "Feng Shui holds those things in high esteem. But it doesn't pretend that those material things are the only things necessary to have a wonderful life." I studied her for a moment. Even in her mid-fifties, Susan had the easy, natural beauty of a younger woman. She also had the look of someone who had enjoyed a comfortable life. Her clothes were simple but well made. Her nails were manicured. Her make-up was modest but very well done. I had always enjoyed Susan's company. And honestly, there were times when I envied her. So many things had seemed to come easier for her than for others. But there were also times when I was happy not to have to live in her skin.

Her husband was extremely successful but also a workaholic. He had gone for years without taking a vacation. He often went into the office on days that should have been days off. It was the price he had to pay when building up his own business. Susan understood it, but that didn't make it any easier being the only parent around to chauffeur three children to a soccer game here, a baseball game there, a dance recital someplace else. There were precious few days when she wasn't on twenty-four-hour-a-day call, in case one of the kids needed a ride or got sick. Sunday mornings, everyone had to tiptoe and whisper; it was the only day that her husband was able to sleep in. Later, when he was finally able to take a little more time off, he developed a passion for golf, rather than spending more time with Susan. It was clear that, despite the many comforts and benefits in her life, there was a hollowness and sadness at its center.

"Look, there's no such thing as a perfect life," Susan said when I pointed that out to her. "No one gets through unhurt or unscarred."

"I'm not talking about a perfect life," I told her. "I'm talking about a balanced life."

She looked at me as if I had expressed the idea in a foreign language.

"Feng Shui incorporates wealth and prosperity into the map. But if there isn't a balance among those and other aspects of life, then there is no happiness," I told her.

Her eyes took on a sad, faraway look. "With the children grown and out of the house, I feel lonely. It's a big house without children, and Larry's either at work or playing golf."

The map of Feng Shui is called the bagua (see page 102). As you'll learn later, by following this map, you can begin to take control of your life again. You are no longer simply a passenger. You are the driver. The feeling of being in control can alter all your perceptions about your life.

The bagua basically creates a checkerboard of nine boxes that can be horizontally transposed over each space you occupy, home, individual rooms, office. Each of the nine boxes contains an area or an aspect of your life. The goal of Feng Shui is to have every aspect of life balanced on all three levels: the physical, the mental/emotional, and the spiritual. A truly balanced person is balanced in all nine areas of the bagua on all three levels.

"That's twenty-seven areas of life to balance!" Susan exclaimed, with some degree of alarm.

I smiled and nodded. "But it isn't nearly as difficult as you might think. In fact, it becomes progressively easier as you become more comfortable with the process of bringing your life into balance. And let me emphasize here that it is the process that is most enlightening and uplifting about Feng Shui."

"Why's that?" Susan asked me. "I mean, wouldn't you want to get into balance and stay there?"

"Sure," I agreed. "But you can't."

Her shoulders sagged.

"All of life is change. It is the process that has to be uplifting. Look, if all you do is focus on the destination, you miss a lot of the joy of the trip," I told her.

Feng Shui is a logical, mapped-out process. And while it is not impossible to achieve perfect balance in all these twenty-seven areas of your life, it is not productive to put too much pressure on yourself to do so. After all, juggling just one area of your life, say love and relationships, is difficult enough on the physical level alone. Seeking to have balance on the mental/emotional level and spiritual level at the same time is no trifling task. Even if your love and relationships are perfectly aligned, there are still the other areas of life to balance.

Susan waved her hands in the air. "Stop!" she begged. "It's all so complicated. I thought Feng Shui was supposed to make life easier, not harder!"

"It will," I told her, "you'll see."

Now About You—The Next Step in the Dance

Determine your quality of living in all the major areas of your life.

Let's quickly inventory your life for balance. It will be very helpful in the process to find if any area of your life is heading in a direction different from where you think it should be going.

Mark with a "−" the areas of life that are taking too much out of you, or leaving you with a feeling of lacking.

Now mark with a "+" the areas that seem to work for you well or you are making good progress. Compare the two on the following map.

Notice areas where you have −'s, and beside those blocks make a note of one thing you can do to improve the situation this week.

Now take a look at the +'s. Likewise make a note of one thing you can do to make that area of your life even better this week, and resolve to make that happen.

Now look at the areas that have no marks at all. Decide what you can do to include this area as part of your life. Write down things you will do beside those blocks also, and resolve to do them too.

LIFE ISSUES	− or +	BAGUA MAP
Finances		Wealth & Prosperity
Self esteem		Fame & Reputation
Significant other		Love & Relationship
Personal health & close relationships		Health and Family
Fun		Creativity & Children
Growth		Knowledge & Self Cultivation
Work		Career
Friends & experiences		Helpful People & Travel

Interaction

CHAPTER **10**

You're Only Changing the Energy

$\mathcal{F}$ENG SHUI IS REMARKABLY sensible. It acknowledges and respects all aspects of life at all levels. It is curious that in the West, we have taken these aspects of life and more or less picked and chosen those that we judged as more appropriate. For example, while we tend to exaggerate the importance of wealth and prosperity, we rarely assign more than the physical aspect to it. We view wealth and prosperity in terms of things. We consider wealth to be a material value. And it is, but not exclusively.

Susan was surprised that Feng Shui gave any credence to wealth at all. "I thought all those Eastern philosophies were against material things," she said.

"Hardly," I replied. "Remember, Feng Shui views each of the areas of the bagua as existing on three planes. One of those planes is the physical, and it is equally as important as the other two. We live in the physical, the material world. To deny that would be foolish. We affect the material world, and the material world affects us. Feng Shui is all about the way life energy flows through things as well as through us."

One of the reasons that Feng Shui is so appealing to so many westerners, once they understand it, is precisely because it does acknowledge the importance of those things that we have always held in highest esteem, the physical, objective reality of the world. However, it goes a great deal deeper than just the physical. Which makes perfect sense, doesn't it?

We can readily acknowledge that there is a physical level where nature prevails in the energy flow. Elements. Objects. Colors. Textures. The movement and placement of things acknowledge, indeed proclaim, the way in which this natural level of our surroundings are affected by energy.

Still doubt it? Then do a very simple experiment. Clear out the clutter in your physical environment, and see how things change. That's it. Don't get involved in the bagua map yet. Don't worry about this corner or that. Move stuff around. Experiment. If you are honest, you will see that more than the placement of things changes. That "more" is the shifting of energy. It is said in Feng Shui lore that if you move 27 things with intent, your life will change immediately. After our conversation and without telling me, Susan did this experiment as I'd suggested, and she was more than a little surprised by the results.

"I didn't have a plan," she explained to me when she told me about what she'd done. "I was mostly trying to disprove what you were saying. It sounded so straightforward, but I was resisting it. Don't ask me why.

"In any case, I chose a small room off the living room. We had always used it as a sitting room, a place for people to gather when we had guests, usually something for Larry's clients. But over time, we had begun to use that room as a storage area. His papers. Books. Projects the kids worked on.

"The furniture was a bit dark and heavy. I decided I would take your little test on that room. I cleared away the clutter of things that had accumulated there. I moved some of the paintings and prints around. I shifted the placement of the chairs and the small sofa." She laughed. "I'll tell you, I was exhausted. And, standing in the middle of the room when I was done, I didn't think much had changed. Sure, I liked the room better now that it was uncluttered. But I was too exhausted to note anything being different other than the placement of the furniture. And then a funny thing happened."

"What was that?" I asked.

"After dinner, Larry was getting ready to leave for a meeting he'd scheduled. I don't know what made him wander into that little sitting room, but when he did, he called me. When I came in, he asked me what had changed in the room. I told him that I'd just moved some things around. He looked around and then sat down in a chair, very strange for him. He said he'd always wanted that room to be something different than what it had become. I told him I had too.

"'Really?' he asked. And then you know what happened, Annie?"

I shook my head. "No, what happened?"

"We started talking . . . about so many things. We talked about how we'd wanted a lot of things to be different than what they had turned out to be. We had the most candid conversation we'd had in all the years of our marriage. The funniest thing was," she added, "that we came to realize that we'd actually used that room for what it was meant to be used for, conversation. Larry never made it to his meeting that evening." She smiled. "I think that was the first business meeting he'd ever voluntarily cancelled in his life."

Not all of these experiments turn out so positively, of course. But simply performing the experiment is a real no-lose situation. If you like the way the changes in a room alter the energy, leave them. If you don't, simply put the furniture back the way it was. Don't worry. When you return everything to it's original position, the energy, too, will return to the way it was.

Beyond the physical level of Feng Shui and the manipulation of objects, there is the mental level. On this level, you think and feel Feng Shui. It is where comfort, safety, beauty, and harmony affect the mental and emotional aspects of life.

The third level of Feng Shui is the spiritual level, the level of creation. On this third level, there are no limits to what you can think or do. Nothing is impossible. Intention is all.

"Okay, that's all fine," Susan said, more than willing to listen now. "But how do I do it?"

"It's a lot like changing a tire," I told her.

She looked at me as if I were crazy.

I told her what my mechanic once explained to me about changing a tire; that is, when replacing the tire, you tighten the lug nuts in a particular order. You tighten one a little, then tighten the one opposite it. Then you move in a star pattern, tightening a little here, then a little there. In this way, the tire is tightened flush, and it rolls true.

Adjusting a space to Feng Shui is similar because we often move to opposite corners to make the adjustments, the balancing, and we seek. Look again at the bagua on page 102. For example, if you are struggling with some aspect of love or relationships, go to the opposite corner—knowledge and self-cultivation—and address the emotional aspect of your love/relationship issue by working there. Or, if your problem is with your health, go to the bagua and find the opposite area, which is joy (creativity and children). Find an activity like walking that will encourage you to exercise without creating any additional pressure on you. If you can enhance your emotional state of joy during exercising, you will improve your physical body because you will do it more often (health and family).

The process is simple:

1. Define the problem and locate that area of life on the map.
2. Look for a physical cause of the problem in that area.
3. Enhance the emotional state of the opposite area on the map.

Now, you have shifted your energy toward a solution. This is what Susan did without being aware of the process. When she cleared out the clutter of the room, she shifted the energy in a more beneficial direction, where it could be focused.

Now About You–The Next Step in the Dance

Understand all the areas of life are interconnected in cause and effect, and too much of one thing often means too little of another, causing imbalance.

1. Having too much fun might result in not taking care of your health.
2. Giving too much in a love relationship might pull you away from who you really are or want to become.

3. Worrying too much about money might result in being blind to opportunities you do have.
4. Working too much might make you feel unappreciated and result in less self confidence in your abilities.
5. Taking care too much of others might result in not taking care of your self first.
6. Too much self involvement might result in not leaving room for a love relationship.
7. Being something you're not might result in making your work suffer.
8. Doing too many things might result in you not enjoying any of them.

Notice in the bagua map on page 102 that each of the previous statements creates a +/- in the areas located in opposite corners or opposite edges of the map.

1. High Creativity & Children and Low Health & Family
2. High Love & Relationship and Low Knowledge & Self Cultivation
3. High Wealth & Prosperity and Low Helpful People & Travel
4. High Career and Low Fame & Reputation
5. Low Creativity & Children and High Health & Family
6. Low Love & Relationship and High Knowledge & Self Cultivation
7. Low Career and High Fame & Reputation
8. Low Wealth & Prosperity and High Helpful People & Travel

PART II

Meaning of the Map

BAGUA MAP

Far Left Corner   Far Right Corner

Wealth & Prosperity *Gratitude*	Fame & Reputation *Authenticity*	Love & Relationship *Receptivity*
Health & Family *Support*	Center *Letting Go (Physical)* *Forgiveness (Mental)* *Surrender (Spiritual)*	Creativity & Children *Joy*
Knowledge & Self Cultivation *Introspection*	Career *Passion*	Helpful People & Travel *Awareness*

\ | /

Door Entrance Options

The Nine Life Areas of Feng Shui

How we use them to create balance or
identify imbalance in our lives.

Wealth & Prosperity (Gratitude)

Defined individually by what we value in life and different for each person.

Fame & Reputation (Authenticity)

How other people see us, but more importantly, how we see ourselves.

Love & Relationship (Receptivity)

Our ability to allow ourselves to be loved, as well as loving and forgiving others.

Health & Family (Support)

How we identify our personal team and how we interact with them.

The Center (Letting Go)

Where we stand, grounded to examine who we really are and what we want from life. Letting go of attachments. .

Creativity & Children (Joy)

How we relearn to view the world with wonder and awe as if through the eyes of a child.

Knowledge & Self Cultivation (Introspection)

What we do to grow and become better people for ourselves and others.

Career (Passion)

The activity that turns us on and gets us excited about living life to its fullest, be it work or not.

Helpful People & Travel (Awareness)

How we recognize the synchronicity of life's miracles, including all the people and events that come to us for whatever period of time, and where these experiences lead us.

發現

Discovery

CHAPTER 11

What You Really Want

THE BAGUA MAP IS at once the most simple, direct, and at the same time, the most confusing aspect of Feng Shui. Once you become familiar with it, the bagua will become an indispensable tool in helping you to maintain balance in your life.

Essentially, the bagua map is all about balance in life. Elemental (physical) balance is about nature. Psychological (mental and emotional) balance is about common sense. Spiritual balance is about being the best we can become. The map is designed to accomplish the purpose of Feng Shui, which is to live a full and balanced life, in harmony with all your environments, both internal and external.

If, in the process of going through the bagua and evaluating your environment, you discover a deficiency, then you can apply an enhancement or "cure" to alleviate that deficiency. It is that simple, that straightforward.

Anything that can be sensed (seen, smelled, heard, touched, or tasted) can be used as an enhancement or cure. It may very well be that the stronger the sensory potential of the cure, the better its effect, for the simple reason that it will affect internal change more quickly and more dramatically.

"But what do you mean by a deficiency?" my friend, Nancy, asked me several years ago. "I mean, on any given day, you can walk into my house and see chaos. The laundry has to be done. The kids are running around. Someone has left a book bag in the living room. Someone else forgot their lunch on the kitchen counter. My husband's glasses are still on the bed stand. Clothes are strewn all over.

"Yet an hour later, that very same house will be relatively calm. Calm, that is, if I got around to washing the breakfast dishes and tidying up, putting in a load of laundry and collecting the various items all over the house before I had to leave for work."

I reassured Nancy that a deficiency is not the result of a pile of clothes left on the floor for an hour or so until you are able to get to the laundry. A deficiency is not dishes on the counter that need to be washed.

In Feng Shui, a deficiency is a pattern of deficiency. It is a continuous item or arrangement that blocks and depletes energy, not one of the thousands of small obstacles that move quickly through our lives. To understand the significance of these patterns, it is sometimes good to think in terms of dreams. A bad dream is disturbing. It can wake you up with heart-pounding suddenness. Such a dream could simply be the consequence of a particular incident, of course. It could be that you saw a movie or news report that disturbed your imagination. Maybe you ate something that didn't agree with you. Perhaps you received upsetting news. Such a dream can mean a poor night's sleep, but it isn't necessarily indicative of something more unless that dream begins to recur.

It is the patterns that matter. You may have little control over the singular incidents that buffet you throughout each and every day. For example, if a supplier has trouble getting a part that you need for a job you are working on, that introduces tension and negativity into your day. But you probably can't influence the supplier's ability to acquire the part. All you can do is have the positive personal energy in place to respond.

Checks get lost in the mail. Tires go flat. Computers crash. Electric power goes out. Vacuum cleaner bags burst, spewing dust and dirt all over. Drains clog. Toilets leak. People become ill. The list goes on and on. Things happen. The important thing to remember about the items on this list is that they are each singular events not indicative of your life.

If, however, that pile of laundry is always in the middle of the floor, if clothes are always strewn around the house, if backpacks always get deposited wherever and whenever, then you have a potential pattern. Then it can be addressed as a deficiency in one of the quadrants in the space in question, a yard, a home, an individual room, or a workspace.

When you recognize a deficiency, you are, ironically, actually recognizing a pattern of comfort. As water seeks its lowest level, so do people also seek to live in circumstances that are comfortable. Unfortunately, here, "comfort" is not a positive attribute. Instead, it refers to that which is easiest, the path of least resistance. What that generally means for most people is an almost blind re-creation of the negative patterns that have dominated their lives. They have always been like this. They will always be like this. People move from place to place, from home to home. The circumstances of their lives change. And yet, the very same negative patterns remain.

"Why am I always the one to . . . ," they can often be heard saying. "Why me?"

Negative patterns inevitably lead to a feeling of victimization, of losing control. When you are trapped in negative patterns, you feel that life happens to you. You don't live, so much as you function as a neutered observer in your own life drama. That is not living in balance!

You are more than just an active player in your life. You are the star! The world is your stage. But you must claim the intention to write the script, to speak the lines, to sing the songs, to accept responsibility for your performance. Are you ready to do that? Then you are ready to look with analytical objectivity at the patterns in your life in order to see what is disturbing the positive flow of energy.

I recently had a client who was at her wit's end. Helen had, according to her, "done everything to change my life." She had changed jobs. She had gotten out of a bad relationship. She had moved to a new apartment.

"But nothing seems to have changed," she said into the telephone. "I have a new boyfriend, but he's just as much a jerk as my old boyfriend." She looked me in the eye. "Men are men, right?" she asked with a shrug.

No.

Although I speak with many women who have or have had difficult relationships with men, the problem is not solely with men. It is also with these women. There are many, many women who have wonderful relationships with men. Did they just get lucky and find the one or two good men in the world?

No.

What they have done is to address their personal energy in a way that creates new patterns that support loving and successful relationships.

Helen had made many changes in her life, significant changes, difficult changes, changes for which she deserved a great deal of credit for her courage. Unfortunately, in making those changes, she kept her negative energy patterns and, in her new apartment, her new job, and her new relationship, the same negative patterns quickly took hold. She argued with or resented coworkers. She was uncomfortable in her new apartment. And her relationship with her new boyfriend was just as unfulfilling as her previous relationship had been.

As we spoke, I asked her some questions about her apartment. "Where did you get the furniture?"

"Oh, I brought all that with me," she said. "I wasn't going to leave any of my stuff with my old boyfriend."

"What did you leave behind?"

She looked at me as if she wasn't sure what I was asking. "You mean, besides my boyfriend?" she asked with a smile.

"Yes, besides your boyfriend," I said.

"Not much," she acknowledged after a moment or two. She had brought the same kitchen utensils, the same forks and knives. She brought her stereo along with all the records and CDs she had collected over the years. She brought the pictures that had hung on the walls, only to re-hang them in her new apartment. At work, she brought with her everything she could, from the small frame where she kept photographs of her niece and nephew to her coffee mug.

"You really haven't changed anything, have you?" I asked.

Her expression was confused. "But all that stuff, that's how I feel at home," she said. "I'd be lost without my things."

I nodded. "It sounds more like you're lost with your things."

Three days later, I visited Helen in her apartment. As she walked me through it, she also described for me where each piece of furniture had been in her previous apartment and the one before that. To my eyes, it was an amazing visit. Helen seemed to embody exactly what I had been trying to teach all my clients not to do. She might as well have packed a huge crate, labeled it negative energy, and had it delivered to her new apartment. The address had changed. The walls were new. The neighbors were different. But everything was the same. No surprise there.

We began with her records and CDs. Helen kept, and continued to listen to, the records that she'd first heard in junior high school, records she associated with her first boyfriend.

"Mostly the records make me sad," she admitted. "They make me think of when we broke up." She shrugged. "But sometimes I like a good cry, you know? Kind of freshens me up."

While it might be true that crying can be cathartic, it is equally true that Helen was replaying negative energy patterns every time she played her music.

"You need to get rid of this music," I told her.

She looked at me with an expression of shock.

"But I love this music," she protested. "I've been listening to this music for twenty years. It relaxes me."

I shook my head. "No it doesn't. It holds you back. Let it go."

I explained to her how her music, her furniture, the posters and pictures she put up on her walls, all defined her space. Until she was able to change that environment, the one she carried with her wherever she went, it made little difference where she lived or even with whom she lived.

"I'll tell you what," I said. "Let's do an experiment. Let's get rid of everything you can. We'll put it someplace in storage. That way, if there's no change, you can always get it back."

She thought about my challenge for a moment and then shrugged. "I guess that would be all right. You know, checking it out for a few days or so."

"Give me two weeks," I said. "After two weeks, if there's no difference, then you can bring everything back."

"Two weeks," she agreed, hesitantly.

Although it sometimes takes as long as several months for new energy patterns to emerge, I knew that I would have to convince Helen in a quick and dramatic way that she could change her energy patterns. If I didn't, then she would never pull herself out of the negative energy in which she was stuck.

After Helen packed up her records, tapes, and CDs, she took down the pictures and prints from her walls, all except for one, which she told me she couldn't bring herself to take down.

"I first saw it when I was a little girl," she told me. The print showed a cottage in a clearing. In the foreground, there was a small lake that reflected the tall, green forest that surrounded it. Wildflowers swayed in a meadow to the right of the house. Lovely flowers filled the window boxes. "I always thought that I would love to live there someday."

I agreed with Helen that she should keep that picture. It clearly held a great deal of positive energy for her.

After we moved out boxes of music and prints, we set about rearranging the furniture. Although it might have been best simply to get rid of much of what she had, Helen was in no position financially to do so as an experiment.

"If you convince me, then I'll do what I can a little at a time," she promised.

We moved a rocking chair from the bedroom after she told me that it was the rocking chair in which her grandmother always sat.

"She was a very religious woman," Helen said. "She went to church every day of her life." She smiled sadly. "She would never have accepted me living with a boyfriend."

I raised my eyebrows. "Then why would you invite her into your bedroom?" I asked.

"Huh?"

"Having this chair in your bedroom is like having your grandmother in here," I explained. Helen colored. I nodded in agreement. "Let's take this chair out and put it in the living room by the window. You can sit in it and read if you'd like."

The more we moved things around, the more Helen was able to articulate what different pieces of furniture meant to her. There was one coffee table that her previous boyfriend had purchased and that she had brought along because "it was such an expensive and pretty piece." It was also the piece of furniture against which he had smashed a vase during an argument. And the piece of furniture over which she had fallen when he'd pushed her.

"I really think we need to get this out of your apartment," I told her. "It will open everything up."

When we were finished, Helen looked around her. "Wow," she said. "It sure looks different." Her voice told me she wasn't too certain she liked that difference.

"It is different. Live in it for a few days. Remember, you promised me two weeks."

"Two weeks," she repeated, as if she would have to suffer through those two weeks before she could go back to what made her comfortable.

A week and a half later, I was surprised by a visit from Helen. "I thought I was going to speak with you this weekend," I said.

She smiled. "I couldn't wait any longer," she said.

I studied her. She seemed to be bursting with energy. I couldn't wait to hear what she had come to tell me.

"I can't believe how different things are," she said. "At first, I hated the apartment. It felt so strange. But then, after three or four days, it started to grow on me.

"And at work, I met this new guy. I hadn't even noticed him before, but he works in my department. We got to talking, and he asked me out. We went out two or three times, and then I invited him over for dinner. He said he loved the way it felt. I was surprised by his saying that, but I was even more surprised when I agreed with him. I told him I did, too.

"I don't know if I'll keep going out with him," she went on. "I like him and he seems wonderful, but I'm so comfortable with things right now that I don't need to have a boyfriend. And he's good with that too. We talked about it. He said that he liked that I was a strong woman who understood what she wanted."

Helen looked at me in amazement. "I didn't know I was a strong woman who knew what she wanted!" She laughed. "But then, when I thought about it, I started to realize that I did know what I wanted. And what I didn't want."

That was exactly what she had become as a result of the changed energy in her apartment: a woman who knew what she wanted and got it.

Now About You—The Next Step in the Dance

Make room for the new by clearing out the old.

Old and undesirable energy patterns or habits are often held in place by outdated memories in the form of sensory activators like music, photographs, clothes, furniture and even people.

At a minimum, temporarily get the source of this old energy out of sight. When it is out of mind, new desirable patterns and habits can be established. Once you see that you can develop new habits by breaking the old energy patterns, permanently remove the source of the problem. For example: a newly reformed alcoholic wouldn't want to continue to go to the bar every night, or a newly divorced woman wouldn't want to keep photos of her ex-husband around, even if they also show the kids.

Visions

CHAPTER **12**

Mapping Out Your Life

*I*F YOU WANT THINGS to stay exactly as they are in your life, then don't move or change anything in your space. But if you want to create the kind of life you've only dreamed of until now, then get to work!

The bagua diagram on page 102 illustrates how Feng Shui divides any physical space into nine squares. Let's take each of these areas and identify its real meaning, whether it's traditionally associated with a horizontal surface or with the whole of our lives. One thing to note before beginning is, when you examine the way the bagua works in a given space, you are not interested so much in direction as in orientation. You are interested in relationships, in how these areas of the room interrelate. Again, remember the tumblers in a lock. When the tumblers all fall into place relative to one another, then the lock opens.

Wealth and Prosperity

In the upper left corner of the bagua is the Wealth and Prosperity square. When we talk about wealth and prosperity in Feng Shui, we are not speaking only of money or material wealth, but quality of life as well. Remember, each of these squares functions on three different levels: the physical, the mental, and the spiritual. You need all three levels to be aligned before you can truly stand in the center and feel more balanced.

Feng Shui respects the physical reality of the need for wealth and prosperity, but physical wealth does not and cannot stand alone, not if you hope to achieve balance and peace with your wealth. Instead, when we speak of wealth and prosperity on the bagua, we are looking at the whole context of your life. In addressing this area, you must address how you feel about your life. Ask yourself, "What do I want from my life?" What has value to me (versus worth)? What are the riches I hold in my heart, not only in my bank account? What does my soul desire? By what do I want to be remembered? How do I want to be remembered? For what am I grateful?

These questions should give you a fuller perspective on the broader meaning of wealth and prosperity than our society teaches. You should be able to see how, in answering these questions honestly, you will place wealth and prosperity in a new perspective. The wealth and prosperity promised in this section of the bagua are the wealth and prosperity that are enjoyed and cherished and not simply coveted.

Fame and Reputation

Next to the Wealth and Prosperity square is the Fame and Reputation square. Of course, this square has a great deal to do with how you are perceived by others. After all, both fame and reputation are relationship qualities. They depend on how others relate to you. Right?

Yes. And no. While it is true that fame and reputation have a great deal to do with how you are perceived by others, there is another component that cannot be excluded: How you perceive yourself! Imagine what you would think about yourself if you were able to step outside of your skin and observe yourself. What would you see? Would you like the person you were observing? Is that person someone with whom you would want to be friends? Whom you could trust? Someone you could love?

When you observe yourself in this way, do you find that you are living the life that you profess to be living, or do you live one step removed, behind a façade? Are you trying to fool others in hopes of fooling yourself? Have you accepted the masks and trappings of the you that you want to be, without really being that person? Who are you fooling? Are you living with integrity?

Abraham Lincoln is reported to have said, "It is true that you may fool all of the people some of the time; you can even fool some of the people all of the time . . ." What he might have added is that, "If you fool yourself all of the time, you're the fool."

Love and Relationships

It is also true that no man (or woman) is an island. We live in relationships with others. We often thrive because of those relationships. The holy person who can live fully, and only, in the spirit is a rarity beyond rarities. The rest

117

of us need relationships. Require them. Want them. Long for them.

In the bagua, the Love and Relationship square that completes the top row is about a significant other. It is not about your relationships with your employer, your teacher, or your students. It is about your romantic relationship.

You don't have such a relationship in your life? There are many reasons for being without a significant other. But ask yourself: Is the most likely reason that I don't have one, or one that works well, because I don't value myself enough to become the person who would attract one?

I know that this is likely to elicit shrieks of protest. How dare I suggest that the inability to find a significant other worthy of your love could be your fault. But it may very well be. And if it is, creating in yourself the positive energy patterns that would attract someone special will open your life to that special someone appearing. Look what happened with Helen, whose story I told in Chapter 11. The same thing can happen for you.

Are you in a bad relationship? Maybe you haven't honored yourself enough to admit that this person is not the one for you and, in fear, you simply settled for what you could get. A bird in the hand, right?

Regardless of your relationship status, if you are without a significant other or if you are with a person who is not the right one, you need to know that to have love, whether in a marital relationship or simply an intimate one, you must exist in a state of honesty and receptivity. If you are not honest enough with yourself to admit that the person you are with is a person you should not be with, why would you expect anything to change? Do you really think that you will be sitting in the diner and a knight will come riding by on a white horse? Or, if you are a man, do you really expect real love to be impressed by a car? Or fancy clothes?

If you cannot begin with honesty, real self-honesty, then you will never know what it is to have a successful relationship. Period.

Creativity and Children

As we continue around the bagua in a clockwise fashion, we come next to Creativity and Children. This square is not so much about children you may or may not have. Rather, it is about that childlike, innocent creativity and worldview within you. This is where you get to do things with your hands and imagination and look at the world with awe.

That is one of the wonderful things about children, they are touchers. Everything gets touched. Childhood is the time for finger paint and modeling clay. It is a time of mud pies and water fights. It is a tactile time.

Childhood is also the time of make-believe and stories, of magic languages and imaginary friends. It is a time when there are no limits to the imagination and therefore, to creativity. Childhood is the time of giants and wizards, the time of flowers that grow to the sky, the time of nursery rhymes, the time when a tea party can be even more amazing than the tea party Alice experienced in Wonderland.

Childhood is the time when you simply are, without being self-conscious of being. You don't care how many people are in the bathroom while you're taking a bath, all you're interested in is showing them how the rubber ducky swims.

Childhood is whimsical. Childhood is about hanging upside down on playground equipment and straining your eyes to see the end of the sky but not being able to. Childhood is about seeing the world through a myriad of colors, when rainbows are magical and chocolate milk is the best thing in the world. Childhood is the time when you look upon the world with eyes that do not judge, when you love those who love you, when your laughter is joyous rather than guarded. When you know how to be delighted.

The creativity and childhood square of the bagua is where you feel that way again, where you recapture that magical energy and bring it to bear upon the patterns in your life.

Helpful People and Travel

Next around the bagua is the Helpful People and Travel square. It is here that, as you might expect, you get connected with the outside world. It can completely change your point of view. This is the nexus, or wheel hub, of the comings and goings of people in your life, those you draw to you for life, and those who stop in for only a season. It is where all the possible emanations of those bonds become meaningful consequences in some manner. It is here that you travel to a distant land physically, or toward new beliefs mentally, or to visit with God spiritually.

It is through Helpful People and Travel that God makes miracles occur in your life, miracles which we refer to as synchronicities. In the orient there are three kinds of luck, earth luck or Feng Shui, man luck which is conscious decision, and divine luck which is heavenly guidance. These types of luck are synchronistic miracles, that cry out to be recognized for what they are, more than chance.

These synchronicities—events that seem related in meaning but without an apparent cause by conventional means—are brought into your life via the people who travel into and out of it and by your own travels, whether physical, psychological, or spiritual. It is our responsibility to be in a state of awareness in order to appreciate them.

Career

For those of you who think that Career is simply what you do to earn your keep, think again! According to the bagua, what you do for a living says a lot about who you are. And what you do and who you are speak directly to why you are here. After all, why are you here, if not to be who you are and, at least in large part, to do what you do? A career is not simply a job, not simply a way to earn a living, it is much more.

Remember, each of these squares on the bagua has to be understood on three distinct levels: the physical, the mental, and the spiritual. A career certainly functions on the physical level. You must earn a paycheck. But if that is the only level on which you understand your career, then you can never find balance or satisfaction in your life.

When you view it with absolute candor, your career is about more than earning a living. This is why I've always been interested in the mental function of how we "name" our careers. What a job is called has become important to our society in the last few decades, both to rectify gender bias and also to lend an aura of impressiveness to what we do. A new name, however, really will not do the latter. What brings impressiveness to your career is the dignity that you bring to your tasks. A maid who works diligently with a true heart has a more honorable career than the CEO of a company who cheats and abuses stockholders.

It represents what you are at your core. When all the layers of who others think you are, are peeled back, what is left is your real life, your spiritual self. This is where the depths of your soul shows through, what makes you unique. Your soul shows through in direct proportion to the dignity and enthusiasm you bring to your understanding of who you are and what you do. It is your passion for life.

Knowledge and Self-Cultivation

The next stop on the bagua is the square of Knowledge and Self-cultivation. This is where you stretch yourself to be more than you ever imagined you could be. This is where you read, where you learn, where you grow. This is where you gaze upon a painting and see things that you never saw before. This is where you contemplate who you are and who you would like to be.

It is where you mentor others, where you discover who you were really meant to be, not what the world has tried to make you. It is here that you step onto a way and make it your own, working it like a potter works the moist clay, watching it with the intensity of a child watching a flower grow. It's here that you sense those things deep within yourself that are sure to blossom if you allow them.

It is imperative for you to find a spot in your environment that creates the feeling of sanctuary. Creating a place to go when the world has taken too much from you will allow you to repair your own wounds and renew your strength and confidence and spirit.

It is here that you experience the inner stillness that will allow action to flow forth and develop an intentional pattern of rejuvenation by meditation, yoga, reading, praying, walking or going quietly into your own soul. Here you begin to nurture and love yourself.

Health and Family

As you follow the map back up toward Wealth and Prosperity, you come to Health and Family. Here you examine your own constitution, from a physical, mental, and spiritual perspective. You determine what needs to be done to nurture yourself by yourself and through others. This is the soil into which you sink your roots for nourishment and from where you derive strength.

Here you explore your family and ancestral roots. It is where you determine who you are intimately close to considering all with whom you associate. They become your support team whether you are related by blood or you simply choose to view them as family.

It is also where you determine your support needs. Support comes in many forms, such as help with the yard, or the household cleaning, or the kids' homework. Another kind of help you receive is the listening ear of a friend or confidant who gives encouragement. Spiritual support can come in the form of gathering with those of like mind or in personal and private study.

The area of Health and Family also makes you look closely at how you treat your bodies. It helps remind you that your body can support you better through proper food and activity such as exercise. It shows you that your mind is fed by reserving time in your daily routine to relax, play and rejuvenate. It also reiterates that you must find a way to care for your spirit that sustains you through times of trouble.

Center

You now have moved completely around the outside of the bagua. Now that you know the general meaning of each square in your life, it is time to look at what they specifically represent to you. What is their significance to you, and how do you understand them and use them to enrich your life?

To do that, you must go to the last square on the bagua, the Center, where balance can be found. At the center, you can begin to measure what is lacking in your life and see where you want more out of life or identify what is overwhelming you. By defining yourself through each of the outside squares, you now have the honesty and the intent to evaluate the deficiencies.

The center is where we all want to be, with all that it implies, all that it means. If you live in the center, then you can reach out to each of the squares on the bagua equally well. Your life will be filled with compassion, pride, dignity, and love. Unfortunately, most often we find ourselves mired in one of the areas, or we want to be too much in another one, and, as a result, we are not in complete balance because other areas then suffer as a result. When you are not in the center, you feel like the little Dutch boy running out of fingers to plug the holes appearing in the dike.

However, you need not feel frustrated by the need for continual adjustments. After all, isn't that what constant change implies, the need for constant adjustment? When you recognize how Feng Shui flows through all of your life, you can begin to understand how the things you do affect the things that follow. Your choices today can set in motion a succession of events and circumstances not seen for years.

Because we have been raised to think negatively, too often when we think of consequences, we think in terms of punishments. But rewards follow action as well. And you have control of your rewards as fully as you have responsibility for your punishments. If you lead a balanced life, it doesn't mean that there will never be problems or challenges, but you will enjoy the rewards that ensue from such a life.

The bagua provides a simple road map. Now that we've come to familiarize ourselves with the "stops" along the way, let's go forward. After all, God made us to be happy. But it's up to us to discover how to find that happiness.

Now About You—The Next Step in the Dance

Identify what must leave your life in order for you to move on.

Refer to the bagua map on page 102 and pretend to stand in the center square. As you look at each of the areas of life surrounding you, honestly write down what you must let go of. In order to move forward with your life, you must clear away the old for the new to come in.

Write a list of the things in any of the areas you must release in order to move on toward balance.

Example:

Wealth and Prosperity

Things & People (physical):
car with high payments

Behaviors, Ideas, & Attitudes (mental):
shopping at stores I can't afford

Opinions, Beliefs, & Judgments (spiritual)
belief that I'm entitled

Fields

CHAPTER 13

Balancing All of You

*O*N THE BAGUA MAP, you will see that each of the squares also has a secondary association. For example, Wealth and Prosperity has Gratitude. Helpful People and Travel has awareness of the state of Awareness. We will use these secondary areas to help you understand precisely how you can find that balance that you seek.

Gratitude (Wealth and Prosperity)

Let's begin once again in the upper left corner of the bagua, at Wealth and Prosperity. If you feel that there is a deficiency or blockage in the Wealth and Prosperity aspect of your life—the area that asks such fundamental questions as, "What do

I want from my life?"—then your task becomes: How can I remove that blockage? If it is wealth and prosperity that is lacking in your life, you must ask yourself what creates that lack. In order to do that, you need look no further than the underlying theme of that square: Gratitude.

Gratitude is the true source of wealth and prosperity. A man can own several palatial villas around the globe, fly in his own private jet, be driven in limousines, but he is not wealthy if he feels no gratitude for what he has. He will feel as if something is missing.

By the same token, a person who lives in a simple apartment, who enjoys only the most basic material pleasures, but who is grateful for them, is far wealthier than the ungrateful rich man could ever be.

With gratitude comes a better wealth and prosperity. Live from a mindset of abundance, and that is what you will see. Share, or tithe 10%. If you save 10% of your income each week for yourself that alone will make you feel prosperous again. Tithe *and* save (even if it's only 3% or 5%) and you will be amazed at what happens. You immediately come from a position of abundance because you are giving to others and yourself. Remarkably there is always enough.

View your life from the opposite, from the viewpoint of scarcity, and that is what you will manifest.

Look at all that you have. Then offer a prayer of thanks and gratitude that you have more than you need. When you can honestly and sincerely do that, your life becomes full.

Authenticity (Fame and Reputation)

Fame and Reputation is not only what others think of you, but what you think of yourself. Everyone gets confused about that at times. When you get confused you say or do things that are opposite or incongruent with who you really are in your soul. Fame and reputation is about being authentic in

128

how you acknowledge yourself which affects the way others see you. You are the only one who can control of the impression you make.

To create the impression you would like others to see, you must first want to see the truth about yourself. That truth will give you an understanding of what your words, actions and beliefs communicate to others about you. Once you see how you are projecting yourself to the world you can decide whether you like how you appear. Simply by taking notice of what you project, you will automatically begin the process of becoming more authentic in who you would like to become.

Acquiring the energy it takes to become the person you want to become is a matter first of deciding what you want. You must define the values and characteristics you would like to enhance and develop in yourself. Also you must get a frame of reference of what that value or characteristic looks like in others in order to be able to develop it in yourself. Then you have to want it, begin it, mean it. Build on your authenticity in who you want to become.

Fame and reputation are not the result of the work of a public relations firm. Madison Avenue is not the place to go for this. The way to be noticed by others is to stand in integrity and authentically to be who you are. When you know who you are, others do not become confused about you because you are not confused about yourself.

One of the most important things we must learn is how to see our own magnificence and power. To be worthy of being known and respected you must be congruent in what you project and how you walk your talk. When you are congruent with yourself others can trust you to be congruent with them. They then can see you as being who you really are and feel comfortable with their own decision to accept you or not. "Walking your tallest" says you are moving through the world in a way that would make others take notice.

Receptivity (Love and Relationship)

If you are having a problem with love and relationships, the question should not be, "Where is the love of my life?" Rather, it should be, "How many walls have I built around my heart?" I would be willing to guess that the answer to that question is, "Several." How strong are these walls? Do they rival the Great Wall of China? Does talking about your walls make you defensive? It does most people.

You may have been hurt in your relationships in the past. That hurt makes it hard to trust again, hard to risk another experience that could result in that kind of hurt. The truth is it does not matter why or how the walls got placed there. You must address the present situation, not the past. All that matters is that you know you will be able to make the walls go away. As surely as the sound of bugles brought down the walls of Jericho, you will be able to bring down the walls that have been built up around your heart. The first step is realizing and acknowledging that the walls are there. You cannot bring down walls that you do not know exist.

We all build walls around our hearts. We all have known heartache. We all know what it is to say to one we love, "I will love you, but I won't let you see this secret part of me because I'm afraid that, if you do, you will not love me anymore." We create ourselves to be the people we think other people will love. Then, we can't be sure whether they really love us or the facade we have created. It is necessary to break this cycle so that you can have an honest, fulfilling relationship. You do that through receptivity.

In order to enjoy the fruits of a wonderful relationship, you have to be willing to be completely and totally receptive of someone else's love. Otherwise, you run the risk of not feeling it. Imagine what it would be like to open your heart and receive the kind of love of which you've always dreamed! Hold that image in your mind. Then remember that desire and never forget how it feels to receive unconditionally. Giving doesn't matter if you can't receive honestly! Anyone can give love to another. It takes an open and receptive heart to receive it.

Joy (Creativity and Children)

Many of the people who come to me as clients are only too familiar with being unhappy or lonely, defeated, or depressed. A person feeling those things is certainly not being creative and assured. Imagine a cup of warm water filled with suds. If you continue to fill the cup with water, the suds will run over the edge and out of the cup. If you fill your cup with sadness and negativity, you cannot have room for remembering a childlike wonder at the world.

Let it go. Throw your hands out and twirl around in an open field until you're dizzy. Walk barefoot through a meadow. Go to a carnival and buy a balloon, for yourself! Watch a cartoon on television. Listen to a silly song. Do the hokey-pokey. Do something crazy and out of character. Take a cake to a friend to celebrate their un-birthday. Rent a funny movie and laugh out loud. Go caroling in June. Wear colorful clothes. Do something you never thought you could: write a song, ride a horse, go for a bicycle ride. Do something no one could ever imagine you doing. Perform random acts of kindness, not for the "thank you" you will receive, but simply to do them! They will put some joy back into your life.

That's the feeling that you're trying to remember: joy. How you get there is up to you, but I will give you a clue: The easiest way is by doing something no one would ever expect you to do. Like making a handprint in the sand. Or playing Frisbee catch with your dog. Or picking flowers.

Better yet, do something nice for someone else.

Awareness (Helpful People and Travel)

So many times we feel stuck in our lives. Stuck in a rut. Stuck energy in our home, stuck energy in our office, stuck energy in our love life. Just stuck period. If that is how you feel, you should know that you're not alone.

We've all been there. Nothing is happening, and worse, it doesn't appear as if anything is going to happen. You notice that you become bored easily and you're anxious to do something, even feeling as if your own skin doesn't fit you well. You wish something would change, but nothing does, because you don't.

Being aware is the way to get unstuck fast. All you must do is begin to believe in other people by appreciating roles they play in your life, and the role you play in theirs. This awareness means noticing the opportunities around you and all the people in every facet of your life.

Opportunities can come simply in the form of going someplace different, meeting someone new, or looking at a challenge from a different point of view. You must then act upon the opportunities best for you at that moment. Choose the opportunities that will give you the highest and best return and change your life the most and the fastest.

There are more than enough miracles and synchronicities of life present for all. When you begin to recognize this simple fact, then synchronicity becomes apparent. Start to look for it. You'll see that chance meeting as an opportunity or make yourself available to new circumstances. Change your perspective and look at something differently. Change in itself will create opportunity for you. Simply be aware and take advantage of the chance to do something you haven't done before or do it in a new way.

This is what the Helpful People and Travel area is all about. Your eyes are toward the world, the people in it, and the opportunities that they represent. You're back and plugged in as a vital participant in your life because you now know how to look for miracles in your life.

Passion (Career)

Not long ago, a young man came to me. He was downcast and weary looking. Most people would have looked at him and seen a successful young businessman. But I knew better. Although his clothes were neat and tidy and his car displayed an obviously healthy salary, he was not happy.

"You know," he explained to me, "I went to school specifically to be what I have become. I knew that if I studied business, I would be able to get a high-paying job out of college. And that is exactly what has happened. Everything has gone according to my plan. There's just one problem," he said.

"What's that?" I asked.

"I hate what I'm doing. I can't stand myself in the morning, and I like myself even less at the end of the day. It takes all my energy just to get myself to the office."

I felt the frustration and hurt of this young man. What could be worse than not doing something you love? A career that you hate affects you more than almost anything else. The question is, How much is your soul worth? That was the question I asked this young man.

"Please," he said dismissively. "Don't tell me that I'm selling out. Of course I'm selling out. I've always sold out. I have a big house. A nice car. My wife is happy." He lowered his head. "I'm the one who's miserable."

"Then let me ask you again," I said. "How much is your soul worth?"

He shrugged.

"You have to think about your value," I told him. "Are you cheap or expensive. This isn't only about your job or profession. This is about who you believe you are.

"You are more than what you do for work," I said, "and the work you do should reflect that more."

If you cannot meet someone for the first time and tell them, with some passion or enthusiasm, what you do, then you need to make a change. Your soul is crying out in pain. Deep inside, it all comes down to who you believe you are. Go deep and look. That young man had stood at a fork in the road when he was in college. He had wanted to study music, but his parents had told him that there was no future in music.

"Music can always be your hobby," his father said. "You've got to think in terms of practicalities."

So he did.

After I spent some time with him, he managed to change jobs to incorporate his love of music into his life and his career. He made less money but he was far wealthier for the change!

Introspection (Knowledge and Self-Cultivation)

"To thine own self be true."

Many years ago, I saw this quote in a schoolroom, and it filled me with a strange fear and excitement. There was something in its direct admonition that rang so true to me. But, how does one come to know oneself enough to be true to oneself?

A teacher once told me that it requires stillness. It took me a long time to understand what it was she really said to me that day. But now I do. To be still, to go to that still place within you, is to become introspective and quiet. It is also the only way to know yourself and ultimately find your faith. This has always been the case. It is even more the case now, when our days move so quickly. When your job makes instantaneous demands, and your cell phone and pager intrudes into every sanctuary you seek. When the kids are acting up, your significant other is moody or simply when you feel the world bearing down on you.

All these pressures make a place to be still even more important, your quiet place where you can seek solace. It is where you can go to shake off the demons of the day and reclaim your spirit. It's a place to be still, to read a book, to listen to music, or to think. It is a place where you can do something you haven't done before, where you can stretch yourself and grow. It is a place where you can seek that stillness inside where only you reside.

It's where being alone feels wonderful. It's a physical place that allows your mental and spiritual needs to be met.

Support (Health and Family)

Deriving strength and support is a matter of asking at times. Often when we need help and don't receive the kind of help we need, it is because we didn't ask. Sometimes we don't ask because we don't know who to ask. Sometimes we don't ask because we don't know what we need or we are not in a good place internally. It is in the Health and Family area that we must develop our support team to help us.

This is the place where you identify at least one person who can hold your highest and best vision for yourself when you can't. They are the person you can allow to see your vulnerabilities without being judged.

Here we also find the people who support you when you falter on your diet or lose your confidence or question your faith. They are the ones you can always count on and retreat to on the really tough days. They are the people who are friends forever. They are the people whom you would tell if you had a terminal disease.

Then there is the matter of supporting yourself. Nurturing yourself is as important as having others nurture you. It is said you need hugs every day but that's not the only way to receive support. It's a kind of support that tends to be very internal and more subtle in nature than physically or mentally doing things for yourself. It is where you develop the resources to sustain yourself when you feel that you have nothing left. It is where you develop what is necessary to dig deep into yourself and summon up all the courage in your body and mind to keep on keeping on.

Perhaps this ability comes from your ancestral heritage, or it may come from your family or close associates. It may come from deep inside of you, from a place that you didn't know existed. In the moment you experience this internal support that is older and wiser than you, grab its strength so you can make it a part of who you are. Once you have experienced having this internal source of strength and support, you will find that quality within yourself every time you need it. You'll remember what it feels like, and that memory alone will make you stronger.

Letting Go, Forgive & Surrender (Center)

Almost by accident we discover that more is less when we begin to assess where we are on the map of life. Too much of any one of the squares makes us tilt too close to one area of life and away from the others, until we are desperate again for level ground. It is this desperation that precipitates our letting go. Letting go of the attachment to the square that draws us too close is the beginning of attaining balance.

For instance, letting go on a physical level in wealth and prosperity might mean giving something away, or tithing, or even throwing something away. Being pulled to acquire more and more material possessions might be taking away from the opportunity to travel and meet helpful people because there is little money left for the fare.

Letting go on the mental level in Wealth and Prosperity might mean adopting the attitude it takes to make a budget and plan out expenditures to match your income. As boring as it sounds, this acceptance of your current situation is a big step in the maturing it takes to balance your life and forgive yourself for allowing the situation to happen. Like the story of the talents, God rewards those who have been good stewards of that which they've been given.

On the spiritual level, the letting go in wealth and prosperity might mean a recognizing of knowing that you will be provided for through your trust in the divine. It is through this inner knowing, this most basic component of faith, that you come to understand that you are never alone and that there are no mistakes.

Everything has meaning and there are no divine accidents. We are always free to choose what to feel or say or do. But it is in the moment when we finally surrender and listen to our inner guidance that we are in synch with the divine and get back on tract.

Remember the ancient oriental story of the red thread that connects everyone and everything: it is still weaving a beautiful tapestry that you have yet to admire.

Now About You—The Next Step in the Dance

Recognize and embody the emotional state associated with a square to achieve what is missing in that area of your life.

Wealth & Prosperity—Gratitude

I will list in a journal (or say aloud) all the things and people I have to be grateful for right now, no matter how small. How can I become even more grateful each day?

Fame & Reputation—Authenticity

Tomorrow I will be the real me with at least one person. How can I show who I am even more authentically?

Love & Relationship—Receptivity

I will not negate the next compliment I receive by saying "This old thing," or "It's nothing." What else can I change to be able to receive even more love?

Health & Family—Support

Tomorrow I will ask for help when I need it and not let anyone cross my personal boundary. How do I ask for more support from others and still continue to stand up for myself even more?

Creativity & Children—Joy

Tomorrow I will find and do one thing that gives me joy. What can I do to have even more fun?

Knowledge & Self cultivation—Introspection

Tomorrow I will thank myself by doing something special for myself that doesn't cost over $10.00. What else can I do to know and nurture myself even more?

Career—Passion

Tomorrow I will show or tell another person about my favorite thing with passion. What can I feel even more passionate about today?

Helpful People & Travel—Synchronistic Awareness

Tomorrow I will start to mentally note or write down all of the tiny miracles and coincidences I experience with things and people. How can I notice even more synchronistic connections and relationships in my life?

Mastery

CHAPTER 14

Finding Your Balance

*I*T IS THE STRIVING that matters. Feng Shui does not help you with that for which you are striving. It is like the currents of the ocean that can carry your ship, it is neither your ship, nor your destination, but rather the medium through which you travel to move forward.

Remember one of the fundamental principles of Feng Shui is consistent and constant change. Change is the only constant in life. As contradictory as that sounds, it is true. Nothing stays the same for long because balance is, at best, momentary. By definition, balance requires that all the many variables in our lives be in a particular relationship to one another. Any change in any of them changes all of them. But change is always happening, so balance is always either about to be achieved or about to be shifted. While some people confront this fundamental reality and come away feeling defeated by it, others embrace it and are invigorated by it. It does not matter where you start or where there was a set back, a challenge, or a blockage. Each of these moments represents a simple turning of the cube.

The cube?

When I am explaining this idea to people, I often ask them to remember the "toy" (It was hardly a toy!) called the Rubik's Cube that was very popular a number of years ago. This cube is designed so that, through the manipulation of all the lateral and horizontal planes, you can align the cube so that each of the six sides is represented by a single color. Without a successful manipulation, each side of the cube is a checkerboard of up to six colors.

In Feng Shui, there is no perfect place. There is no once and for all perfect space defined by harmony, health, wealth, and happiness. That sense of perfection and contentment is a fleeting feeling that results from moments when the aspects of your life seem to fall into place, when your life is like the solution to the Rubik's Cube.

There are wondrous moments when your life seems to be in perfect harmony, when everything is as close to perfect as it could get, when it is so near perfect that it almost hurts. At those moments, the cube of your life is solved, each side having its own pure, perfect color. When you experience those moments, you want to hold onto them. You want to freeze them in time and space forever. You even fear that your very breathing will shift the balance, so you whisper a prayer simply to stop the shifting of the many faces on the cube. Stop twisting. Freeze frame. It may freeze, but only for a fleeting moment. No matter how wonderful it feels to finally get it right, the inevitable shifting of the cube eventually begins anew. When that happens, when the cube starts to turn again, you can only remember what it was like to have it all right, then rely on that feeling as an inspiration to continue to strive for that balance again.

It is like a dance. A constant to and fro. If you are intimately involved in the dance, you react automatically to the subtle and not-so-subtle shifts in life. You are always engaged in the process. Then the shifts do not seem to be such dramatic lurches. Events and circumstances do not throw you horribly off balance because you are already in the process of engaging in remaining in balance.

That is the beauty of Feng Shui. Once you have begun the dance, the map shows you the steps for balancing your life. You don't need gurus. You don't need special beads, mantras, or blankets. There is nothing mystical or strange about it. You can engage the Feng Shui process of living while continuing to enjoy the faith in which you are comfortable.

Feng Shui is completely rational. You can sort it out using your mind. It does not require a leap of faith, only an acknowledgement that the energy of life flows through everything, that you share a connection with the rest of the living world. The logic of Feng Shui is the logic of life: All things change. Feng Shui helps identify the tools you need to maintain balance in the context of this change.

When the energy in a room is completely balanced, it is a feeling unlike any other. It is calm, yet ripe with potential. It is exciting, yet comfortable. It is completely alive, yet completely serene. Imagine the sensation of the most comfortable sanctuary combined with the excitement of a first date. Imagine the juxtaposition of sitting still in a quiet room while riding on a roller coaster. All things are possible in a space that is completely balanced, and all things are realized.

To experience such a balance is to alter your perspective on the world in which you live and the space through which you move. It is to change how you react and respond to your world and your space. And, as you will discover, when you change how you react to the world, the world changes how it responds to you.

To experience a balanced space is to become your surroundings. This inevitably leads to a closer attention to detail. The phrase, "God is in the details," takes on incredible meaning, because its truth is not simply trivially true but profoundly true. If your home is cluttered in certain areas, particular areas of your life will likewise be cluttered. If your office or your desk is in chaos, it should not surprise you to discover that your business or your finances are in a similar state of confusion. If you haven't shifted your furniture for years, you may, upon reflection, realize that your relationships are likewise stuck and not moving forward.

"Alright," one of my clients said, "suppose I accept what you're saying. How is Feng Shui more than simply moving things around and feeling better about it?"

"Feeling better about it is the result of the change in energy," I explained. "As for how Feng Shui relates to your life and not only your furniture—well, Feng Shui is all about leading a balanced life, a life that allows you to realize your goals and your dreams. The goal of Feng Shui is for you to get whatever it is you truly want from life. Using the tools of Feng Shui allows you to create the physical surroundings that will support getting what you want from life."

Surroundings speak to us as clearly as any person. We only need to learn how to listen in order to understand what our surroundings are saying. Paying attention at all times is very important so we don't miss a very important lesson. For example, every time you walk by that unused treadmill, it is whispering to you, "Aren't you getting a little thick around the middle?"

"That's guilt," my client argued. "After all, I might have purchased that treadmill knowing that I was a few pounds overweight. I might have resolved to use it regularly. I might even have begun doing so but, over time, I fell back into bad habits. So, that treadmill is a reminder of what I should be doing but I'm not. It's natural to feel guilty."

"Of course it is," I agreed. "The difference between your understanding and mine is that you believe that the feeling of guilt begins and ends within you. I know that the feeling is also the result of the energy blockage in the space that is the result of the unused treadmill. Removing the treadmill will free up the energy in the room and in your mind by not reminding you constantly that you are not exercising."

That treadmill is obviously an ever-present reminder of goals unmet, as are other examples that speak just as clearly in other ways. The heightened stress created in offices by misplaced desks and workspaces, for example. A simple adjustment in which every desk is situated in the power position so that it faces the entrance to the room will reduce a tremendous amount of that stress and anxiety. The fight, flight or freeze syndrome is no longer something activated by having your back to the door. Simple adjustments in furniture or cubicle workspace can enable the redirection of energy so that a calmer atmosphere prevails.

Everything in your home and work environment talks to you constantly. It is your responsibility—and to your benefit—to ensure that your environments speak to you in supportive and positive ways. Negative space is as damaging in your life as being around negative people.

Have you ever spent a lot of time with someone who constantly complains? Have you ever "mapped" the way you try to react and respond to that person? At first, you try to be supportive and suggest methods to improve the source of the complaints. Then you become worn down when that is not successful. Then you feel drained of your positive energy. You begin to complain about the complainer. You resent the time you spend in their presence. You become miserable. Your negative feelings begin to seep into other areas of your life, even if only by virtue of the fact that you complain about that person even when you're not around them!

Negative energy in your home or work environment accomplishes the same thing. It wears you down. It drains you of your positive energy. It exhausts you because you have to use up so much energy just to maintain some equilibrium. Over time, your body takes on the energy patterns of your home or your office. Is your home worn down, overwhelmed, or lethargic and stuck in negative patterns? Are you?

The opposite is true when you are around a creative and positive person. You are enriched and enlivened by his or her presence. You are up and filled with energy. Likewise, when you are in a space that is filled with unobstructed positive energy, you are energized yourself.

A simple example of what I mean by this was quite literally brought home to me by a new acquaintance of mine who had come to my home as a guest at a holiday party. She told me later how it felt to be in a Feng Shui consultant's home.

"You know, Annie, it just felt so comfortable. The moment I walked into your home, I felt like I could take off my coat and go straight up to the guest bedroom and take a nap if I wanted to."

I laughed. "You wouldn't have been the first to take a nap up there," I told her.

"It wasn't that I was tired," she went on. " I felt relaxed and comfortable, safe. I knew I would be fine. I told my friend how you had told Emily [the young child who had come with her] to go upstairs and see if she could find the cats. You explained to her how they liked to hide under things, and to see them, she'd have to find them.

"Your house gave me a feeling of comfort, that I was more than a guest. I wasn't only welcomed there, I was embraced. It felt good, and I wanted to stay. And Emily was thrilled to find the cats."

I was very pleased by what she was sharing with me. Certainly, my hope and intent were for my home to have exactly that positive energy.

"I couldn't quite put my finger on why your home felt so inviting," she went on to say. "Your furniture is nice, but nothing particularly noteworthy. I told my friend that I didn't feel any limitations, any barriers in the house. Your house seemed to reflect exactly who you are . . . open, and honest.

"With you and your house, you get what you see. There's no pretense. No masks. No blocked areas. You don't have any hidden agendas, and neither does your home."

Those comments were wonderful to hear. They were certainly rewarding to me as a Feng Shui consultant. After all, the feeling that she described got right to the heart of what Feng Shui is: Being comfortable. Being balanced. Being safe. Feeling welcome enough to live in your own skin, wherever you are. My guest felt it. She felt the absence of boundaries and obstacles. She felt the consistent, calm, balanced energy throughout my house.

Let me be perfectly honest with you. Even as a Feng Shui consultant, I had never before achieved quite this level of balance in my home. I know from experience that living and working in a balanced environment is a heavenly feeling. I love being in my home, and yes, it is Feng Shui-compliant. As a result, I don't need to go anywhere to find stimulation or to relax. Needing to get out of the house is now a foreign idea to me as I am complete right here. The fact that I also work from my house is a bonus for which I am grateful each and every day. I find that working from my home is like being in a warm, comfortable bath.

It was not long ago that my body had first felt this complete sense of total relaxation and peace, so you can imagine my delight in re-capturing the feeling I now enjoy in my home.

That first time was during a walk on the beach in Jamaica. The day was perfection. The sun's warmth caressed my skin as I walked along the shore. The crystal blue water rolled up over my bare feet. The breeze brushed back my hair and rustled through the nearby vegetation. I felt as if I had been placed there to enjoy a moment of God's loveliest creation. There was perfection in nature and form. It was balanced, calm, and peaceful. That stretch of beach was the essence of Feng Shui.

As I walked along, I was conscious of not having a care in the world. I was aware of thinking that life doesn't get any better than this. But these conscious thoughts receded with each footstep as my body responded more and more to the environment. My body responded to the energy of that place the way a baby responds to the gentle rocking of its mother. I was totally safe and secure.

The only other time I came close to such a feeling was during a seminar I attended. The speaker invited us to close our eyes and to create a safe place. The instructions were simple: Conjure up a place where we could go to be free of the stress, the fear, the exhaustion of the world.

Once again, I found myself on a beach, this time in an A-frame house. I was aware of the duality of my reverie, a mountain cabin with large windows, set in the sun and the sand and an exquisite garden, lush with tropical plants. Perhaps it was an odd combination—the mountains and the sea—but it worked wonderfully for me. Imagining myself there allowed me once again to feel those feelings of safety, harmony, peace, and contentment.

My home now recreates the feeling of those places. Not because it physically resembles either of those places—neither the real beach in Jamaica nor the imaginary place that brought together the mountains and the sea—but because the unencumbered energy of all these places is equivalent. I was able to free the energy in my home by following the process laid out in Feng Shui. Over time, in the process of making my house Feng Shui-compliant, I have become more and more like my surroundings: easy going, content, and calm.

You, too, can create an environment that makes your body respond to the surrounding energy. To create such an environment, every move should be deliberate and conscious. Every item and piece of furniture should be put in place with clear intent. Each and every accessory should be put in place for maximum impact, using only the things you love. And, most importantly, the space should be completely designed to make you feel the most pleasure and harmony possible.

This ability to create such a space is what the application of Feng Shui offers you. You can work and live your daily life in a sense of peace and awe at how magnificent and precious your body and life really are. You can design how you want to act in the world by designing your surroundings with specific and deliberate choices.

To begin to create such a space, you must slow down long enough to pay attention to your surroundings. You must learn to listen to the objects that exist in your space. By taking the time to listen, you can determine what your home currently says to you. Then, you must decide what you want it to say. Would the person you want to become have this art work on the wall? How would they live? Would there be a week's mail accumulating on the kitchen counter? What about their laundry habits?

You can then make a conscious decision about where you want to go and what kind of life you want to live. Once you have made that fundamental decision, you can adjust your surroundings to support the energy that will attract this kind of life to you.

You must create the space that you envision the person you want to be would live in!

Remember, the destination is not so important, it is the walk that has meaning. It's what you do with your life while you are traveling that makes all the difference. Feng Shui gives you a map that will help you get to where and what you want faster. It will help you make the decisions that will create your surroundings to become representative of the you that you want to become today.

When you incorporate those tools and those changes, when you create your world to manifest who you want to become, you will find that you will become that person, and more quickly than you thought possible.

Now About You—The Next Step in the Dance

Imagine how you will change yourself and your environment to match the kind of home and work life of a transformed future you.

Many people find it challenging when asked, "What do you want?" This exercise is a proven method that makes it easier not only to get excited about the process but to determine what you would like. Know that any choices you make can be changed so there is no such thing as not knowing or not choosing because there may be something better.

When determining what you would like to be, do, or have in life, use phrases like: I have; I appear; I feel; I take; I ask; I act; I deal with; I do; I say; I let go of; and any others that help you define yourself, what you want to accomplish, or what you want to have.

What do you imagine the home or office of the person who you just described look like? Go back over each of your answers and then identify at least one thing in your current home you could change that would more represent the kind of person who has that same thing.

Transformation

CHAPTER 15

Alleviating the Blockage

ENG SHUI IS AN external catalyst that triggers an internal change in the perception of an event, a circumstance, or a desire. By adjusting the interaction of the three levels—common sense/physical, psychological (mental/emotional), and spiritual—you are able to bring them into balance.

But don't assume that this balance is a once-and-for-all thing. Balance in life is a lot like balance on a tightrope. Each step changes the dynamics and requires adjustments to maintain balance. It is the process of seeking, finding, and maintaining balance that is important. It is this process that puts us in control of our lives. We are not balanced, we are in balance as a result of our intent to maintain balance. We are in charge of our lives. We have infinite choices.

In Chapter 10 Susan accomplished more by her decision to make small changes in that one room of her house than she did in any of the specific changes she made. She didn't force her husband to cancel the meeting and stay home, he decided that on his own. Moving the furniture got them talking because it was the fact that there were changes, not what the changes were, that first caught Larry's attention. It was clear in the shift in Susan's personal energy that she had been the instrument of change. Susan had accomplished that simply by her determination to make a change. In other words, the intent to incorporate change is the first and most important change that you can make. Decide to change. That, in and of itself, is change and, by itself, is the first and most difficult step to take.

The thought to create a different outcome in any life area creates not only decisions about that area but physical activity in that space to support your new intentions. Sometimes you can do all the right things and nothing happens because there is an outside event over which you have little control that has upset the energy flow in your life. When this happens, a blockage has occurred.

My friend Jane experienced such a blockage not long after first working with Feng Shui. Jane had been married for more than twenty years when she discovered that her husband had been spending a little too much time with his secretary. The divorce, while amicable on the surface, was deeply painful to Jane. Perhaps most difficult was the fact that her two children were both out of the house at college. Suddenly, she felt very alone and vulnerable.

"At first, I liked the fact that the house was unchanged," she told me. "It was comforting. Oh, I was plenty angry with Rick, but still, it was the life I was most used to."

When I began working with Jane, I helped her rearrange the space of the house to allow her energy to flow through it.

"It was wonderful, Annie," she told me when I saw her again not long ago. "The whole sense and excitement of renewal. My house was "my" home. Not "our" home. The rooms were open and free. I felt so wonderful being there. And then, I don't know what happened. The room that I loved the most, my bedroom, just lost its energy. I was having trouble sleeping. I couldn't concentrate on the things I was reading."

The more we spoke, the more I came to understand what had happened. The changes that Jane made in her home reflected the energy and needs she had after going through a difficult divorce. Her renewed energy helped motivate her to return to school and finish a degree that she had put on hold in order to raise her two children. Along with her degree, she was able to find a more interesting and exciting job.

"I was in a management position for the first time in my life," she told me. "There were plenty of mornings when I felt nervous and scared, you can be sure of that. But every evening, I was able to come home and realize that I had accomplished most of what I had hoped to accomplish that day."

The problems began to occur when she realized that she was no longer the person she had been right after her divorce.

"I was still young, after all," she said. "I married Bob when I was twenty. I learned about his relationship with his secretary when I was forty."

Jane not only was relatively young, but she also had taken care of herself, exercising, eating well, doing things that she found interesting. As a result, she was still very attractive, both physically and intellectually. Needless to say, however, she didn't feel particularly attractive right after her divorce.

It was only by brightening up her house and filling it with things that had meaning for her that the positive energy around her restored her confidence in herself.

"Right after the divorce, when I went back to school, I was so self-conscious of being older than the other students. One of my teachers asked me if I'd like to have coffee after class. My mind was so far away from any thoughts of romance that I thought he wanted to discuss my work in class. I declined, telling him that I would try to improve my test scores."

Jane smiled when she related that story. "He was good-looking too. I liked him. But in my wildest imagination, I couldn't picture him interested in me."

As time went on, however, the positive energy in her life, coupled with her accomplishments, helped her begin to see herself as attractive on several levels. She realized that she missed the positive things about a close relationship with a man. A man with whom she worked began to attract her attention. They spoke often at work, and as time went on, their conversations often strayed far beyond work-related matters.

"Ed was interested in so many things I'd always wanted to learn more about—art, music, the theater. And he clearly was interested in me."

They went out a few times. Then, feeling the attraction growing more powerful, Jane invited him to her house. And the relationship lost its spark.

"It wasn't that anything went wrong," she said. "It was just that . . ." She couldn't quite find the words. "It didn't feel right."

What happened, quite simply, was that the balance Jane had worked so hard to achieve after the divorce had been altered by the changes in her life, even though they were positive changes. As a result, the space that she occupied had also been thrown off balance. In order to accommodate the change in her life, she needed to turn her attention to the bagua once again and adjust her space accordingly.

Not all change is bad. Certainly, the changes that occurred in Jane's life were anything but bad. They were a positive step. She wanted to have a relationship again, and she deserved to have one. However, when she invited someone new into her life, that new relationship threw off the balance that she had worked so hard to gain. She was, in short, nearly thrown off the tightrope.

"I could understand my divorce throwing me for a loop," she said to me. "But this?"

I nodded my head. "Yes," I told her. "Anything and everything in life is variable. Everything keeps changing. That's not a bad thing. It just is. Most of the time, we focus on the changes in life that are due to sad events, but both kinds of change are an inevitable part of life."

A mother raises her children and they grow up and leave for college. When they leave, her life is very different. The dynamic that has defined her for so many years has changed. The change, while filling her with a kind of nostalgia, is anything but a bad change. It is the result of the inevitable growth and development of her children. It is the result of her doing a very good job. But, with that shift in balance, comes the need for adjustment, for rebalancing. Put another way, with that shift comes the need for continued maintenance of the energy flow.

We are, first and foremost, physical beings. We live in this material world. When we reach a blockage, the only thing to do is to go back to level one (the physical level, the bagua itself) and begin anew in that area of our lives.

Eliot, an old friend of mine, found himself struggling against a very significant genetic reality, he was going bald. And this was in the days before Rogaine!

"I couldn't stand it," he complained to me. "Oh, I know it is only vanity but every time my drain clogged with hair I felt defeated."

In an attempt to combat his thinning hair, he used every sort of concoction he could put his hands on. He took vitamins. He applied ointments to his scalp. He used special shampoos. He had his hair cut to maximize its remaining thickness. He became one of those people who combed the hair over from the side.

His determination—his wife said, obsession—with hiding his baldness began to limit his activities. He refused to go swimming. He hated going out on windy days. He felt self-conscious meeting new people.

He hated seeing people he had known when he was young, convinced that they were snickering about his hair loss behind his back.

Finally, he came to realize that his vanity was throwing his entire life out of balance.

"It was ridiculous," he said.

So, he shaved his head.

"I figured, if I couldn't beat it, I'd join it."

His new look not only complimented his features, but his wife found it incredibly sexy.

"I don't care about the wind, the rain, pools, oceans. None of it matters now."

Now, his lack of hair was something he exerted control over. Not the other way around.

As women age, we face similar kinds of adjustments. We can become slaves of youth, submitting ourselves to everything from simple beauty treatments to plastic surgery, but it is not until we realize that real beauty, and I mean physical beauty too, comes from being in balance where you simply "live better in your own skin" than you used to. Our bodies gracefully accommodate those changes into their lives and the results of balance begin to appear. Trying to force ourselves to be what we once were or what we never were is a sure recipe for imbalance, and therefore, for unhappiness and stress.

For so many, divorce or death is the most apparent example of such a blockage. Like Jane, such a moment is the moment to stop and go back to square one to reevaluate the intent of your life and to refocus. Once your intent is clear, it is time to act, to do something about it.

We all have the tools. We've always had the tools. Common sense enables us to deal with things on a mental and emotional level. Faith and belief allow us to understand that there is a higher spiritual purpose to what we need to do. The challenging part is that, in this process of going back to square one to reevaluate and refocus intent, we need to apply our new vision of ourselves to every one of the nine areas of our lives, at all three levels. Feng Shui is a process. It is not a destination.

I am sometimes reminded of the conversations I had with friends when I was young. We would get together and imagine what it would be like to be grown up, with our own families. The answer to the question, "What do you want to be when you grow up?" usually was, "I want to be happy." But happy is not a destination. It is the nature of the process. Feng Shui as a process that contributes to happiness even as we deal with unhappy events and circumstances. Once you have "Feng Shui'd" your space, you can begin to experience life in a new, vital, and exciting way.

You're not "there" yet, because there is no "there" to get to, but you are "on the way," and that is exactly where you need to be. Happiness is not a destination, but a byproduct of the process. Feng Shui is the process.

Now About You—The Next Step in the Dance

Understand that letting go of things, people, behaviors, ideas, attitudes and judgments makes room for you to move to the next level of life where you can begin to attract what you desire.

Wanting change and attracting the energy of your desires takes planning in order for the new energy to stick. As you decide what you want to attract you must make room for that new energy to stay. List all the things you have put off and begin doing them one by one. You will not only immediately improve the quality of your life, you will begin to develop the personal energy necessary to hold on to what you attract.

Write a "Change My Life" list. This will immediately help you to begin changing the things in you home and office that do not match the energy of what you'd like to attract into your life.

My list of things to change as soon as possible:

Example: fix the broken garage door, clean out my office, finish my book, take a vacation, go to see my parents; tell _____, *"I love you;" tell* _____, *"I forgive you."*

PART III

*More Stories That
Could Be You*

Austerities

CHAPTER **16**

Letting It Go

L OOK AROUND YOU. WHAT do you see? A sofa? A chair? A bed? An end table? Look closer. What do you really see? A lamp? A television? A rug? A computer keyboard?

In order to really get to know your space, you must pay attention to detail, become intimate with this space you inhabit, listen to what it says to you. But what does it mean, really mean, to do this? What does it mean to become so familiar and intimate with your space that you can hear everything that it says to you? And about you.

For me, it meant touching everything in my space. Everything. From A to Z. This is what I advise my clients to do. Touch everything that inhabits their space. I do not mean to run your hands lightly over tabletops and along upholstered chairs. I mean everything.

In order to know exactly who my surroundings said I was, I had to get to know everything in my surroundings and to know everything intimately. I had to touch everything in my space, see each thing's size, shape, color, texture, and function. And, with each thing that I touched, I reinforced the decision of who I wanted to become. Which meant that, with everything that I touched, I also had to decide its fate. Would I discard it? Keep it? Cherish it? Let it become a part of defining who I was to become?

The process of touch allowed Feng Shui to change my life, again.

I knew, of course, that this thorough examination of everything in my home would not be accomplished easily, and it would not be accomplished all at once. In fact, I divided my house into rooms and approached each room distinct from the others. Only when I finally had worked my way through each room did I evaluate my entire home as one space.

I touched every knickknack I owned. Every dishtowel and potholder. Every half-used container of makeup. Every article of clothing. I touched every cleaning agent that resided under my kitchen sink and in my bathroom cabinet. I touched every towel and every blanket in the closet. I touched every pair of shoes. Every CD, cassette tape, and record album. I touched every video. Every pillow. I touched every dish. Every knife. Every fork. Every spoon. I touched every container in the pantry. Every box of cereal. Every box of pasta. Every jar of jam or jelly. I touched every pot and pan in my kitchen. Every utensil. Every spatula and measuring cup.

And I touched each of these things considerately. I was in no rush. I lingered over each and every item, for I knew that, with each, I would have to make a conscious decision as to whether it would remain in my space or whether it would be discarded, whether its time had passed in my life or whether it could help me become the person I wanted to be.

I did not evaluate anything as a group. I did not think about forks; instead, I considered each and every fork in my cutlery drawer. Why? Because the decision to have ten forks or twenty forks or twenty-five forks said something very profound about the person I wanted to be. In that respect, there was no difference in emphasis on quantity and quality. One bar of soap or three? Was I storing things up for some distant winter, or was I living each day as if it were the only day in creation? I lingered over photographs and letters, knowing that I would have to decide what their fate would be. So many things that had come to occupy—clutter?—my life would have to go. It was up to me to decide.

There were keepers, of course, things of such warmth and value that I would not part with them under any circumstance. And there were goers. Many of them. More than I could have imagined. However, I found it was relatively easy to say goodbye to these goers, once I used a deliberate process with which to judge them. Whatever value or interest they had once had for me, they were clearly no longer relevant to the person I had become, or more importantly, to the person I sought to be.

Of course, there were those things that filled me with phantom guilt, things that made me shiver to get rid of them. Things that were so rooted in the person I had been that they seemed to grip me with clenched fists. What would I do with these? Would their rootedness in the past lock me into old energy patterns? Or were they so essential to who I was that they could be roots from which I could nourish the person I would become? How could I decide?

In general, patience was the answer to any dilemma. Items for which a decision seemed impossible were simply put aside for three days. Invariably, after three days, I was clear about what to do with the previously undecided item because my energy had changed, based on the many other decisions I had made during those three days. There was no urgency. I had time to be patient, as long as I continued to move forward. As long as I remained in the process, I was fine.

Throughout the process, I came to realize how much stuff had come to clutter my life. I had matchbooks from restaurants that no longer existed. I had postcards that had been written by people I had not spoken to in a decade or more. I had drawers full of menus from Chinese and Italian restaurants.

"My heavens, where did I get all this stuff?" I asked myself over and over.

I knew the answer. Like the barnacles that cling to rocks at the shore, these things had clung to me and, because I didn't bother to shake them loose, they stayed. Life had rolled them all into my life like the tide brings the barnacles to the reef. I was constantly amazed at how much stuff was in my home that had absolutely no meaning to me whatsoever. No practical benefit. No spiritual aspect. No psychological relief. Some of that stuff was just taking up space, taking up energy. My energy.

Well, I wasn't sharing anymore!

All that stuff defined who I was, and I wasn't happy with the definition. Not one bit. If I didn't know why something was there in my space and in my life, I could not think of a reason to keep it. So I didn't. After all, what good could it do for me to cling to something like that? The criterion that I worked with was not that I would keep something if it did no harm. It was: If it does not contribute to who I am now or want to become, then I will let it go. I wanted only positive energy, positive contributions to who I was and who I wanted to be.

I asked the question as I touched every single one of the hundreds of items in my home. Does this contribute to who I am now or who I want to become? If not, then it was gone. It became a compulsive mission for me to practice exactly what I preached and taught to others. I was determined to do more than simply talk the talk of Feng Shui. I was determined to walk the walk. That was the me I wanted to become, a me who was consistent with what I believed. I wanted to *be* the talk.

There were many times that I felt my energy flag, when I wanted to say, "Enough! I have done enough!" But I would not allow myself to cut corners or stop short of my goal. Facing what I would come to refer to as my catharsis, I knew I had to keep on until the task was complete. If I did not, then I knew I was doomed to fall back into the negative energy patterns of my previous surroundings. And that, I was unwilling to do.

So I continued going through each and every one of my possessions, one at a time. I kept only those things that made me feel good. No matter what the cost, financially or emotionally, I held to that standard. I threw out, sold, or gave away everything that had no place in my new life. I prayed to God for the strength to make it through what was an emotionally arduous process. When I have been asked what that experience was like, the only analogy I've come up with is that it was like going through a divorce—a divorce from myself, a divorce from the me I no longer wanted to be. And, as in a divorce, I went through moments of sadness, anger, determination, and exhilaration. I did not call it my catharsis lightly!

I faced what was, perhaps, the most difficult task when I came to my bookshelves. I have been a lifelong lover of books. I love to read, and I enjoy the sensation of having a book in my hands. Over the years, I had acquired thousands of volumes. I had novels, biographies, autobiographies, reference books, poetry books. My shelves were lined with stories as old as The Canterbury Tales and Greek Myths and as new as last year's bestsellers. I enjoyed books about gardening and basic hardware. I had several copies of the Bible and the Koran, plus the Bhagavad-Gita, and several other sacred texts. I collected how-to books about everything from candle making to macramé.

When I stood and faced my books, I realized that they were like visas in a passport. They were physical reminders of the places I had been, and the people I had been! How could I decide which to keep and which to give up? I stepped away from the task and instituted my three-day waiting period. During those three days, I thought long and hard about what it was that I needed to do.

"Annie, you must stick to the strictest of standards," I told myself. I could allow no waffling. I realized that, in my decisions about my books, I would be face to face with the most difficult decisions of intent. I resolved to accomplish what I had set out to accomplish.

The first to go were the novels. Then the old school texts: the psychology books, the biology books, the sociology books, the books that held me back to the person I was so long before! The poetry went next. Then the histories and the biographies. Curiously, the trashy romances were the last to find their way to the trash heap. In the end, the only books I kept from the thousands that had taken up space and energy in my home were those books that spoke to who I was now and who I wanted to become. I kept most of the sacred texts. I kept my books on Feng Shui. I clung to books that sought to address life's deepest meaning and to proclaim its greatest secrets. When I was finished, I looked at my bookshelves and realized that I had kept exactly those books that defined what I wanted to absorb from them, and I had let go of all the rest.

When I was finished with my touching, I knew perfectly what harmony felt like. I had created a new energy in my home, and my body began immediately—and unconsciously—to absorb it. Despite the physical demands of the task I had completed, my body felt light and energized. As I walked through the rooms of my house, I felt a sense of release that quickly turned to joy.

The new me also was apparent to others. From that day forward, people commented on how much more relaxed I appeared. And it was true. I was more relaxed. I was calmer, more focused. And accepting. After all, I was not being held back by someone I no longer was, someone who had become something of a stranger to me. Now, no longer burdened or constrained by the energy patterns of my former self, I was also able to accept the person I had been and to love her, which allowed me to move beyond who I had been.

Let me say this again: The task was not simple. It was rigorous. My body went into near shock during this process because of the incredible energy shifts. But was it worth it? Absolutely! I came to enjoy a sense of calm unlike anything I had ever known before. My old, destructive energy patterns had been completely banished from the new me. Living in my own skin was easier now.

Truth be known, however, it did take a while to become comfortable with that new reality. I was like a newly divorced person, glad to be rid of my former spouse and of the old me. I knew the divorce was the right thing, but honestly, there were also times I missed the marriage. Still, with each passing day, a new realization and understanding grew in me. I came to realize that all my life, I had lived in chaos, a prisoner of its unpredictability. That rattled me, but now that my space no longer supported that chaos, it could no longer claim me. I was amazed and delighted. My body shifted as the energy did, and I even lost weight—which had not been an immediate goal.

This touching process allowed me to create an environment of harmony. I still find myself in awe of the new me as I see how I react to events, situations, and people. My new energy is so much more alive than my old energy. I am forging new ground and becoming the person I have always wanted to be, the person I had always promised myself I would be. Anger no longer has a hold on me. Frustration is losing its grip day by day. In their place, love and acceptance have come to reside. Love and acceptance have changed the way I relate to the new—and old—people in my life.

It is amazing. Now, I make a point of going through the same process three times a year. (Don't worry, it gets easier each time). Each time I do it, I am reminded that most people have never known what it is like to live or work in an environment of total harmony. We simply assume the bad things are the way life is because that is all we have known. We are confused when something goes right! But that isn't the way we have to live. It isn't the way we ought to live!

Nor do our bodies usually know what harmony feels like. Feeling harmony is often confusing and frightening at first. It's like finally falling in love. At first you feel the fear of trusting. But the joy does follow and the comfort does come. The cleansing acts of letting go and forgiving do work.

Stripping away all the pretense of who you thought you were is a necessary catharsis. Once you do it, you free yourself and your body to be affected by your new, energized space. You free yourself to become your surroundings. Literally. If the fame and reputation area of your home is cluttered with dirty dishes, how can you expect new appointments and clients to come in? If something is broken or the toilet is leaking in the wealth and prosperity area, there's a slow drain on your money. If the exercise equipment is still in the love and relationship area, then you're still working too hard at loving, rather than letting yourself be loved.

Everything in your life is there for a reason. There are no mistakes. But you must supply intent to make sure that you have control over the reasons, that the reasons are reasons you want to keep in your life. Your things define you. Make sure the right things define the right you! The you, you want to become.

Walk around your house and listen. Everything there talks to you. If you really study some object in your home, you will begin to feel the meaning that object has for you. If it is a good feeling, that object stays. If it is a bad feeling, it goes. Be strict in your intent. Be certain in your faith about your ability to hear what your space is saying to you. The one thing I told myself whenever I reached an impasse, when I didn't think I could go on with touching the things in my house, was that everything I was dealing with was only stuff. Things. I could keep this thing or get rid of it. I was in control. That was an amazing realization.

This same imperative applies to other areas of your life. You must also rigorously examine your relationships. If they are good, they stay. If they are bad, they go. If you do not make this decision about everything in your life, you will live your life at the mercy of your environment, or at the mercy of other people's whims and energy.

Once you have changed your energy pattern by changing your space, you will have changed your presentation of who you are to the world. And, once you have done that, the world will respond to the new you rather than to the old you.

Feng Shui is not magic or mysterious. Feng Shui simply gives you the tools to reshape your present and your future. And you will have created it all. This is the real power and secret of Feng Shui. It requires you to decide who you are and who you want to become. Then, with your intent in place, it gives you the tools to make those changes that are necessary to transform yourself into the person you want to become. It provides a map to help you make those changes. You create it all. You are the ship. Feng Shui is the current that carries you.

Now About You—The Next Step in the Dance

You do not have to throw anything away, or give it away or sell it, but you must have a defendable reason to keep it, a place for it, and understand the ramifications of holding on to it.

Clearing out is more than de-cluttering your spaces, it is also emptying out emotional baggage you no longer need for protection, and accepting that the arrival of your heart's desires maybe on a divine timetable not in sync with your own.

When beginning to de-clutter, start small: medicine cabinet (15 minutes), top of kitchen table, linen closet (25 minutes), top of dresser (8 minutes), top bathroom sink, bathtub area (4 minutes), under the sink in the kitchen, the fireplace hearth and mantel (14 minutes), etc. Take a 5 foot radius around your favorite chair, or your bed which includes the night stands.

Do only what you can finish in one sitting: always leave the site looking better than when you started. Never leave an area messy, because it will generate even more negative clutter energy which will be absorbed into your body.

Touch everything: Everything that remains in your space needs to have a current purpose in your household, it is symbolic of a treasured memory, or contains enough positive energy that you can feel in your body.

Stack small wins: Complete one de-cluttering job and acknowledge yourself for it. Stand in the door and admire your work. Then move to the next area and do the same. Tell a friend. Pretty soon a whole room is done.

- *Three "tops of things" I can de-clutter quickly:* Nightstand, dresser, kitchen or dining room table, etc.
- *Three closed things I can de-clutter quickly:* Medicine cabinet, refrigerator, under kitchen sink, etc.
- *Three five-foot radiuses I can de-clutter quickly:* My side of the bed, beside the TV chair, etc.

殿

Sanctuary

CHAPTER 17

Remodeling Your Home and Your Life

R EMODELING OR REDECORATING ANY room in a home is a significant decision. Our homes are so much an extension of ourselves and our life force that any alteration is fraught with positive and negative potential. Even people who have no knowledge of or appreciation (at first!) for Feng Shui have an instinctive sense of this. They approach decisions about changing their home with caution and care.

What I have learned is that people frequently have a difficult time articulating what they want in the addition of space or the redecoration of a room. They want more room, but often it is not really room that they are after. They are really seeking to re-create a certain feeling that doesn't currently exist in the home. This can mean they need to find a way to tap into energy from a home where they lived previously or visited, a desire that isn't so much about space or geography as about spirituality. But how does one talk to a contractor about the spirituality of a room?

Contractors are many things, but it's expecting a lot to also require them to be attuned to the spiritual needs of their customers. The same goes for architects, who are expert at bringing issues of space and engineering into agreement, but may not be as knowledgeable about spiritual needs. As a consequence, they might not be the people to consult when it comes to the psychological consequences of a particular layout or room décor.

Not long ago, I received a phone call from Ben, a very successful businessman. I did not know this man personally, but I recognized his name immediately. He and his wife were well known in the community for bringing together disparate groups of movers and shakers. Their wealth landed them on the newspaper society pages with great regularity.

"Could you come to my home?" he asked, not beating around the bush. "I'm having a problem with my architect, and a friend of mine suggested someone who is well-versed in fung shooey." I giggled and asked him when it would be convenient for me to come over.

"Go right now if you can," he exclaimed. "Mt wife is at her wit's end there. This remodeling job has taken a turn for the worse and my friend believes you can help us."

When I arrived later that day, I found he was telling the truth. His wife, Ruth, was indeed at her wit's end. While her architect and her contractor sat at her kitchen table, examining plans, she was flitting about, very emotional. Although I had never met her before, she greeted me as if we were best friends.

"Thank God you're here!" she cried out when I walked in. "Could you please explain to these men what it is that I'm after here?"

The two men looked at me with a mixture of annoyance and expectation. I shrugged my shoulders at them and turned to Ruth. "Why don't we start with you telling me a little about what you'd like done here?"

She sighed deeply. "I simply hate our kitchen and dining room. I have since these two redid them nearly five years ago. My goodness, five years! Oh, we had the most glorious parties then!" She went on to mention the names of actors and lawyers and authors who had once visited their house, enjoying their unique hospitality. "But since the kitchen and dining room were redone, there is simply no frisson. Our parties even bore us! I don't know how we've put up with it until now. But we can't bear it another moment. Now, we are determined to redo it right. The problem is, I am at a loss to explain to them what it means to do it right."

I glanced around the rooms to be redone. As I might have expected, they were constructed and decorated in exquisite detail. But they didn't feel right.

"Why did you have the rooms redone five years ago?" I asked her.

She told me about an unfortunate kitchen fire, something to do with clumsy help and baked Alaska.

"Most of the damage was smoke related," she said. "But the fire department also had to damage some walls to make sure the fire was completely out. I had no choice but to redo everything."

The problem was clear to me as I walked through the rest of the house while we talked. Although she'd had no choice but to redo the rooms in question, her architect and contractor had talked her into a different tone, a different style. And that tone and style did not fit the house or her.

Ben and Ruth's home previously had been a very true extension of their personalities, but the fire remodeling work had somehow disconnected what had once been a harmonious whole. Now, they were determined to get that harmony back.

As I spoke to the architect and the contractor, they expressed frustration with Ruth.

"No matter what I suggest, all she says is that it isn't right," the architect complained. "Well, I can appreciate her difficulty, but it is nearly impossible to design something based on someone telling you that something else isn't quite right."

"May I see the plans?" I asked.

Both men stepped aside. "Feel free," the contractor said.

"If you have any questions, please ask," the architect said.

The difficulty Ruth was having with explaining herself put her architect and contractor in a difficult position. They were good at what they did, but they were not therapists, and they were not sensitive to the same things that I was sensitive to in her space. Feng Shui helped identify the energy patterns and the flow of the space. The feelings that Ruth was having so much trouble articulating were more about the atmosphere she wanted her parties to have.

The problem is, when these expectations are not articulated they cannot be reflected in the final work. Then everyone is left feeling let down. Rather than solving the problem the work was designed to solve, the construction makes matters worse. And everyone is disappointed, builder, architect, and client. The builder mutters about why the client is never satisfied, and the client complains that the builder doesn't understand.

The reality is the contractor/builder often does exactly what he said he would. He creates the physical structure that the architect has designed, and more often than not, he has created it expertly. The trouble is that it is never only the physical space that is important. Equally important is the feeling that the client wanted the architect and the contractor to bring into reality. Ruth and Ben were happy with the quality of the work that the architect and contractor had performed. However, this time they wanted to be happy with the final product.

They realized that it lacked a certain feeling they wanted, and they desperately did not want that to happen again.

"Maybe it's me," she confided to me. "Look around you. The work is lovely. Everything. But it just . . . it just doesn't feel right. And it isn't only us. Our parties are mere shadows of what they used to be—no matter who is here."

Ruth was anxious to move forward with the construction, but she also was afraid of moving forward with it. Ben had suggested that she meet with the contractors to express her specific ideas. But the truth was she didn't know what she wanted the kitchen and dining room to be like. All she knew was that she wanted them to bring back a reality into her life that had been there once before.

"Oh, I thought about redoing them exactly as they were before the fire," she said. "But somehow that didn't feel right either."

On that point, she was correct. Duplication isn't the answer in such a situation. Even if she wanted to recreate the same feeling the rooms had had years before, she was not the same person she was then. Simply replicating how the rooms looked before the fire would not have allowed the energy to flow in the way that Ruth now needed, because she had grown and so had Ben.

The first thing I decided to do was to adjust her current kitchen and dining room space. I went around the two rooms, moving things, rearranging things, allowing for a more successful flow of energy. When I was finished, she said one word: "Yes." In the process of making those small, often subtle adjustments, I demonstrated to the architect a clearer way to achieve Ruth's goals. With only a few small changes, he was able to adapt the new plans to allow for the kind of energy flow for which Ruth was looking.

"Yes," she sighed, closing her eyes and standing in the middle of her soon-to-be-remodeled space. "Yes, I can feel the new energy already."

Although she, the architect, and the contractor were all amazed at how much difference small changes could make, she was perfectly comfortable with it. I had managed to make concrete the feeling for which she was groping.

Several months later, I was invited to a dinner party at Ruth's home. It was an eclectic gathering of people, some well known, and others, like me, not known beyond their own neighborhoods. The architect and contractor were there as well.

"Can't you feel it?" she asked me at one point.

I smiled. Of course I could feel it, that frisson, that shudder of excitement that Ben and Ruth had been hoping to recreate. It was back. The kitchen and dining room were very different than they had been five years before, but the energy was the same.

The feeling is all about the energy, not the construction. The vision of the client has to match what the architect designs and the builder builds or there is incongruence. It's that incongruence that makes a space feel wrong.

Charles was one of my favorite clients. He was one of those computer people who could make laptops sing. I envied his technological abilities as I watched him manipulate my website like I move furniture. Little did I realize that his proficiency with computers was where his office proficiency stopped.

"Annie," he said on the other end of the telephone, "this is a business call about my office at work. I'll probably talk to you about my home office also, but it's the one at the company that's the issue right now."

"How can I help Charles?" I said.

"Well, I've hit a wall," he replied.

"What do you mean?" I asked.

"I've hit a wall like the one that happens to marathon runners," he added. "And it's a literal wall of papers."

What a great analogy I thought. Paper for some people becomes their great Achilles' heel, their downfall. I arranged to go to his office on the weekend because during the week his company is alive with all kinds of technical people like a beehive.

"I see what you mean," I said when I got to the door of his office.

He had a window, though you couldn't get to it to pull the blinds. And I think there was a credenza somewhere behind his desk. I was glad he'd bought the file archive boxes I had requested he get.

As he cleared a chair for me to sit down he said, "Do you think there's hope?" We both laughed out loud and that broke the tension of his nervousness.

"Of course," I said, "We'll have you back up and running by tonight. You may have some homework, but I guarantee you'll feel 100% different." Then we went to work.

First I had Charles explain what kinds of things he did in the office, how his day started and what happened as it progressed. We talked about the specific tasks he accomplished and what he needed to do. I needed to get a sense of what the priorities were and how they would best fit into his space.

We did some basic things first. We moved the paper intact from it's various locations in the office out to the hall. We grouped all the papers on the desk together, all the papers on the credenza were handled the same, and lastly the papers from the office floor were separated by area.

The next step was to move the furniture. The desk went into the power position facing the door. The credenza was not placed behind the desk, but to the side, to allow for more mobility behind the desk and room for two short bookcases. The computer area was adjacent to the desk area and now had more free floor space around it and more horizontal surfaces nearby to spread out.

I explained to him that we were going to set up the room according to how he needed to work with task specific areas. The desk would have a work function as would the computer area. The credenza would be used for something specific not just as a flat surface to collect papers.

Charles had gotten so used to having so many papers in front of him that he had resorted to putting the important stuff on the floor. We changed that procedure by using the tops of the bookcases behind him. Now he would know that whatever was on the top of the bookcases need to be done first.

Other projects—of which he had many—went on the shelves below. Now he had a project area for hot projects to do right away, and a separate area for the ones that were important but not critical. When they became critical he would bump them up a shelf.

I knew the desk would be a challenge to keep clean so we talked at length about finding a place to put everything where he could see it. He is one of those people that has to see his work or he doesn't remember having what he has to do—out of sight and out of mind!

Slowly we began to bring things back into the office, starting with the projects, placing them one by one in the place we decided would house them best. There wasn't much paper left as we continued to empty the hall, and I noticed that Charles was beginning to become more relaxed as he sat every chance he got behind his desk.

"Come on keep bringing papers in Charles . . . you're supposed to be sorting." I said.

"I know, but I like sitting at my desk now . . . see?" he laughed.

Yes I knew. That always happens. We broke the old energy patterns that were being stuck in the corners and everywhere the papers prohibited movement. By now he was left with only three boxes to sort. Not bad for a complete office.

"I'll be able to do more work now," he said.

I replied, "But now it won't feel so much like work Charles."

Now About You—The Next Step in the Dance

Making the space reflect the energy you want to feel is the first step in a remodeling or decorating project.

Define what you want the feel of the space to be. Collect pictures from magazines; write out a description of the result the end product will produce. Work backwards in fitting the space to your needs, dreams, and desires rather than letting the space dictate to you.

Go to building expos to get additional ideas of what the result will look like, and remember store displays and models are always designed to have good energy. You want to make sure the energy you are buying/designing will work for you back in your home, that you are not buying the store energy.

How do I want this space to feel?

What am I going to do in this room?

Who is going to use this space? For what purpose?

When did I start wanting to make this change?*

Why do I want to this change?

---

* If the desire to make this major change began around the time of a major life event, wait three days. Ask yourself these questions again before proceeding, then go with your gut, because your body never lies. The energy of your desire may be mixed up with the energy of the event and you will be either trading or substituting energies, still not getting what you want.

Chameleon

CHAPTER **18**

Subtle Effects of Floor Plans

*D*INAH AND I HAVE known each other a long time. We live in the same community and cross paths often. We have never been close friends, but our interactions have always been friendly and pleasant.

Not long ago, I went into a local bookstore in my constant search for interesting, new things to read. As I prowled the aisles, I almost tripped over someone who was on her knees, studying the titles of the books on the bottom shelf.

"Dinah!" I exclaimed, surprised both at almost tripping over her and at discovering that I knew her.

"Annie!" she said, smiling almost furtively.

"I'm sorry, I didn't even see you there," I apologized. "I was reading the back cover of this book I'm interested in."

She waved away my apology. "Oh, don't worry. I shouldn't have been huddled like that on the floor."

"What had you so interested down there?" I asked.

She sighed deeply. Then she glanced up at the sign that indicated the section of the bookstore we were in: Nutrition and Diet.

I had always had the sense that Dinah was a cook. I don't know if I had overheard someone mention to me what a wonderful cook she was or if in one of our brief encounters we had discussed food, but I was sure that that was something that I knew about her. In truth, she was the exact image of someone who loves good, nutritious food.

She is not particularly tall but a good size for her frame, which is a little wide at her hips and with the kind of comfortable weight that comes with eating and living well. She is always dressed in comfortable, loose shirts and blouses and flowing skirts so I certainly could never make a more detailed impression regarding her body type or size.

"There are so many wonderful cookbooks here," I noted, glancing at the shelves and recognizing a number of books that were familiar to me, some of which had even found their way into my own kitchen.

There were bread making books, oriental and middle-eastern cooking books, vegetarian books—a full range of the kinds of cooking and baking that makes you breathe deeply on a brisk, autumn day.

"Yes," Dinah nodded, none too happily. "There are a lot of wonderful books about cooking."

I frowned. "What's the matter?"

Dinah made an attempt at smiling. "Well, I don't know if you remember but I do love to cook . . ."

"Of course I remember," I told her.

She managed a genuine smile then, "Well, the problem with loving to cook is that I also love to eat . . ." At that point, she glanced down guiltily toward the titles that she'd really been looking at.

As I followed her glance, I saw the rows of diet books. All kinds of diets. Low fat. Low carbohydrate. Eat all you want diets. Diet on less than 500 calories a day. The co-dependency diet. You name it, there were diet books for everyone there. The only problem, as I came to learn from Dinah, was that she'd tried most of them and none of them worked for her.

"And I do exercise," she said, a real urgency entering her voice. "But no matter how much I exercise or how little I eat I can't lose any weight. It is so frustrating."

Her frustration was not only evident in her voice but also in her facial expression. I felt terrible for her, not the least because I didn't think she was particularly overweight. As I've suggested, she wasn't petite by any means but she carried herself well and she always had a healthy glow to her skin.

Part of the problem is, of course, we live in a culture that nearly deifies being skinny. Body image is a big concern for many people, not only women, and not only young women. Dinah, when I bumped into her that day, was in her early forties and had two grown children, one in college and one a junior in high school.

"Feel like going for a walk?" I asked her.

She shrugged. "I'd love it," she admitted.

The fresh air outside the bookstore washed over us as we walked along the sidewalk at the shopping center. Although, on most days, I might have suggested stopping for a cup of tea or even lunch, I knew that such a suggestion would not have been welcome that day.

As we walked, we talked. At first, our conversation strayed far from dieting and diet books. This was intentional on my part. I felt that she needed a little space before she could discuss that issue objectively. However, when we were talking about her husband, the issue of her weight became part of the conversation.

"Bob's gotten onto this health and exercise kick," she explained. "And I'm really glad. I guess when he went to his doctor for his last physical, he got something of a wake up call. The doctor told him that his blood pressure was a little elevated and that his cholesterol levels were too high. The doctor suggested that, before discussing medication for those two things, that Bob evaluate his diet and exercise program and, lose a few pounds."

I had never met Dinah's husband but in our discussion, I came to recognize in him a great many men like him. A professional, he had been very focused on his career most of his life. He had managed to achieve many of his professional goals over the course of the years, rising to a position in senior management.

Of course, that rise had not been without some cost. He worked too many hours and was under too much stress. He spent too much time in a chair and on the phone, or traveling through airports where the food was anything but good for you. Despite the fact that Dinah had spent so many years cooking healthily, the main beneficiaries of her efforts were her two kids. Bob was out of the house so much that he ate most of his meals on the run, in fast food restaurants, and as snacks. The practice had resulted in too much weight and other discomforts.

But now, as he found himself firmly entrenched in middle age, he was confronted with the potential costs of his lifelong bad habits. With the same determination that had helped him become successful in business, he was goal-oriented in addressing the problem. He ate better and he engaged in a regular exercise program. When he next went to his doctor, he had lost five pounds, his blood pressure was down a bit—although not as much as the doctor would have liked yet—and his blood cholesterol levels were back within the normal range, if still "high normal." In other words, he was making positive progress.

Unfortunately, Dinah felt that she was being left behind. Like so many people who are reformed from their bad habits, Bob became nearly religious in his determination. And he expected, and wanted, Dinah to join him.

"But I can't seem to lose weight. I mean, I am so thrilled that he's eating better and taking better care of himself. I can't believe after all these years of trying to take care of myself and my kids that I'm losing ground."

Dinah and I stopped and sat on a bench next to a green area. The changing of the leaves was glorious on the thatch of trees and the lush green of the grass was uplifting. Yet, Dinah seemed not to be interested in anything at all. She seemed utterly and completely defeated.

I asked her about some of the diets she'd tried since she'd become determined to lose weight.

"I feel like I've tried them all," she said. "Carrot juice. Carbohydrates. Even the all-protein diet, which was particularly hard for me after a number of years being a vegetarian."

"Can I ask you a difficult question?" I queried.

"Go ahead," she said.

"Are you sure you have to lose weight? Maybe you are the perfect weight and body type for your frame. You certainly look healthy and fit."

"Well, thank you for that. I think that I'm honestly evaluating myself when I say I need to lose about fifteen pounds. Maybe a couple more. I don't know. This isn't about some adolescent idea of beauty. This is about my health and, frankly, it's more about my relationship with my husband," she added in a voice that dropped to a whisper.

We were both quiet for a moment. Then she suddenly brightened.

"This is terrible of me," she said. "All I'm doing is bemoaning my own fate. How rude of me! You know, I seem to remember that you were involved in something I thought was very interesting . . ."

"Feng Shui," I said.

"Yes, that's it! There was a brief passage in a book I was reading about it. It sounded very interesting."

I couldn't tell if she was simply being polite or if she'd really found such a passage to be interesting. In any case, I said that I considered Feng Shui to be a bit more than interesting.

"I had an idea of what it was about," she said. "I'm sure that my home is all wrong," she went on. "Cluttered and blocked off. I'd love for you to come by and help me with it."

Apparently, she wasn't being simply polite. She really was interested in my coming to her house and helping her address its arrangement according to the rules of Feng Shui.

We made a date for me to come to her house a week later.

I arrived at a nice, modest home situated on a nice-sized lot. The house was well-cared for and the garden was clearly one that had received a great deal of love. Although there were only a couple of things that were still blossoming this late in the season, the leaves and plants were all neatly pruned.

Because of the way the house was situated on the lot, I walked up the driveway, and, instead of using the "formal" front entrance, I immediately felt that the side entrance was the one to approach. I knocked on the door and a moment later, Dinah came and opened the door with a bright smile.

"I'm so glad you could come out. Come in, come in," she said, opening the door.

I had no sooner stepped into the house than I realized the reason that she was having so much trouble with her weight. "Dinah," I said.

"Yes?"

"Is this entrance the main entrance to your house?"

She glanced at the door behind me. "Well, it isn't the front door but it's the one we always use. It's convenient from the driveway and the garage."

I nodded solemnly.

"Is there anything the matter?" she asked, her expression clouding over with concern.

"Oh no, not the matter really. But, do you see how this entrance opens up immediately into your kitchen?"

"Absolutely," she said happily. "That's exactly the way we planned it when we remodeled the kitchen." With that, she took me on a quick tour of her kitchen, the professional stove and oven, the huge refrigerator, the food preparation area and the sink.

She had every reason to be very pleased with her kitchen. It was gorgeous. It was obviously a food lover's kitchen. It was both beautiful and utilitarian. It was obvious that a great deal of care and thought had gone into its design.

"Is there something the matter?" she asked again, seeing how I was pivoting and looking at the kitchen and the entryway.

"Has the entry way always led directly into the kitchen?" I asked.

"No," she said. "Before we remodeled, there was a little mudroom before the kitchen and another door. But we opened the wall to create more open space for the kitchen."

Although the kitchen benefited from the additional space, the Feng Shui of the area did not. Remembering that in Feng Shui everything is interrelated, I knew that the open space had not come without a price. With the way the entryway opened up directly into the kitchen, the chi, the energy of the space flowed directly into the kitchen, the cooking space. This invariably means that the emphasis in the home will be on cooking, and possibly weight gain or poor nutrition.

I broached the subject with Dinah shortly after we sat down.

"Oh my goodness, you mean my new kitchen might have something to do with my dieting problems?"

"Didn't you tell me that you have always been in good shape and that you didn't used to have the same problems keeping weight off as you do now?"

She was thoughtful for a moment. "Well, yes, yes I did."

I explained to her the way that chi-energy moved into her kitchen and how that might be having a direct impact on her weight problems. She could hardly believe that her decision to redesign her kitchen could have resulted in such an outcome, but the timing matched.

"What do I have to do?" she asked. "I don't have to take apart my whole kitchen, do I? My husband would . . . well, you know!"

"Oh, no," I said quickly. "Nothing so dramatic. What you do need to do is to find a way to break the flow of energy directly from your entryway into the kitchen."

She was quiet as she thought about what she could possibly do. "What would you suggest?"

"Hmm," I said, getting up from the chair. "Let's go have another look."

We went back into the kitchen. Where the former mudroom had been removed and there had been a doorway into the kitchen, there was still an open space. "Actually, there is a very simple solution," I said, nodding toward the open entryway. "A string of beads along here would not only block the energy but it would also capture the kitchen light and add a lovely touch to the room."

She smiled. "You're right," she said.

I saw Dinah about a month later, in the very same bookstore I had seen her previously. This time, I managed to avoid nearly tripping over her. She greeted me warmly when she saw me.

"Annie! I've been meaning to call you," she said, her voice filled with warm enthusiasm. "Several days after I saw you, I put up a rod and beads like you suggested." She smiled.

"Not only were you right about how lovely they look in my kitchen, but I've lost five pounds!"

"That's wonderful."

"I feel great," she went on. "And Bob is happy because I'm happy."

"So, what are you looking for today?" I asked her, glancing at the bookshelves.

She laughed. "Why, a book on Feng Shui of course!" Then she leaned a little closer to me. "Now that I've lost a little weight and Bob's exercise program, I think I should consider some adjustments in our bedroom as well."

"That sounds like a great idea," I said to her. Then I smiled a smile broad enough to match hers. "You look radiant, Dinah."

"Thank you. I really owe it to you," she said.

I shook my head. "You deserve the credit. You made the necessary changes . . . "

"I find it so remarkable how things work out. You know, how I bumped into you that day and how you were able to give me some insight that really has had a very important impact on my life. I'm only now beginning to realize how interconnected things truly are," she added.

"It is amazing, isn't it?" I smiled.

"Yes, it is." Then she looked at the shelves. "You wouldn't happen to be able to recommend a good book, would you?"

I was able to do exactly that, and more. Not only did I offer to come to her house and do an entire Feng Shui consulting, I also told her that I was writing my own book about Feng Shui's ability to transform lives ergonomically. Placement and neatness is everything.

"Now that's a book I want in my library!" she said.

Now About You—The Next Step in the Dance

The things, people, attitudes, beliefs, or ideas you consciously choose to allow into your environment influence who you are now and who you will become.

Understand that your space and your things are silent communicators constantly speaking to you literally, metaphorically, and symbolically. The literal intent of rooms is often established by personal and corporate history dictating their use; dining room, play room over garage (no closet), or master bedroom because it has a bath.

The metaphorical intent of the art on the walls needs to serve your highest vision of yourself. And the condition of your space may symbolically be reinforcing who you don't want to be. Your future will be determined by choosing consciously, and with intent, who and what you allow in your space. Ask yourself what your home says about you.

Site

CHAPTER **19**

The Land, the House
and the Trees

RICKI CALLED ME LONG distance while I was at a conference. She had tracked me down through my website and numerous telephone messages. She had a crisis, in her mind.

"I don't know which home to buy," she said breathlessly. "I wish you were here so you could go and see them for me. I got scared when the agent said we have to make up our minds quickly, because houses are selling so fast. What do you think?"

"First, Ricki, calm down. You'll get the right house for you. It always works that way. I used to be a real estate broker you know," I said calmingly. "There are no mistakes."

"I know! That's one of the reasons I called you for Feng Shui advice. You had a professional background in real estate for 20 years. I need all the expertise I can get!" she exclaimed.

"Tell me about your concerns," I said. Ricki then related how the first house, which was priced best, was on a cul-de-sac where the lights shone right into the front windows as people drove their cars down the street. The land was also hilly and rolled away from the house all across the rear of the home. Both things concerned her from Feng Shui books she'd read, and rightly so.

The second house was on a corner with much more traffic, but had a nicer floor plan. It was also a little more expensive, but her major concern was it had a big flat yard with too many trees and was much darker inside.

We talked for a moment about how the reason a buyer buys a home, is normally the same reason that the seller bought the home originally. So if price and low traffic were major points of her purchase, that's who she'd look for when selling house number one. If the floor plan, yard with trees and Feng Shui principles were more important she'd be better off with the second home. The resale marketability of a home is always a point in question during the purchase decision. My experience has always told me not to worry about resale, as there will always be another buyer wanting those same things when you go to sell.

"Well that doesn't help me one bit," she chided impatiently. "My agent is waiting for an answer, Annie. She thinks there may be other bidders."

"Okay Ricki, listen," I responded.

I explained the benefits of choosing the second home, even though it was more expensive, because you can change things easier. Trees can be trimmed or cut down to let light in and permit energy flow around the home. Walls can be painted in order to brighten and lighten rooms, to break up stagnant energy stuck in the darkness. And with the floor plan already very good, it sounded to me that the changes were relatively cosmetic in house number two.

In house number one the difficulty with the cul-de-sac and the car lights were permanent, as was the yard rolling away from the home. You cannot move the house, or change the topography, so any Feng Shui correction, like the symbolic hanging of a Bagua mirror outside above the door to reflect the car headlights, would only serve to remind her of the problems and the compromise she made for money. The not-quite-right floor plan was an even more complex problem, as it meant either adding-on or remodeling, not to mention major terraced landscaping in the back yard.

To me it seemed like a simple solution, but to her the price was a large factor. We then briefly looked at the potential costs associated with curing the problems of each house, and home number two proved to be the better deal and more cost effective.

Intrinsic problems aside, like the corner lot, we talked about the various solutions she could make on the interior to assure the alleviation of any depressive feelings. The ideas she got most excited about were choosing color for the walls, texture and pattern of the new window coverings, and carpeting.

"I've always wanted a bright home, and I'd love to paint the major public areas of the house a pale yellow or maize. What do you think Annie?" she asked.

"That would have been one of my solutions! You've been reading up on Feng Shui," I remarked laughing.

Pale yellow is a happy color that, in and of itself, nearly precludes depressive thoughts. That was a perfect suggestion for some of the main rooms. Also, I suggested she take a close look at relationship colors that are representative of any human skin tone for other more intimate areas such as the family room or bedrooms. Relationship colors can range from pale peach to deep terra cotta and chocolate browns, all of which provide a resting feeling to oversize rooms or rooms with vaulted ceilings.

"You can literally change your mood by alleviating darkness and cold colors or conflicting textures and patterns from a room," I explained.

Ricki, or any of us, need our Feng Shui knowledge to transform our world into what we'd like it to become. We should think about how we want to feel in a room or a house. Then we need to recall a place that made us feel that way in the past, since we can re-create that feeling in our bodies simply by remembering it. All that's left is to discover why a particular memory remained so strong in our bodies and duplicate the key reasons through décor, position or symbolic associations.

This is the beauty of using Feng Shui in a transformational way. We are creating our own sanctuaries one step at a time from our own memories. We throw out the negative associations and incorporate the positive memories into our spaces. In that way, we truly make our living and working environments part of our most positive and pleasant experiences.

Ricki bought house number two and I visited her after closing. She'd done a beautiful job. She had painted the walls cheerful maize yellow, installed a beautiful Berber textured carpet in a lighter shade, and opened up the windows with light breezy curtains. About a half dozen trees were cut down and now she has a cheerful, bright home on a great lot with a very livable floor plan, all accomplished within budget using Feng Shui principles.

"Thanks Annie. You must have thought me crazy that day I tracked you down while you were halfway across country, but as you can see, all this was worth it," she sighed.

After being in the Feng Shui consulting business only a short time, I realized much of my success had been directly attributable to an innate knowing of the principles of Feng

Shui, but I never understood that fact while I was in real estate. The scientific and energetic reasons why some homes feel better than others are the same regardless of whether or not you acknowledge Feng Shui.

For example, in the real estate industry it is a known fact that homes where car lights directly shine into the front windows are harder to sell and bring less money than those that don't. Little did I realize the technical principle is that the lights are an actual form of energy traveling or flowing down the street (like water), right into the home, disturbing the peacefulness of the inhabitants.

Betty and her husband Todd had a similar problem. Their two story home was located on an interior corner lot of a large subdivision. It did not sit exactly square on the lot and car lights moved across the front of the home where the foyer, living room, and master bedroom were located. They had tried blinds, sheers, and finally heavy drapes to keep out the lights. The blinds and sheers still let the movement of the lights into the room and yet the heavy drapes made the rooms feel depressive. In addition, they'd spent extra money buying a beautiful cut glass front door which they couldn't enjoy.

"I've tried everything I can think of except Feng Shui. I'm even considering selling and I don't really want to. We can't sleep. The living room is either like a carnival or a cave. I need help," Betty lamented.

"Okay Betty I'll come out and take a look and we can discuss your options," I replied knowing that there are almost always a couple of different approaches available in situations like these.

Upon arrival at Betty's I could see the exact problem. Unknowingly the developer sited that lot oddly and the builder didn't realize the angle of the home was in partial line with the traffic flow. This could have been one of those houses that a car crashes into when the driver loses their brakes.

As we walked the lot perimeter next to the street we talked about many things. Their lifestyle. Their sleep patterns. Even how they wanted or would like to use the living room. Betty and Tom wanted to be able to use the living room in the evening while the kids used the den. They also wanted to block out the lights from the windows in the bedroom without creating a cave-like effect. And to top it off, the evening was the only time they had together because everyone was off and running at the crack of dawn.

"There are two best solutions Betty. One for the downstairs living room and one for the bedroom. I'll explain," I told her. "Then it is your decision."

"Okay, shoot," she said with anticipation, notebook in hand.

I went on to explain that the best solution for the car headlights problem affecting the first floor was to change the landscaping. Betty's driveway actually crossed through the lights' path, but since it was flat, the lights kept coming through the windows. We took her site plan and actually drew the raised landscape beds or berms that would frame the driveway entrance on each side, and fade to ground level in a gentle slope. The landscape beds would hold specific fast growing evergreens with some flowering bushes that would shield the house as they gradually faded to ground level. This would accomplish the light solution and protect the home should a car come racing down the street with no brakes.

The upstairs solution was a little harder. Betty and Tom were somewhat traditional in their décor. As we talked, I first considered some of the more austere and simple accordion opaque shades that pull up from the bottom, but they didn't seem right for this space. Such shades would have solved the problem with the car lights at night, and in the day they would still have allowed for privacy while allowing natural light coming in the window top, but the style of these shades would not have matched their traditional décor. Then we hit on a combination of two solutions. Plantation shutters would look great in both the downstairs living room and here in the bedrooms, and they would keep out most of the car lights. With the addition of the new window glass tinting materials, the family could have exactly what they needed: They could see out during the day, have no car lights shining in at night, and they would have appropriately attractive window coverings.

Feng Shui is about comfort and safety as well as all the other factors we've discussed. Stepping back from the problem allows you to see the situation like a consultant. There are no pat answers that work in every situation. Each home or office is as different as its occupants, and the solution to a problem must fit your needs, as well as those of others in close proximity.

Building a house from scratch is exciting, satisfying, time consuming and nerve racking depending on who you talk to, builder, buyer, architect or consultant. There are specific things that you can do to make a home out of a new house that directly relate to Feng Shui principles which make a dwelling live better.

Linda came to me early on, right after they bought their lot in a development of 5 acre lots. The land was mostly clear and flat with a gentle treed roll at one side and an old farmhouse near the center. They were planning their dream home and she'd been sketching floor plans since the inception of the idea. Her immediate concern was to decide where on the property to build the house, and secondly to give her design a Feng Shui tweak before taking it to the architect. I was thrilled. This was the ideal time for her to think about potential problems that later would have required retrofitting if she hadn't called at the beginning.

"Well, what do you think Annie?" she said quizzically. "I think the house should be here and the pool there, and the guest house here and my husband's workshop and extra garage there."

"Whoa, Nelly . . . hold on, Linda. Let's slow down and take things one at a time," I teased. "The first thing we need to do is walk the lot. Let me see the survey."

As we oriented ourselves using the survey, we started walking the lot beginning at the original entrance. It was beautiful land. Majestic almost. They were fortunate at this time in their lives to be in a position to buy such a place and carry out their dream plans. I was impressed. The old farmhouse stood at the crest of a small rise and nicely overlooked the rest of the neighborhood which was already developed. It was obvious this had been the home site of the original landowner.

When we had covered the entire property we went and sat on the porch steps and started sketching options for positioning the house not to mention all the other outbuildings and pool. As we talked I explained my reasoning for my first and second choices. Both called for the house to be near where the old farmhouse had been located, but not perpendicular to the road. I proposed that the house sit a little off center in order to capture the full impact of viewing the house as you come up the hill, driving deeper into the neighborhood. And I explained that frankly, the original owner had already given us part of the answer because that was where he had constructed his home. The land begged for its new home to have more than a plain vanilla orientation on the lot. Linda took copious notes for her architect and builder's consideration.

"Okay, now let's take a closer look at your floor plan sketch," I said.

Linda had obviously done her homework. I could see that she had incorporated a number of Feng Shui principles into the basic shape and flow of the house. What we were doing was truly tweaking. We started in the kitchen and utility area near the 3-car garage. She had created a large and multi-purpose utility room that had great enclosed storage for all kinds of things like pantry, golf clubs, vacuum cleaner, mops, cleaning buckets, etc. She had also put in a small work area near the window in this galley shaped room. Across the hall was a small office, or task area I like to call them, for mail and things coming into and the leaving the house. She had put cabinets and lots of drawers everywhere.

I asked Linda what she planned to do at the little work area, and she said it was for wrapping things like presents or things to be mailed. So I suggested making the window a different shape and much higher, putting the desk all across the end of the galley for a larger work space. This left room for a different sort of cabinetry on the side that would house tall wrapping paper and boxes. Since this meant that someone seated at the desk would have their back to the door (a Feng Shui no-no), I suggested a mirror above the desk so anyone sitting there could see behind them. Across the hall, I recommended putting a phone/DSL line in the little task area where the mail was going to land, though Linda resisted this suggestion. I reasoned that it might prove convenient to pick up email there or pay bills as well, while cooking or doing laundry.

The kitchen was wide open and had a lovely center island where she proposed having the sink. I recommended taking the cleaning sink and dishwasher to the back wall and adding a small vegetable sink on the island. It's never attractive or comfortable for a kitchen person to have a sink full of dirty things during dinner or a party, right in the line of sight of the grand foyer and great room. I also suggested the addition of a very large wall mirror above the sink to reflect the other two rooms and make the dishwasher feel like part of the gathering. Adding a couple of bar stools and a counter for relaxing, quick meals, or talking to the cook, was a finishing touch.

Before we left the kitchen, as we walked the floor plan in our minds, I asked the purpose of the cabinets she'd placed on the wall near the utility room entrance. She said they were regular drawers. I suggested she make a closet where she could hang her pans and shelve her pots and large appliances easily. Then near the utility I proposed a small vertical space for a broom and electric sweeper. She objected saying they were in the real utility room, but I asked her to think about her functional intent. Vacuuming and mopping are very intentional actions, but sweeping . . . well you might do that simply because you spilled the sugar. She agreed.

The great room was great except for where she planned to place the sofas. Again I adjusted the furniture positioning to be on a slight angle to take advantage of seeing the entrance and to create a little more drama in this very intentional floor plan.

"I'd never have done that," she laughed. "I guess I'm too conservative."

Then I laughed, "Well, it's that conservative nature that can really appreciate what we're doing here by making people more comfortable not having their backs to the entrance doors."

There was only one more area of concern for me, and that was what I called the cubby hole office off her husband's den. Even though it was small by the standards of other rooms it was still bigger than many walk in closets. When I asked what the purpose of the room was, she said "their" office. Two people. But with room hardly enough for one with all the built-ins.

She further explained, "We work too much. I want this house to be about us. Since we own our own business, it's easy to fall into a pattern of constant work. And I want to leave all the work at the office this time. That's why I even resisted the DSL line."

"I understand." I said. "But you need to be realistic also."

When I told her that no one would ever go in that office because it would feel like a windowless tomb, she said, "Good!" Explaining again that a built-in desk facing the wall would not work well, I got her to agree to a prettier free standing desk with lamp for the lap top computer facing out into her husband's study. She could have bookcases or cabinets above the built-in file cabinets. Then it could become a more cozy area near his den without being so isolated. With the desk facing out, they could actually see each other. Again she agreed.

Building a home is not for the weak willed. You must be able to take a look at what is not working in your life right now and intentionally plan solutions to those challenges into the design. Feng Shui principles help do this. As builders and architects across the country start to embrace the concepts, the buying public will begin to see homes available that will help empower family life, enrich relationships, and eliminate clutter. I can't wait.

Now About You—The Next Step in the Dance

Understand that buying a home is less about the house than it is how you want to live, and who you want to become.

Evaluate how you want to live, and how you do live currently, before you build or buy a home. By being aware of and melding how you live now and how you want to live, you can make your new home better support the kind of lifestyle you would like to lead.

Examine the parts of your current home that do not support you, or cause you difficulty, and include a solution to them in your next home. Common problems are: lack of sufficient or specific item storage, entrance clutter, kitchen counter clutter, cable and computer hookup locations, and flexible use space, etc. Annoying small problems in these areas that can often be retro-fitted using Feng Shui principles.

Essence

CHAPTER 20

It's All in the Details

NOT EVERYONE IS IN the position to spend any amount on a remodeling project, much less to do it twice. In fact, the cost, time, and hassle of such work often are the things that put off many people. For Lizzie, it was the cost that kept her from making the changes in her home for which she longed.

"No, no, sit right here," she instructed me when I came to her home. Dutifully, I took a seat in her living room.

"Don't you feel closed in?"

She was right. The living room had a small, confining energy to it, and the chair in which I sat was the spot where that energy was most focused.

"What I really want to do is to knock down that wall," she said, pointing to the wall directly in front of me. "I'd open this space into the dining room. It would make it so much nicer in here. But I've had three people come in to give me estimates, and all three were much more than I was hoping to spend." She lowered her eyes. "Apparently this wall is a supporting wall, so knocking it out will require a lot more than simply getting rid of it. What am I going to do, Annie?"

Lizzie was constrained by her budget, but her thinking also was constrained by her not realizing that the reality of Feng Shui isn't about physical space alone, but also about energy. The solution I gave Lizzie was simple and inexpensive. Rather than knocking out the wall and engaging in a very expensive project, I advised her to put up a wall-to-ceiling mirror to create the illusion of space in the living room. In addition, I suggested that she remove the leaf from the dining room table.

Although the table could seat six, it needed to do so only during holidays and special occasions. Most of the time, Lizzie really only needed two chairs there, for her and her significant other.

Creating a space that was more comfortable for the two of them solved a number of concerns. Her partner had a terminal illness, and their first concern was having as much time together, in comfort, as possible. In addition to making both rooms feel larger, the more effective use of energy helped give Lizzie's partner a sense of support and Lizzie more courage and a feeling of well-being.

What Lizzie had really wanted to achieve was more openness between the two of them during a very difficult time. It was much less about the living room. With Feng Shui, we were able to accomplish that without adding a major and stressful renovation to the challenges facing them.

Sometimes my clients are looking at the wrong things when they ask me for a consult in their homes. A year or so ago, I was asked to visit the studio of Sharon, a local artist. She wanted to do something with her studio, but she wasn't sure exactly what.

"I haven't been able to work the way I want to," she complained to me when she called. "And the work I've done . . . well, I'm not satisfied with it."

Before going to her downtown loft studio, I met her at her home, and Sharon showed me around. One of the things that struck me immediately was in her bedroom. There were many pictures and photographs on the walls— pictures of her children, her parents, her husband Don's parents.

"Oh my," I said with a slight shudder. "These shouldn't be here."

She looked at me curiously.

"The energy is all wrong," I told her, absolutely convinced about this.

"What do you mean?" she asked.

Rather than tell her, I showed her. I went along the walls and took down photographs. In their place, we put up a couple of her more abstract works. These changes, as it turned out, quickly turned the bedroom into a more intimate space for Sharon and her husband. The last thing they needed in their bedroom was an audience of children and ancestors.

From the house, we went to Sharon's loft, where we worked together to create a flow for displaying her work in a meandering sort of way that led through the various twists and turns we created in the large open space. The point was to draw the energy and attention to her artwork. I angled a very large mirror to monitor any comings and goings through the entrance. This created a very private space for her to paint in, with a lovely view. To further enhance the intimacy of this creative space, I hung colorful silks from rods attached to the fifteen-foot-high ceiling.

Our efforts were so successful that Sharon asked me to turn my attention to her husband's home office. Don had recently retired from a company for which he'd worked for a long while. His plan was to find another position, perhaps part-time, and to do some consulting work. Unfortunately, he had been having a very difficult time finding any other work.

When I examined his home office, I wasn't surprised to discover the reason why. His office was like a rummage sale of thirty years of professional life, papers, files, books, stereo equipment that no longer worked. His desk was shifted so that it faced away from the door, conceding its position of power and vision. Things were tattered and old. Even the pen in the pen set had no ink. In short, the office was the perfect reflection of how he was feeling about himself professionally, old and no longer useful, which wasn't the case at all.

In the same way that we can work to create energy in spaces, spaces can exert their influence and energy on us. We cleaned Don's office thoroughly. We created a "success wall," where we displayed his numerous awards. We brought in two good chairs, changed the lighting, brought in some fresh, cut flowers, and I moved the desk to its position of power, facing the door. Within two weeks of our changes, Don's job search became infinitely easier and more exciting when the right job offer came along.

One of the lessons that my efforts in Don's office brought home was that *we all become our surroundings.* Our surroundings have as much influence over our behavior and our sense of ourselves as any clothes we wear. We've all seen the truth of the old saying about the clothes making the man, or woman, or child. We all behave differently when dressed in school uniforms, "appropriate" business attire, or our "Sunday best," because we are different. Our living and workspaces have the same, perhaps even more, impact on who we are and how we act. We are extensions of the spaces we occupy, and the spaces we occupy are mirrors of ourselves. Change one, you change the other.

Not long ago I was involved in a marathon appointment with an artist and sales executive. Betty was a driven woman. She wanted to paint more. Be more creative. Make more money. Have more in the way of a great, new relationship. She wanted more and she wanted it now.

In order to address her desire, we moved nearly everything in her home, including all the accessories. We stripped the walls and replaced everything with more than twenty-five of her own paintings where she had hung none of her own work previously.

"Oh my," she said when she saw her work on the walls, shown in the ways we'd set up. "I'm dumbfounded."

The placement of her paintings had brought them to even greater life than she'd first seen. And she felt more inspired by being surrounded by her own work than she ever had being surrounded by works of other "acknowledged" artists.

We took a guest bedroom she had never given too much thought to and turned it into a personal sanctuary that became her private reading room, filled with many of her favorite things. And her bedroom, we turned into a romantic and personal boudoir, a place where sensuality was never confused with mere sleeping!

By the time we were finished that day, we had changed enough. She had to stop on occasion and take deep breaths whenever she looked around.

"I can't believe what we've done," she said, walking through her house.

I heard from her about a month later. She had been painting more. She had already made a number of new business contacts which had proved to be quite beneficial to her.

"My favorite thing is entertaining," Betty told me. "I never used to entertain before. I always thought of my home as the place I kind of collapsed in, you know? But now I feel as if I inhabit it completely. I want others to share that."

She confided in me that she had even enjoyed a couple of romantic evenings with candle lit dinners.

As much as all these things were wonderful to hear, the thing that was most rewarding was the way she simply beamed. Where she had come across as a driven, hard person in the past, now she presented herself as she was, a very ambitious, energetic and enthusiastic woman for whom the whole world was ripe for the picking.

"I was ready for a change," she said to me several months after we'd redone her house. "I didn't realize how great a change I would experience. Thank you."

One of my most satisfying experiences was helping a young couple who had a child who had been diagnosed with an attention disorder.

"He just won't calm down," the mother said when she called me.

I could hear the tension in her voice, as if she was stealing a couple of minutes before "the other shoe dropped." In that house, it turned out, they were always waiting for that other shoe to drop. And it generally did. In a most unpleasant way.

By changing the furniture in their son's bedroom, we created a space where he felt more safe, and we took away almost all of the stuffed animals.

"But he always loved those," the mother protested.

"These are a lot of eyes looking at a child," I said. "That could make a child uncomfortable."

We muted the colors in the room. I know people generally like primary colors with children but those colors are very hot and active, which fed into the boy's hyperactivity.

My goal was simply to calm the room down and, in the process, calm the child down. The changes worked. The boy now feels more comfortable in his room and, as a consequence, he plays there more. The result: a calmer house.

Kids get the Bagua Map. They understand that their hamster belongs in Health and Family and that the bed might go in Wealth and Prosperity. They instinctively understand how the desk belongs in Career and that the dresser goes in Fame and Reputation.

Homes. Bedrooms. Living rooms and kitchens. All change according to Feng Shui, and, in changing, change the people who inhabit them.

Few places are as susceptible to the laws of Feng Shui as the workplace. Correctly arranging an office can be critical for a successful career. Performance and acceptance of the individual is critical upon how the person feels about himself and how he is perceived by others in the office.

This is where Feng Shui can be critically important. Putting the desk and accompanying furniture in power positions. Flanking the back and sides of the office to "protect his back." Hanging art that reinforces the intent of the job and the passion of the executive.

Not long ago, I helped a newly retired FBI agent who would continue working in electronic surveillance. I instituted all the benefits of Feng Shui to aide him but nothing was as powerful and effective as the art we chose for his walls. These all showed animals, predators. The hawk after the mouse in the sand. The leopard. The eagles. The lion.

The symbology was powerful and effective. These animals are sleek, powerful, smart and swift. They attack, but only with reason. This was exactly what he wanted to communicate, exactly what he did.

One of my advanced students recently asked the question, "How can I keep the Thanksgiving Day holiday from becoming another major meltdown?"

In her home it seems that the combination of adult children plus grandparents often makes for a soup bowl of prickly emotions for the entire family. The teens and college age adults pick on each other and everyone else gets in the way of the battle lines. No one ends up happy, and the turkey's not well digested.

In her words, "It's too much work to have it turn out so wrong." I agree.

I assured her she was not alone in her dilemma. The holidays are hard for many families. But there is something you can do to make it better. Here is a summary of her story, blow by blow from two days before Thanksgiving to the Saturday after!

In that initial call, Janie said, "Well, it's already started. They aren't even here yet and they're fighting. I told you Annie, for the last few years Thanksgiving is always a meltdown!"

After consoling her, I asked Janie if she could smooth over the immediate crisis of getting everyone home for the holiday by doing something different herself. I suggested that she drive 1½ hours on the day before Thanksgiving to get her stranded son rather than use guilt to persuade her daughter to wait for him to finish work and pick him up. She agreed to that, and one problem was solved.

Next I asked, "Did you remove all those childhood pictures of the kids from the main foyer wall?" She actually called it the "Wall of Children." It documented each one from the age of infant through high school, but displaying no current age pictures.

"No," she replied, "I told you in class I love that wall. It's been my life. I love my babies. I don't really want to take it down."

I explained again to Janie, that those pictures could represent something very different to each of the kids. And certainly they were not demonstrating very mature attitudes and behavior when they came home for the holidays for the last few years.

"They see those pictures and immediately revert back to the emotional state of 10 or 13 or 16 or what ever the ages were!" I reminded her.

I again suggested she remove the pictures, even if they were only put in a box until after the holiday and then re-hung after everyone went home. She agreed to do what I asked.

The following week I received this message on my voice mail from an ecstatically happy Janie.

"I'm officially declaring a Thanksgiving Day Miracle! It was great Annie. There was no fussing or bickering. There were a couple of close moments; however, it seemed as if they miraculously blew over."

She continued, "The kids came in like little puppies, sniffing around each room to see what was different. It was amazing. They even sat in the living room and civilly discussed the difficulties of modern day dating!"

This was music to my ears. She had listened to me and was able to change an established destructive pattern in her home by a little manipulation of the environment. Taking down the pictures of the kids at an age that no longer represents them had a positive effect on them. In their minds subconsciously, those old pictures affected how they saw themselves or how they wanted their parents to see them. This theory worked yet again!

"In fact, it took hours for them to even notice the 'Wall of Children' was down!" she said. "And then each of them asked, 'Where did you put me?' Annie it was so interesting, that's all each one said. Once they found out I put them in the basement near my desk that was the last of the comments! I would have never believed this possible! Thank you. And my husband says thanks, too. He even considered it such a triumph that he suggested going out dancing when we left my parents at the airport!"

When I called Janie back she went on to explain that up until the time they loaded everyone back into the cars and onto the planes, there was compete harmony. I wasn't surprised.

Changing our everyday patterns and habits that don't serve us really allows us to create the kind of life we do want. In other words, Janie took the old environment, which fostered the meltdowns and made it new by Feng Shui principles.

When we change patterns and habits in this manner physically, it brings our conscious mind into active play, living, thinking, and reacting in the present moment. When we act in the present moment, we usually don't respond negatively to situations, people, or events.

Everything is interrelated, and little things can trigger big changes.

One of my students recently came to me with a question about "those women and their perfect homes."

She was referring to the women who keep their homes in such a state that *Better Homes and Gardens* could show up on a moment's notice and begin to photograph. This student is an older woman who had always felt that her own home never quite measured up.

"Not a damned thing out of place," she added with disdain. "Like everything's been hair-sprayed into place." She paused. "Do you think that's a good energy?"

I explained to her that it was as easy to get stuck in "perfect" as anyplace else. It's just a different kind of stuck.

Generally people who are so exacting that they present such a perfect face to the world are people who are terribly fearful. People who never have a hair out of place or who always look perfect are frightened of losing control. Or they are frightened of never being good enough, or of being abandoned.

That determination to be perfect is a symptom.

I told my student that I sometimes do get asked to come to these "perfect" homes and when I do, I do manage to move things around. Usually, there is a great deal of resistance. Things had been placed where they were for very particular reasons, just not sound ones.

"Are you *sure* you have to move that?" they say.

I always look at my client, quietly reminding them that they were the one who had asked me into their home. I hadn't come barging in. It is amazing at how a very small change—turning a table off center, or placing the seating furniture in a new configuration—is enough to break their thinking free and allow them to address what they really want from their lives.

I always remember that if the people who seem to have it all really had it all, they wouldn't have asked me to their homes in the first place.

"When I think of these perfect homes," I told my student, "I think of pine needles with ice frozen all over the outside. Inside, it's alive, but you would hardly know it. And, if you try to change it too quickly, it might break. So the movements have to be slow and deliberate, coaxing the ice to melt and allow the life inside to blossom naturally.

We become aware that our words and actions all have consequences, right now. Feng Shui fosters this living in the present moment. Not worrying about or reacting to past events, nor worrying about future outcomes. Feng Shui is all about setting up your physical environment to support you physically, mentally, and spiritually right now for the future. You can't change someone else by "doing" Feng Shui, but you can make their environment feel more harmonious Besides, turkey tastes better with a smiling face!

Now About You—The Next Step in the Dance

Remember that you do not have to reinvent the wheel, because what has worked for someone else may very well work for you.

Modest alterations can contribute to substantial life and behavioral changes as much as major modifications. Most adjustments in flow or symbology have very subtle affects on you that can result in very different habitual patterns in body, mind and spirit.

Look at the problem areas or habits that are causing the difficulties and see how other people have solved their situations in similar circumstances.

Imagine your desired outcome and see what would have to be different physically, mentally, and spiritually in you and the space to achieve that outcome.

脈

絡

Context

CHAPTER 21

Changing Patterns
About Men, Money & Romance

*P*ATTERNS MATTER.
Wake up from a disturbing dream, and you might
have difficulty getting back to sleep. Your heart may pound;
your thoughts may turn brooding. But a disturbing dream is
usually just a dream. It was probably something you ate.

Have the same disturbing dream over and over, however, and you've got something important to consider, a pattern. Your dream is like a thread that, should you pull on it
enough, will help you to unravel a tapestry of some hidden
and troublesome aspect of your life or personality.

Our lives tend to be a series of ongoing patterns, routines,
and rituals that give our lives order and meaning. They say a
lot about who we are and what is important to us. Too often,

however, we fail to see that patterns may repeat themselves in ways that limit who we are as people. Similarly, there are patterns that repeat in our homes, at our work, in individual rooms. We often block out our perception of these patterns and what they really say, relying instead on their predictability to create the illusion of comfort. But predictability and illusion are not worth the harm that negative patterns can cause in our lives.

We often block or deny our pain. These denials and blockages then manifest themselves in our physical space, our bodies, and our emotional and spiritual selves. Denial itself perpetuates patterns. Overcoming denial can help to remove the negative patterns in our lives. By the same token, removing some of the physical patterns that occupy our physical spaces can also help to open our eyes and make us aware of our blockages.

When I first met Jesse, she was twenty-three years old. She was, by her own admission, a little bit "out of control." She was seeing three different men, going out almost every night, and having a good time. The first time we spoke, she told me that her favorite song was the Cyndi Lauper song, *Girls Just Wanna Have Fun*. The trouble was, Jesse wasn't having fun. If she had been at some time, that time was long past.

"I don't know how to turn things around," she said honestly. "I'm going out more and enjoying it less."

Despite her appreciation for the futility of her search for "fun," she couldn't figure out how to make her life enjoyable without the constant distraction of dating, parties, clubs, and dancing.

When I visited Jesse's workplace, I found a space that was cluttered with all sorts of knickknacks. There were papers and files everywhere. Her file cabinet was stuffed full, and she had cardboard boxes with other files on the floor. I learned that many of the files were long dormant and, at the very least, could have been warehoused someplace far,

far away from her office. The clutter created a challenge for anyone having to navigate their way through the office.

"Are you all right?" she asked me, as I stumbled while making my way to the chair opposite her desk.

"Oh, I'm fine," I said lightly. "Sure you have enough stuff here?"

"This is nothing," she told me. "You should see my apartment."

Sure enough, when I went to her apartment, I found a similar situation. There were boxes loaded with papers and things. Every available tabletop seemed to be weighted down with . . . things.

"Jessee, what is all this?" I asked her.

She shrugged. "Stuff."

"Do you need it all?"

She smiled and shrugged again. "I'm a packrat. I can't get rid of anything. I can't help it."

That was an understatement. She had even kept class work from when she was an elementary school student, not special projects or artwork, but everyday work such as spelling sheets. Yes, she held on to things. The patterns in every part of her life—her personal life, her professional life, and her home life—repeated themselves over and over. Just as she couldn't let go of even the most trivial piece of her past, she couldn't let go of old boyfriends, and she couldn't say no to an offer of a night out.

"Saying 'no' is one of the most important decisions any of us can make," I pointed out to her. "It's like the tail is wagging the dog around here, not the other way around."

"I know, I know," she said, her voice colored with disappointment in herself. "It's so hard for me."

I am not trained in assisting someone psychologically, but I do believe that I am sensitive to people's emotional needs and that I have helpful insights. With Feng Shui, I can use my sensitivities to help others, even Jesse.

"I'm not saying you should throw away anything," I told her. "However, you must remove it from your immediate space."

Together, we went through everything in her apartment. We packed cardboard boxes of papers, photographs, stuffed animals, toys, everything she had brought with her when she moved out of her parents' home. We took those boxes and stored them in a public storage facility.

"Wow," she said when we returned to her apartment. "I didn't realize the apartment was this big, or this empty."

"We're not finished," I told her.

We rearranged her furniture to allow the free flow of energy. I removed the heavy blinds from the windows and convinced her to get lighter, though just as private, drapes. The result was a lighter, airier apartment. When we finished, she drew a deep breath.

"Wow," she said again.

Although the apartment looked completely different, Jesse said she felt very comfortable and at peace there. I noticed her better posture, her chin held up.

Then, after we had managed to go through her things at home, removing many of them to clear her space, she went through her office at work with similar resolve. Soon, a curious (but predictable) thing happened. Once the clutter was removed from her home and her workplace, the clutter began to clear from her personal life as well. She made decisions about the things she wanted to continue doing and the people she wanted to continue to see. She set boundaries. The other people and things, she let go. She called me six months later with the news she was getting married.

"Really?"

"Yes, to a man I met at work. I guess I'd known him for a long time, but I never really got to know him. I suppose there was too much clutter in my life, blocking my view of him."

I smiled to myself. "That's exactly what it was."

Jesse was able to cast off her "party girl" image and become the person she really was, a caring, committed adult. Her pattern had been to hold on to so much at each step of the way that she had carried her adolescent personality into adulthood. Changing the spaces in which she lived and worked had changed the way she lived, and allowed her to mature gracefully.

"I never told you this," she said, several weeks after she told me about being engaged. "I don't tell many people. But when I was a little girl, my dad left my mom and me. We ended up having to move around a lot. I was always the new kid. Always scared. And always thinking that if I only could have stayed at the last place a little longer, everything would have been great. So I kept a little something from each place . . . to keep it alive. I guess I've been doing that all my life, huh?"

It seemed that she had. She'd been holding on to the past in order to protect herself from the future. Now, she was free from clinging to the past and to all the clutter that it had created in her life, and she was ready to face the future with hope and confidence. Jesse's pattern of not letting go was finally broken.

My friend Bill has long been intrigued with Feng Shui. Intrigued I said. Not convinced. But he's not unlike many of the men I encounter in my practice.

Most of the partners and husbands of women that bring me in to their homes, are, shall I say, in a tolerant mode. They've heard a little about Feng Shui in the media, have listened to their wives curiosities, and wondered whether moguls like Donald Trump and Richard Branson really do pay attention to such things.

But Bill, ever since I have known him, has always wanted the "perfect mate." You know the one I mean. Beautiful. Classy. Professional. Independent. Not too tall, but not too short. Sexy. Laughs a lot. Nice. Romantic. Great in bed. It's that same list that most of my women clients have.

"I don't understand it, Annie," he said. "She has to exist, but I can't seem to go to the right places to meet her, or at least I haven't found her yet." And with a sigh he added, "Please help me, I'm not getting any younger."

"You know this is not about her, don't you Bill?" I answered. "You're looking for that perfect someone, and if you found her, what makes you think she wouldn't slip right through your fingers?"

"No way," Bill replied. "We'd recognize each other, I'm convinced of that. And besides," he said, "I'd do everything right."

"Well, you might be convinced of the recognition, and you might think you're doing all the right things, but if you don't have the proper energy it would take to hold on to her, she'll be gone in no time," I responded.

I explained that in order to attract and keep a woman like that, you have to have the complimentary energy that would allow her to stay. Like energy does attract like energy. So what you want, you have to be.

"If your energy is not congruent with her energy, then eventually she will be repelled away," I offered.

"Bill, listen, it's like that Porsche you've always wanted. You're desiring something that you do not have the energy to hold onto yet," I said.

"Porsche? What are you talking about?" he quizzed. "I'm talking about a woman."

"I know Bill, just listen," I sighed.

I explained that, while he had always dreamed of owning a Porsche, he did not know what the energy of owning a Porsche would be like. He didn't have a concept of what driving it would feel like. He didn't even know how it would make him feel to sit in it. In fact, he knew very little about what owning a Porsche would be like. All he knew was that he wanted a convertible and what color he wanted.

Similarly, he knew very little about what *she* would be like. Or what he'd feel like with her as a couple. Not *what* she'd be like, but how'd he'd *feel* with her. That was what would be important.

"It's hard to recognize what you want, if you haven't ever felt how it makes you feel before," I said. "You have to become a vessel for the feeling you want to have. So you can hold onto it."

Bill chastised me, "So what do you suggest I do, Miss Smarty Pants?"

Laughingly I said, "Go drive a Porsche a week for the next 9 weeks, and then tell me what it's like. How does it makes you feel? What parts touch your body? Do people treat you differently? What's it like? All that."

"Oh," I added, "Then go out on nine dates with nine new women. A pretty one. One that's not too tall and not too short. You get the idea. Then you can report back to me what it feels like to be with a beautiful woman. Or a funny gal that's professional. And a classy girl that looks like she'd be terrific in bed. Or a woman that's adventurous enough to take a joy ride in her date's dream Porsche? Get the picture?"

"Okay, but why do I have to do that? I'm still not clear," he groaned.

"Because Bill, you need to feel the energy of what it would be like to be in that position with a woman or the Porsche," I explained. "Otherwise, you won't recognize the personal energy it will take in you, first, before you can attract either the woman of your dreams or the Porsche into your life."

"I'll try it, but I'll feel a little silly," he commented.

"You'll only feel silly until you meet her, and drive up to introduce me to her in your new Porsche!" I said.

Many times I've seen people try to attract something or someone into their lives that comes in very quickly and leaves just as suddenly. And it's hard to explain to them that in the laws of attraction there is a requirement to act as a good vessel or steward. You have to take care of what you have in order to attract more or new.

Lottery winners face this dilemma all the time. They had little money. They win. They have lots of money. But most of them have lots, only for a little while. And it's only because they do not know what the feeling of being judicious with money feels like.

They have not been good stewards of the little money they had before winning, so they didn't know what it was like to be a good steward of a lot of money after winning. The same kind of thing happens many times to women in a divorce. They get a settlement that should set them up for life, and it disappears in a few years. Divorces don't happen to people who have been good stewards of their marriage.

As for Bill, the last time I was in his office his whole world had changed. He had a more prestigious job, paying five figures higher, an office with a window, and a new home he's started to renovate using Feng Shui principles. I glanced to the right rear corner and smirked.

"I knew you'd walk in and see that corner first thing," he said laughingly about his love and relationship corner.

The corner was neatly stacked with boxes and equipment from his business. He could tell from my expression that I did have a question about his intent for a relationship.

"I decided to do what you suggested. I needed to work on myself first. I want to make sure when I do attract Ms. Right that she sticks around. So I stuck up a Post-It that said, 'Soon it will be time.'

"And besides, I'm not the best Bill I can be for her yet. My energy level is higher, but she's going to deserve so much more," he explained. "I want to make sure that there will be no question as to the quality of the man she'll be getting."

I smiled. My work was done.

It's not about the people or the money. It's about their energy. Like attracts like, in every way. If the vessel is cracked it will leak. Love or Money. It makes no difference. We need to be good stewards of our own energy first.

Now About You—The Next Step in the Dance

Seeing yourself where you are, simply as a starting point in the change process, removes the stigma of failing.

There is no failure, there is no right and wrong way of doing things, only a way and its complement in energy. You are where you are by virtue of the choices you have made and the actions you have taken and not taken in your life. You are where you are supposed to be, so do not get frustrated.

The key to going forward is to keep moving in a fluid manner like flowing water. Even if you become frozen with panic about the possibility of making a wrong decision, there is always movement underneath the surface of the ice.

The energy it takes you to go to the next level or to the next phase is always available under the surface of your awareness. Through the support you have implanted in your physical, mental, and spiritual environment you will be able to achieve your desired outcome.

Time

CHAPTER 22

Blending Your Past, Present and Future

*C*YNTHIA WAS A TALENTED and highly respected physician with a very successful practice. However, she would have been the first to say that the reason she was successful, and the reason she enjoyed what she was doing, had less to do with her professional standing than with her personal life. She was one of those very fortunate people who found her soul mate early in life and had the good sense to hold onto him. In his late fifties, Cynthia's husband suffered a fatal heart attack. The pain and grief of her loss were sharp and difficult.

"I felt like I was just going through the motions," she said, describing what it was like when she returned to work after taking off two weeks to mourn. She talked about hearing things patients and staff said, of understanding the words and performing the appropriate tasks, but feeling as if everything in her life was happening "in another room."

"It was almost a physical sensation," she said.

Cynthia tried not to wallow in her sadness. As a physician, she had dealt enough with death and dying to understand (intellectually) that there are stages to grieving. She went to a group of recently widowed women to share her feelings and to listen to the feelings of others. She tried to take up new hobbies to occupy the many empty hours she now faced alone.

"But the hobbies never stick. The only things I loved doing were the things I loved doing with Matthew. Without him, it didn't seem like there was any point," she sighed softly.

Human emotions are complex, and what Cynthia was going through was perfectly normal for any loving, grieving person. The acute stage of her mourning took several months. When the flowers bloomed in the first spring after Matthew's death, however, she began to feel that she wanted to live again, that he would have wanted her to. But she found that, no matter how determined she was, she couldn't find a "groove" to get back into. Nothing felt normal or good to her.

"Matthew and I spent a lot of time together, and our relationship was very physical as well as emotional," she said, considering her words carefully. "I miss that physical contact. Holding hands. Hugging. Sitting across from him at dinner. And all the rest, too. But once I admitted to myself how much I missed that contact, I didn't know how to begin again. Dating?" she laughed. "I never dated. Matthew was always there, even in school."

She did accept a couple of dinner invitations from people she knew through other friends. But nothing came of them.

"I invited one man to my house. He was very nice. I liked him. Although he was nothing like Matthew, something about him reminded me of being with Matthew. Maybe it was just being comfortable again with a man. But when we got to the house, that sense of comfort quickly disappeared. It was the weirdest thing. I felt . . . awkward. It was almost as if I wasn't in my home at all, but in someone else's." She was quiet for a moment. "I had the feeling he felt awkward too."

When I visited her home, I discovered that, as she said, nothing had changed since Matthew had died. A year later, the house was still very much the home that they had shared. It was no wonder that she felt she wasn't in "her" home. She wasn't. She was still in "their" home. The only problem was, there was no longer a "they."

"I think," I said softly, "we have to make this your home."

She looked at me, horrified. I knew what it was that concerned her.

"We're not going to take Matthew away," I reassured her. "He will always be part of your life and your home. But we have to give you some space."

To that end, we removed some of the things that were uniquely Matthew's from display on the fireplace mantel, things he had collected when he traveled the world on business. In their place, we put things that Matthew and Cynthia had shared, along with some new things that Cynthia had acquired.

A large five foot folding screen frame that contained a number of photographs of Matthew was on prominent display in the living room.

"Hmm," I said, studying it.

"I couldn't get rid of those," she said.

"I don't want you to," I said quickly.

What I did want though, was for them not to define her space at home in such a prominent position. I suggested that we move them to her office for the time being, and, in their place, that we put one nice photograph of him. That was it. It was unnecessary to move furniture or rearrange anything else. All we had to do was to create a space where Cynthia could be just Cynthia and not half of "Cynthia and Matthew." By doing so, we also created a space where a new man that she brought into her home could feel comfortable as well.

A month after we made these changes, Cynthia attended the wedding of a friend's daughter. There, she met a man who was "charming and nice, funny and intelligent." That evening, she danced again for the first time in over a year and, "I felt as if I were dancing on a cloud."

Although beginning to let go of the past was not nearly as difficult a reality for Cynthia as it was for Jesse, in both cases, the presence of the past inhibited their ability to fulfill themselves in the now. By addressing the past in their living and working spaces, we were able to open up the present to them, and help them to realize how happy they could be.

Sometimes we clutter our spaces not so much with the past but with negative messages to ourselves.

Suzanne was about twenty-five pounds overweight. In an effort to "encourage" herself to exercise and to lose weight, she had brought a treadmill into her bedroom. A short time later, she added an exercise bike. Then weights. A number of exercise videotapes were piled up on the television.

The result was that, every time she walked in or out of her bedroom, she thought she was being bombarded with a message: Exercise! The trouble was, that wasn't the only message that was being sent. The other message she was receiving constantly was much less uplifting: You're overweight. You're unattractive.

Needless to say, her bedroom ceased being a place where she and her husband enjoyed any real intimacy. Over time, she didn't much use the exercise equipment either.

She tended to hang clothes on it. Oh, and lose weight? Forget it.

When I visited Suzanne's home for a consult, the very first thing I did was get rid of that exercise equipment. Not only did that remove those negative thoughts, but it also opened up the bedroom for some fresh energy. Physical intimacy became a reality in her life again, not only because the negative energy was removed from her bedroom, but because, with those negative affirmations gone, she began to lose weight. She felt she was more attractive and, as such, behaved more attractively.

"My husband doesn't read in bed anymore," she confided to me with a smile. "That's for sure!"

The loss of intimacy is a powerful sign that we need to make some changes in our lives. Yet, too often, we fail to see the signs. Tina and Ted were like that too.

Shortly after Tina gave birth to their first child, she and Ted realized that they had to do a little better at saving money. In order to make a contribution to the family finances, Tina worked in Ted's law office while her mother came over to watch their little boy.

"It was exciting at first. I mean, we got to have more time together. But then, he began to treat me like he would any other employee," Tina complained. "I guess he can't show any real favoritism, but I am his wife."

Ted wasn't unfair to Tina while she was at work, but he didn't show her the consideration that she expected.

"She was there to work," he said in defense of his behavior. "It wasn't like we were on vacation or anything."

At home, the baby had a bassinette in their bedroom. Toys were scattered all over the house. They'd set up the playpen alongside the chair where Ted used to relax and watch television after a long day at the office. The office also had became an extension of the home, and both were dominated by tension and a sense of frantic childlike energy.

"I reached a point where I felt I couldn't hide anyplace," Ted said.

"Hide?" Tina demanded. "Hide from what?"

The tension between them became so uncomfortable that, one morning, Tina threw down the gauntlet. "If I have to go in that office one more time, I swear I'm going to ask for a divorce!"

"Go ahead," Ted said coldly, as he turned to leave for work.

Tina was crushed. They had recently had a baby. They'd finally begun the family to which they had both been looking forward. And now it seemed as if everything was crashing down around her. The problem that they were facing was normal for any couple who has just had their first child: finding a boundary between their new role as parents and their lives as a couple and as individuals.

It is not easy to do. It was made more difficult by the fact that they were together at work as well as at home. Not only did Ted lose his "sacred" space at home, he'd lost it at work as well. As a result, his sense of who he was got damaged. Tina's frustration had little to do with how Ted treated her at work. It had everything to do with their changing relationship at home.

For them, the "future," their baby, was infringing on their ability to enjoy the present. In order for them to establish some successful boundaries, we arranged their home to create a child area as well as to enhance the adult living areas for a better energy flow. We removed the bassinette from the bedroom as soon as possible. The playpen and child's toys were banished from the den where Ted watched television and relaxed.

"And this room is absolutely sacred," I told them, referring to their bedroom. "This is your space as a couple. It is not an extension of your baby's playroom. It is not his bedroom. It is for the two of you, together."

The changes worked. Not only were they closer physically, emotionally, and spiritually, but they also were more prepared to enjoy life as a family of three instead of two.

The past, the present, the future. These are always in flow, one into the other. Often, the flow is relatively orderly. Sometimes, the flow is interrupted by emotional trauma, death or divorce, for example. Sometimes, we fight for the things that will only drag us down, making living in the present even more difficult.

For example, I know of one divorcee who went through a bitter divorce. As part of the divorce settlement, the woman fought long and hard for all the furniture they had shared. Some of it she believed held real emotional value, the glass dining room table from the fancy beach house; the cherry bedroom set she'd loved the moment she set eyes on it; and she wanted the couches from the living room where so many hours had once been spent happily. She wanted it all. She associated whatever happiness that had ever existed in the marriage with the furniture itself. The nice pieces she associated with previous social and financial status. She still pictured them in homes in which she no longer lived.

Over time, she began to buy new pieces. These pieces not only failed to match the ones she claimed from her divorce, but they also created a crowded feel in her home. What she didn't realize was that holding onto the older furniture was holding onto a life she didn't live anymore. Although there had been more money and social status in her previous life, that wasn't where she was now. It was better to drop down a notch or two on the social scale than constantly to suffer the negativity of "ruing the day" that her life changed.

She began to turn her attention to more positive things. For instance, the oil portrait that she had loved as a young woman, but which had never occupied a place in her home during the twenty-five years of her marriage because her husband didn't like it, now found a prominent place in her home. The portrait cries out, "I am myself, and I am still spiritually connected to that young, excited, and wonderful woman I always have been!"

Along with the furniture filling her much smaller house, she had a garage filled with the various things she'd collected during her married life, things she had "won" in the divorce. She held tightly to all those things because she knew that they were truly valuable. She was loath to let go of anything of monetary worth if she, in her new, more difficult circumstances, could gain something from the possessions. It was her Great Depression mentality at work, a gift to her from her parents and from her husband: Hold onto everything.

But the burden of holding on was so devastating that she finally had to let go. At first, she thought she could realize some gain from selling everything in a garage sale. In her mind, she conjured up the money she would make. Hundreds of dollars, she reasoned. Hundreds of dollars that would benefit her greatly in her new circumstances. But then, something snapped. She didn't want to sell the furniture. She didn't want the equivalent of "blood money."

"This has been my life. I'm not going to sell it," she told herself.

Instead, she decided to give it all away. And give it away she did! To new friends and those she knew wanted and needed different pieces. All day long, they came to pick up the pieces of her past to place in their present.

As she witnessed her old life being depleted, she retreated to her bedroom and began to cry. But why? she wondered. She was scared, as scared as she'd ever been. Even the divorce, which had frightened her to the core of her being, hadn't frightened her in the same way this did. There was anger and hurt in that. Here there was the fear that came with being emptied out. With each piece of furniture, she felt as if her heart was being torn from her chest. It was as if each pain and loss she had ever experienced was being multiplied over and over in her soul. And then it was over. Everything was taken. Her friends, grateful for their gains, wished her luck and love. She was left with what?

With space. And slowly, as she walked around the space, she realized what a good thing it was to rid herself of all that "stuff." Now, her space was a canvas upon which she could paint anything she wanted. Her new world was now hers to build.

Frightening? Yes. Exhilarating? Absolutely!

Oh, by the way, that divorcee who struggled with that pain and that fear? She was me. I know what it is like to struggle with the past. I know the need to re-create space to allow positive energy to flow. I have learned what I've learned as much from the reality of my own life as from any book or seminar. That is why I know that Feng Shui can help you. It helped me.

Another woman, named Bonnie, came to me not terribly long ago. She was about my age. Yet, in her words, she felt "a hundred years old". Her "age" had little to do with her physical health. In fact, she was the picture of health.

"Oh, I've been to my doctor plenty of times. He says I'm fit as a fiddle," she said half smiling.

Her problem was not physical. It was mental and spiritual. She had lost her husband two years earlier after a brief period of illness.

"He passed away about six months after being diagnosed with the cancer," she explained. "I took care of him as long as I could. Then we had a visiting nurse and then hospice."

"He wanted to be at home, and I wanted him at home. Jim and I had always had the best relationship." She sighed. She clasped her hands and placed them in her lap. "He told me that I would have to move on after he was gone. But I haven't been able to. Not yet."

I listened intently to what she was saying. As I did, I watched her. She was still a very attractive woman. Nice hair. Great smile.

"I do feel alone. You know, when Jim told me I'd have to find someone else, I didn't believe him. I didn't want to believe him. I still wanted to believe that he would get better." She lowered her eyes. "Of course, he didn't."

"Do you feel you're ready to move on now?" I asked quietly.

She looked at me for a moment, then nodded. "Yes, I think so. But I don't know how."

"You don't have to know how. You just have to allow that outward-seeking receptive energy to be freed up."

She looked at me quizzically, "I don't understand."

"First, tell me about your wardrobe," I said.

As she spoke, it became apparent that the dark browns and blacks that she was wearing to my studio made up the entirety of the clothes that she'd been wearing since her husband had become gravely ill. And frankly, she admitted they had been the staple of her wardrobe for years before.

"Here's what I want you to do," I began. I told her to go out and buy new clothes. I didn't care what kind so long as they were bright colors—yellows, reds, oranges, rich blues. Then she had to put all her current clothes in shopping bags to give to the poor.

I wanted her to cut the ties with the association of the clothes. The dress she wore the night they spent on the dinner cruise. The dress she wore to their granddaughter's christening. The bathing suit he chided her into getting while on vacation in Jamaica.

"Dress to be cheerful," I told her with determination. "It's similar to dress for success, but the intent is a little different."

"But ..."

"After that, in say two weeks, we're going to talk about your house too," I said.

"Do you really think all that is necessary?" she asked.

"Absolutely," I told her. "Color matches mood, or more correctly mood matches color. You've been dressing in these mourning colors for all this time because you have been mourning. Now, we're going to change the colors to bring you out from that state of sadness."

"That'll work I think," she said.

I nodded my head. Yes, I knew it would.

We have to establish balance. Inside and out. The clothes we wear reflect how we feel inside. In the same way, the way we feel inside is reflected by the clothes we wear. When you want to feel better, you must wear something that matches the mood you want to feel. You'll be surprised at how quickly your mood changes to match the bright and festive colors, textures and patterns you're wearing. Your body never lies, and bright colors feel happier than dark ones. "And, it's the same in your home. Dress your house for success, or at least decorate your home for your cheerfulness," I added.

When I returned to Bonnie's house, more than her wardrobe had changed. So had the curtains all over the house. She had even bought beautiful bright new linens for the master bedroom in a bold flower pattern that shouted, "Look at me." There was a new set of dishes and glasses in the kitchen and we drank tea from delicate English tea mugs. She had grasped the concept of changing things, not only for the sake of the new décor, but in order to break the very natural associations that connect us with the past.

"Thank you Annie," she said confidently. "I never would have done this without your suggestion and encouragement. I guess I almost needed to get permission to let go. Now I'm glad I did."

Bonnie was typical of so many women. Widows and divorcees that feel left behind when their life changes and they face challenges they've never considered having to face before. The principles she enacted in the physical space are good psychology, but more importantly her actions were a great lesson in learning to live with grace.

Now About You—The Next Step in the Dance

Creating your ideal environment is a crutch to give you physical, psychological and spiritual support on the days you are less than your peak self.

Once your environment is re-created to reflect your higher self and best self, the intentions are embedded into the physical structures through energy flow, psychological metaphors and spiritual aspirations. Subconsciously on the days you are feeling less than your peak self, you have a built-in personal support system in place without needing others to give you a hand.

明
示

Manifestation

CHAPTER **23**

Working the Power Positions

$\mathcal{R}$ ECENTLY, I HEARD AN advertisement for mattresses in which the announcer pointed out that fully one-third of our life is spent in bed. "Shouldn't you be comfortable?" the announcer asked. The answer is obvious: Yes! Who wouldn't want to be comfortable for such a large percentage of their life.

By that same argument, you should devote a great deal of care to your workplace. Not only is the place where you work the source of your material wealth, but it also is the place where you spend at least as much time as you do in bed. Unfortunately, Feng Shui is too often an afterthought in decisions about the work environment. I cannot tell you how many times someone has come to me and introduced their interest in Feng Shui with, "Well, I've tried everything else. Why not try this?"

That was certainly the case when Edward came to my studio one afternoon. When he arrived, I was greeted by a tall, dignified-looking man wearing a dark business suit.

"Hello," I said, inviting him in.

"Hello," he said, clearing his throat, the only gesture that betrayed his discomfort.

We were both quiet for a moment. "Can I help you?" I asked.

He gave an almost imperceptible shrug. "I don't know," he said. "I hope so. Frankly, I don't see how you can do any harm."

I thought that was as close to an invitation to help as I was going to get from him, so I forged forward. "Is there a particular question you have?"

He spread his hands in a helpless gesture. "I have a hundred, but the bottom line question is, 'Why am I not making the money I know I should be making?'"

Ed went on to describe his store and the products he sold. In listening, I had to admit that it sounded like the kind of endeavor that should have been very successful. But, as he admitted, it wasn't.

"I've tried everything I can think of. Advertising. New lighting. Having my sales staff wear uniforms. Giveaways." He shook his head. "I'm in a very good location. Good foot traffic. Everything should be perfect." But it wasn't.

Unfortunately, most businesses and corporations have no real vision, and, lacking vision, they tend to go nowhere. This is not to confuse vision with a goal. Every business has the goal of making money. But a vision is necessary to actually see where the business is going. In other words, all "money" is not green.

As I began to explain to Ed, a business is like a person—and—a person who has no goals or vision of where they want their life to go doesn't make progress.

"Well, I wanted to be a major league ballplayer," Ed countered, "but that's not where I ended up."

"A vision keeps you moving forward," I suggested. "That is not to say that the vision you have for yourself as a young man is the person you ultimately become. But without a vision, you are left to be formed by circumstances, rather than influencing circumstances yourself.

"For example, your wanting to be a ballplayer taught you many life lessons. You learned about teamwork, competition, performing under pressure. You learned about winning, and you learned about losing. In a very fundamental way, you are a ballplayer."

He viewed me with some suspicion, as if he wasn't sure he was willing to go along with the argument I was making. However, after a moment, he softly clucked his tongue. "Interesting point," he suggested. "So, what does Feng Shui have to teach this old ballplayer about making his business more profitable?"

I began to explain the flow of energy, but Ed put up his hand to stop me.

"Look, I know you're well-meaning, and I do want to find out if this Feng Shui stuff can help. But you should know, I've gone through hundreds of different management workshops and courses."

"I understand," I told him. "I really do. Yes, I know, there are a million motivational speakers out there to tell you what you're doing wrong. The thing about Feng Shui is that it works with all those various approaches. When you think about what you want your business to do, how you want to relate to your clients and customers, how to develop company teamwork, etc., you're doing strategic planning. What Feng Shui does is free up the energy to allow you to be more successful in implementing your specific strategy."

I asked Ed if I could come visit his offices. "I'd love for you to come by, but I don't see what good that would do."

Ed, like most business people, had a lot to learn about Feng Shui.

Manipulating energy in an office is, on the one hand, a very simple task. Energy flows like traffic on a roadway. When you are in an office, you want to be in the position of a pedestrian on that road, facing oncoming traffic. You want an unobstructed view of everything in front of you. You sure don't want some tractor-trailer barreling down the road behind you, hidden by a curve until it is too late. You want to be able to anticipate things coming at you. That's the same kind of situation you want to create in a place of business—a place where energy is free-flowing and where it is possible to anticipate things coming at you.

Obstructing energy is like walking along a roadway with the traffic coming behind you. You know that you are vulnerable. Your body is stressed and on alert. You are functioning at a higher degree of tension than is healthy. We are "hardwired" to react this way. After all, facing out from a cave enabled our ancestors to mark the approach of lions and tigers and either fight, flee, or freeze. Shouldn't we respect our instinctive need to do the same?

Rearrange the office space so that everyone working there is facing the "cave opening," and you will see a complete change in the way business is conducted in that office.

What does this mean in a practical way? First, by setting up desks or workstations in a way that allows your staff to "see what's coming," you give each worker a stake in the energy of the office and, by extension, a stake in the business itself. The next step is to look at the locations of the various tasks that are performed within an office to make sure, for example, that financial tasks are being done in an area that is functionally related to the other tasks nearby. Office space should be designed so the form of the space follows the function of the task for efficiency.

Think of this as managing traffic flow. After all, you don't want a sports car stuck behind a huge truck, right? Get those sports cars out onto the open road! In other words, open up the flow of energy so that each individual can maximize his or her potential, from the person with the lowest job description to the highest-ranking executive. When you allow people to maximize their potential, you begin to see a corporate environment that maximizes *its* potential. Remember, you become your environment. Therefore, the structure of that environment, the things you put on the wall, the color of the walls, everything has an impact on the physical and mental well-being of your employees or customers—whether you realize it or acknowledge it or not.

Corporate environments can be read physically by how they are set up, the condition of the facilities, where the executive offices are located, and how the employees are related to them in availability and concept. All this can give a clear indication of the status of the company and how it is doing. Correcting deficiencies or things that are amiss in the physical environment of a business brings about structural changes in how that business gets conducted.

That was certainly the case with Ed and his office. As soon as I walked in, I shuddered. There were desks where there should have been hallways. Walls where there should have been doors. People working with their backs to one another and facing a variety of directions.

"Oh no," I said. "This is all wrong."

He looked at me. "What do you mean?"

"Let me show you."

First, I had him explain the flowchart of his business, how decisions were made and how they were communicated. Then I asked him about the various tasks his employees did.

It turned out that there were several people assigned to similar tasks but who worked in different parts of the building.

"Rather than thinking of yourself as the Chief Executive Officer, you have to begin visualizing yourself as the Chief Energy Officer," I told Ed.

"Energy officer?"

"Sure. After all, you are responsible for motivating and inspiring your employees, establishing the direction of your business, and promoting change. All those things take energy, right?"

Of course they do. By paying attention to the unobstructed flow of energy in the office, the strategic and operating plans subconsciously support one another throughout the day. In the same way that there is a natural order of energy in a home, there is a natural order of energy in a place of business, and that order is unique to that business! You cannot necessarily take a bagua map from one business and impose it on another! However, understanding the map's plan can guarantee that the sales or marketing department is not located in the quiet introspective corner of the business. Or that the controller is not located near the kitchen amidst all the noonday noise. It is important that you align your offices to support the energies and the tasks that your employees are expected to perform.

Clutter can be a problem in a business as well as a home. Paper, books, office equipment, furniture, and general clutter often impede the flow of energy. There is no question that records retention and document storage are important aspects of any successful business. However, acknowledging that does not diminish the fact that many businesses collect more things than are necessary for their successful operations.

It goes without saying that the correct placement of office furniture is essential to the free flow of energy. Most of us instinctively place our desks so that we are facing the door. However, we may be less sensitive to desk placement in multilevel buildings, bullpen office cubicles, manufacturing spaces, shipping floors, and retail shops. Each employee's space should support that person's energy and the collective energy of the business. You want energy to accrue and grow, not be inhibited or obstructed.

"Ed, change your energy pattern by changing your surroundings," I told him. "In that way, you change your presentation of who you are to your employees, and you will find that the employees will respond to you differently, and that goes for your customers too."

Ed listened intently but with some degree of skepticism. However, when I finished going through his office with him, he shrugged his shoulders and admitted that, "It makes as much sense as any other advice I've gotten."

Three months later, he was more surprised than I was when he came to visit me to inform me how much things had changed for him.

"It's like night and day. You can feel it in the office," he said happily. "And I'm seeing the change in my bottom line results too. Happier workers. Happier customers. More profit. I don't know how it works and, I've got to admit, it all still sounds a little weird to me, but it works, and that's all I care about."

Feng Shui principles work in homes, home offices, offices, even in retail establishments. You can take that application one step further to meetings themselves. I had occasion to work with a newly appointed and very distressed director on a condominium association board. It seems their association was having some major communication problems around reserve funds, replacement of limited common elements and an assured increase in condominium dues. She was the only director left. All the other directors resigned at the last condo meeting after much yelling and screaming and fighting from the residents toward them.

It seems as if the financial problem had grown over the last year into a nearly insurmountable standoff between homeowners, the board of directors and the management company. It was a legal issue and the board knew they were going to "win" at the proposal for increased dues, but they were trying to make it more palatable to the owners by arranging financing etc. When all their cooperative plans failed and the heat got even hotter, they quit. Maria was left alone on the board.

The management company and Maria announced another meeting and solicited new volunteers for board members. They needed to have members to conduct business and proceed with the running of the association. When I got the notice I knew they had experienced trouble at the meeting I had missed, so I offered to ergonomically set up the room to precipitate a better reception of the board by the homeowners. I think they thought me nuts, but because they knew I had a major background in property management they acquiesced and told me to go ahead.

I explained to them that the room had to take on a totally different form than it had in meetings past. Nothing, not one position of one chair or table could be the same. And I suggested they let me facilitate the discussion period. They agreed to let me ergonomically adjust the room for better rapport, i.e. "Feng Shui it."

That evening they helped me place the tables and chairs in a specific arrangement. The head table was at a different end of the room. It was placed in the power position for the new board of directors to see the door, but it was also angled so the residents could also see the door. The sign-in table was on the opposite side of the door and a rolling rack of extra chairs was in the rear in case more people came than the board anticipated. More did come. Many more, and ready to battle.

Everyone signed in. The meeting started and seemed to progress, and the tension slipped from the air. Discussions were held. Questions were asked. Concerns were voiced and facilitated by being written on flip charts. There was no yelling and no one quit. This night was a huge success all around. As people left (even before the end of the meeting) they quietly picked up their chairs and placed them on the rack. Even I was surprised at that response. Someone said it was the best condo meeting ever!

What happened here is not uncommon. The bad feelings about previous meetings had been anchored into the placement of the furniture during the meetings and then all the animosity was transferred to the board of directors during the course of the meeting. In order for the new board of directors to avoid the potential of the same animosity being transferred to them, they had to change something. By putting themselves and the homeowners both in power positions, opening the channels of communication by introducing a disinterested third party with flip charts to collect the negative comments, and re-arranging the sign-in sheet table for the management company, it was clear this condominium's meetings would never be the same again.

It's worth repeating the major point of this story: If you do what you always did, you get what to you always got. Become aware of how your surroundings affect you and everyone else around you and understand that this happens constantly. When you want to affect groups of people in a positive light, you might remember this story.

Now About You—The Next Step in the Dance

Structurally breaking old patterns in your environment will intentionally change your circumstances and situations to more desirable positive experiences.

Your new altered environment will begin to produce changes. All energy, including yours, reacts swiftly to input that has been altered physically, often with immediate results. Psychological and spiritual input produces a much more subtle reaction with different results over time.

Your brand new environment now promotes fresh patterns and desirable habits through new thought and new ways of doing things. Environmentally negative patterns will no longer hold back your progress because they have been structurally or metaphorically broken.

顋

Emerging

CHAPTER 24

Becoming the Lover
You Already Are

*I*N THE '60S, THE Beatles told us that love is all we need. And it's true. All you need is love. However, there's a problem with that simple observation. To put it bluntly, many people don't have it. We have entire industries that seem to revolve, to a large part, around our longing for love: Music. Movies. Greeting Cards. Romance novels. All we need is love, but all these commercial endeavors seem to do (in addition to generating a lot of commerce) is to highlight the reality that many of us don't have what we need.

What does this have to do with Feng Shui?

Love is a powerful emotion. It holds remarkable energy. Love. There's that important word again, and its connection with Feng Shui, which, as we've discussed, is all about energy, and, as you've learned, the free flow of energy has to do with orientation and relationship (as opposed to geography). Which is to say that, when you really get down to it, even when talking about something as powerful as love, you cannot speak about only one aspect of your life because adjusting one aspect of your life means you have to adjust every aspect of your life. The goal is always a more balanced life.

Still, for many of us, our lives are out of balance because we do not enjoy enough love energy. That was certainly the case for Sarah. Sarah is a pretty woman in her early thirties. She is energetic, enthusiastic, a real "go-getter." To meet her, you would be stunned to discover that she struggled with her love life.

"Oh, it's not a problem getting dates," she confided to me when we first met. "That's always been easy, but I'm not a kid anymore. I want more than just a night of dancing and physical attraction."

Although Sarah, like many women her age, had enjoyed the freedom of relationships without permanent attachments, she had reached a point in her life where she had finally decided that it was time to find something more lasting.

"'Settle down' isn't the right term," she said, furrowing her brow with a thoughtful expression. "It's not that I'm interested in settling down. I like my life. I like my job. I like my friends, but I would like something a bit more real in a relationship."

It was hard not to be charmed by Sarah. She has a wonderful sense of humor, a quick smile, and a self-deprecating perspective on her own attractiveness that, ironically, added to her attraction. I asked her if she'd ever been in love.

"Have I ever been in love?" she repeated. "When haven't I been in love? I've had boyfriends since junior high. Sometimes two or three at a time."

I shook my head. "I don't mean that. I mean, have you ever been in love?"

"I guess when I was in junior high school." She looked at me with a questioning expression.

"Sounds like puppy love to me," I said.

"I still think about him."

"Then maybe you did love him. In that innocent way of first loves."

She recounted two or three people she believed she really did love. "But, you know, the world is so difficult . . ." She left the thought to trail off, satisfied that, at the time, the pain of the end of each relationship was somewhat assuaged by other things going on in her life.

"What's changed now?" I asked her.

"I don't understand."

"What's changed that has made you dissatisfied with the kinds of relationships you've been having?"

"I don't know," she answered honestly. "Maybe it's biological. Maybe not. I just think I'd like something more."

Though she apparently had been content for a long time to have only relationships that didn't last, it sounded as if Sarah had reached a point where she understood—even if she didn't know the words to articulate it—that her lack of a satisfying loving relationship was affecting other aspects of her life. Although she continued to be successful in her career, she was no longer deriving the same satisfaction from that success. Her other relationships were also suffering, not because she was not still close to her friends, but because the balance of their lives pulled them away from her. She was the last one who was still single. They were all married or in long-term, monogamous relationships. They were focused on houses, not clubs. They were focused on "play dates," not romantic dates. They knew that Barney was not just a partner in a financial firm.

"Everything used to be so simple," Sarah sighed.

I explained to Sarah that I found an interesting teacher named Santos a few years ago. He was hardly the Hollywood image of the "wise man." He was tall. Wiry. And he was a little different. Or maybe it wasn't so much that he was strange looking as that he dressed in a way that accentuated the fact that he viewed the world differently, more deeply, than most people. He wore baggy old clothes and a baggy old hat. Add to the picture the fact that he drove a ratty old pick-up truck, and you get the image of a man who was completely unconcerned about the face he presented to the outside world.

Santos was not interested in masks. Quite the opposite.

When I first met him, I was taken aback. From reading his books and hearing about him, I had almost a "guru" image in my mind, an image that did not in any way fit with the person I met. However, as soon as he began to speak, it was clear that he was extremely wise. One of the first things he spoke about was love and loving relationships.

"It's like shattered glass," he began.

Then he smiled when he saw the confused look on my face. He was used to that reaction. "You've got this shattered glass piece, and you've got another shattered piece of glass, and when you find the shards that fit together, they match. Trouble is, the shards are still sharp, and they cut each other. Cut each other to death."

Suddenly, his analogy made sense within my own understanding of relationships. I had always thought in terms of finding the piece of you that was missing, a similar analogy to his shards of broken glass. But he had a new angle on relationships, for glass remains hard and sharp, even when the broken pieces fit.

"What you have to do is make yourself like a cotton ball. That way, when you attract someone who is shattered, they eventually soften and become like a cotton ball too."

"Why would they become like a cotton ball?" I asked.

"Because they can't cut you. And, because they can't cut you, you start to bounce off them, and they bounce off you."

I was stunned by the simplicity and the wisdom of the analogy. Listening to him, I thought, "My gosh, how many times have I, in my own life, met someone and thought that everything was going really great, but then, at some point in the relationship, I suddenly looked at them and said, 'This person's worse than me. I have to get out of this relationship.'"

The reason was very simple. We had been attracted to one another, the way the broken pieces of glass managed to find one another. We fit, but it was our broken edges, still hard and sharp, that fit.

We all are attracted to energy. It's the energy that attracts us to other people and that attracts others to us. How our energy fits determines whether we're attracted to one person as opposed to another. Sarah's energy had always been a certain kind. As a result, the men she attracted recognized their match in her, but the "broken shards" kept cutting away at her. Psychically, she was bleeding, and she didn't know how to stop the bleeding. When she came to me, she only knew that something wasn't right.

Whatever energy we put out, that's the energy that we're going to get back. The energy that we put out can only be changed one way and that is to change it within ourselves. For most of her life, Sarah had put out a particular kind of energy, and the world had responded accordingly. Now, she had to decide how she wanted to change that perception. Once she did that, she would have to "walk the walk."

"I'm not sure I'm getting this," she said to me. "I've always tried to be myself. I haven't tried to put out one kind of energy or another."

"When you're at work, how do you dress?"

"I dress well," she said.

"What exactly does that mean? Give me an example of what you might wear on a given day."

She thought about it for a moment, and then she described a very classy business suit, the kind that did not

hide her beauty but didn't flaunt it either. Her dress was neither too short nor too long.

"So, what you're really trying to do is to communicate
your professionalism, right?"

"Absolutely," she replied.

"When you're doing that, dressing like a professional, do
you feel like a professional?"

"Of course," she answered. "Look, I don't want you to
get the wrong idea. I like to have a good time, but I'm very
professional. I'm very good at what I do," she added with
some obvious pride.

I smiled. "I knew that the moment I met you," I said
honestly.

"What does all this have to do with Feng Shui?" she
asked.

"In Feng Shui, we try to alter our external environment
in order to allow energy to flow more freely. If I want to
change myself in some way, I need to re-create my environment to allow that energy to flow."

She looked at me strangely. I thought for a moment,
trying to find the analogy that might help her understand.
I decided on an experience that had once been shared with
me by a man I'd met at a lecture. He was telling me about a
time when he was in college and had gone to a party, where
he met a woman who was studying to be a dance therapist.
It sounded interesting, but he didn't really understand what
that meant.

"What exactly does a dance therapist do?" he asked.

"I work with autistic children," she told him.

He immediately conjured up an image of a group of
autistic children line dancing. As he told the story to me,
he couldn't keep himself from laughing. "Of course, I was
completely off base. What this young woman did was to sit
opposite an autistic child and mimic his behavior. By mim-
icking his behavior, she drew him out of his internal world."

As soon as I heard this story, I was struck by the power of the example in helping others to understand Feng Shui. There is a direct and powerful relationship between the internal and external world.

In the case of the dance therapist, by mirroring the autistic child's external behavior, she hoped to draw out the child's internal reality. In Feng Shui, we recognize that the external world has its own energy and that we can use that energy to alter our internal energy, the same way changes in our internal energy alter the energy around us.

"So," Sarah said, an expression of understanding beginning to show on her face, "you're saying that my clothes make me feel more professional, and when I feel more professional, I present myself in a more professional manner. And in the same way, by changing my external environment, I can change my love life too?"

I nodded yes.

"But isn't that changing how I feel about my love life, not changing my love life itself?"

Good question.

"When we're talking about energy," I said, "how we perceive ourselves is part of it. If you perceive yourself as a loving person, you are a loving person. Your energy becomes that of a loving person."

"Okay, so what do I have to do? Dress differently?"

I smiled at her quick wit. "Remember, you may not be perfect at first. But soon, you will get what you want because you will get where you want to be because you've decided that's where you want to be. If you're looking for the perfect job, it will come to you when you put out the right energy. In the same way, you will not have to look for the perfect mate because the perfect mate will come to you when you put out the right kind of energy. It's matching the internal and external."

"I was never good at that introspection thing," she laughed.

"You don't have to be," I emphasized. "That's the power of Feng Shui. By fixing the stuff out here," I said, waving my arm around to indicate the external world, "you automatically change the world in here," I concluded, pointing to my heart. You can fix all the junk in your unconscious by looking at your external world and fixing the junk there.

Sarah took a deep breath. "Okay. I'll try it. Where do we start?"

For most people, the answer is: Everywhere. As I said earlier, it isn't possible to balance one part of your life without balancing all the parts of your life. That said, "everywhere" isn't a very helpful answer. So, we start at the beginning. Start with the easy things, and then move to the harder things. My own strategy for moving forward involves what I call the Three Cs.

First, everything you do, you have to do *consciously*.

Most of us sleepwalk through our lives. We are like automatons. We watch the television programs we're told to watch. We purchase the foods we're told to purchase. We wear the clothes we are told to wear. And we don't even think about it.

I remember being in high school when my school considered having students wear uniforms. This was during the 1960s, when everyone was an individual and no one was interested in being told what to wear.

"Why should we have to conform?" one of my classmates asked, challenging the principal in a school meeting.

The principal smiled at him and then pointed at us. "You already do conform. Look at what you're wearing now."

He was right. As we looked around, we saw that the boys, with only minor variations, were dressed alike, right down to the style of shoe they wore. The same was true of the girls. Within small variations of clothes and hairstyles, the vast majority of us conformed completely. And we thought we were all being nonconformists! As high school students, that was a learning opportunity, and the reality is that most people do not become less conformist as they get older. In fact, they get worse, becoming even more fixed in their patterns and their ways. In other words, they become more "unconscious."

The next step is to *clear the clutter*—the clutter that you have unconsciously allowed to gather in all areas of your life. Clutter inhibits the free flow of energy. It blocks energy. It makes you stuck in the problem.

Finally, you have to consciously *create what you want*.

Sarah and I made an appointment for me to come to her house so we could begin the process. Sarah's home was a nice, small house, located in a clean neighborhood. In other words, it was a fair reflection of her material success in life. When she met me at her front door, she smiled a broad, if somewhat nervous, smile.

"Ready?" I asked, returning her smile.

"I think so," she said.

Because her concern was her love life, we had decided to deal with her bedroom first. Bedrooms should have two primary purposes, sleep and intimacy. That being the case, the first task in removing clutter is to remove everything that is not directly related to those two purposes.

"I have to take out my bookcase and desk?" Sarah complained.

"Everything in its place," I said cheerfully. "And nothing where it doesn't belong."

Bedrooms are all about relationships. If you share a bedroom, it is about your relationship with that person. If you live, or sleep alone, your bedroom is about how you relate to yourself. It is that awareness, that consciousness, that must infuse everything you understand about your bedroom.

I attended a class not too long ago in which a group of people were talking about becoming "minimalists," removing everything from their lives that they could. Their goal seemed to be make their lives monochromatic, physically and emotionally.

"Anything I put on the wall—and I can't imagine what that might be—will have to mean the world to me," boasted one woman.

My only problem with that approach is that sameness does not equate to balance. However, there is one thing I admired about their minimalist approach: their determination to clear away clutter and keep in their lives only that which had personal meaning. What most people don't realize is that your body absorbs the energy around you. So if your bedroom is gaudy or plain, masculine or feminine, that's the energy you absorb. Everything counts. Everything around you affects you. So the first things that we decided had to go were Sarah's books and desk. There would be no more confusing intimacy with learning or business.

On her night table, there were a number of photographs, many of them of herself with men she had dated.

"You can't keep these here," I told her simply.

"But they're all my friends," she protested. "That's one good thing I'll say about my relationships: They hardly ever end on a bad note. I stay friends with most of the men I've gone out with."

I wasn't impressed. It's great if you're able to have warm, ongoing relationships with people with whom you've previously had a romantic relationship, but when those relationships block the energy for new relationships, then there's a problem. For Sarah, that meant that her former relationships were like ghosts hovering around any new relationship.

"You're not really looking for just a friend with whom you can also have a physical relationship, are you?" I asked her pointedly.

"No," she admitted.

That is the reason we had to remove the clutter of all her past relationships from her bedroom in order for her to be able to move forward.

The same was true of her "hidden" clutter, the clutter in her closets and drawers. Old lingerie. Old shoes. Old clothes. The clutter of the person she no longer wanted to be, of the kind of life she no longer wanted to lead, had to be cleared away. Everything of the old Sarah, the old life, amounted to clutter that blocked her energy.

The cleanup was difficult for Sarah. I suggested that we put many of the things we were clearing away in cartons and she could put them in storage for a while. She was relieved by this middle step, but I knew what would happen. I knew that, when the energy blocked by these things was released, she would get rid of that clutter from wherever it was in her life.

Dealing with what I call "baggage clutter"—the clutter that piles up on the end of a nightstand or at the bottom of the closet—is not easy.

"How do I know what to get rid of?" Sarah asked.

The rule of thumb is, put it on. If it doesn't fit, doesn't feel right, doesn't look as good as you thought it would, get rid of it. If you haven't worn it in six months, put it in a carton and store it somewhere. If you haven't retrieved it in a month, throw or give away the carton.

I even recommend getting rid of any clothing that is associated with a negative event. I was in South Carolina on September 11, 2001, where I was to speak at a breakfast meeting and motivate people to return to my seminar at one o'clock. I got up. Got dressed. Went downstairs.

"Just live," I began. "Don't let the moment slip by."

I don't know what got into me then, but what had been scheduled as a ten-minute teaser turned into a thirty-minute talk. Sadly, we all know the tragic events that occurred later that morning. The group of fifty to whom I spoke that morning quickly turned into nearly three hundred that afternoon. More people drifted in, wanting to be together, wanting to find some sanctuary against the fear that had so suddenly gripped us all. They wanted hope. They wanted to know that they could go on.

I told Sarah that story and how the suit that I wore that morning, which was brand new, I wore only that one time. I was never able to bring myself to put it on again without reliving the horrible reality of that morning. Even though I thought it lovely I gave it to the woman's shelter as an interview suit for someone less fortunate. It's the sort of thing, I explained to Sarah, that will mire you in the past. You cannot move on if you are mired in the past. I don't care how beautiful a dress is. If it locks you in the past, you have to get rid of it, or the past won't let you go.

The questions you need to ask when you're clearing away the clutter and other things are: What energy does it carry? Is that energy a reason to keep it or get rid of it? How does it make me feel?

The problem is that, if you're looking at an object only from a practical standpoint, you will tend to look for reasons to keep it, and, in coming up with those reasons, you will end up exactly where you started. But if you honestly answer the question of what energy it carries, then you are more likely to see when there are reasons to get rid of it, and that enables you to free yourself of that energy from the past.

The questions are sometimes as important as the answers. If you touch it and you get a bad feeling, get rid of it. If it reminds you of something negative, get rid of it.

"What about this?" Sarah asked, showing me a ring.

She pinched it in her fingers. "A boyfriend gave it to me once. It wasn't an engagement ring," she explained. "But he wanted me to know he was serious."

The ring was beautiful, a diamond surrounded by rubies in an elegant setting. It was clearly an expensive ring. For many of us, the monetary value of an item will dictate how easily—and even whether or not—we can get rid of it. In addition to the emotional and spiritual value, we factor in the commercial cost. Then we debate within ourselves. Selling it on consignment will likely bring only a modest return. Giving it away, well that's even worse. We feel guilty about wanting to get rid of something that cost a lot even if its real monetary value is now somewhat diminished. It's that guilt that will bring you down faster than anything else.

My advice to Sarah was simple: Put the ring in a box and look at it for three days. At the end of three days, you'll instinctively know what to do. Your gut will tell you. I reminded her again that the body doesn't lie. The ring either will stay, or it will go. She'd know.

I told Sarah about another circumstance where a woman, who I'll call Lynn, went through a very painful divorce. It wasn't bitter. In fact, in most respects, it was very amicable. Both she and her ex-husband cared very deeply for their two children and were determined to make the process as positive for them, and each other, as possible. But it was still very painful.

Lynn had a great deal of trouble moving past the divorce. She didn't enjoy dating. She couldn't stop thinking of herself as a "divorced woman"—something she'd never imagined herself being. One day, she was talking to me about her engagement ring, a beautiful piece of jewelry.

"Should I return it?" she wondered.

"What do you want to do with it?" I asked.

Unfortunately, returning it wouldn't free her from the pain with which she was struggling. Nor would keeping it.

"I'd like to bury it ... you know like a funeral," she remarked, "I want this done once and for all."

"Well that's a little drastic don't you think?" I asked.

Lynn explained that she'd like to take it to the beach she and her husband used to frequent and bury it in the sand in hopes it would have a new life with someone else. But I wanted her to be sure. Burying is a ritual that gives closure like a funeral, however, in the sand it becomes potentially retrievable with a metal detector. To create complete closure she could also give the ring to charity or sell it and give the money to a good cause. Burying it in the sand means your intent is only for your closure and leaves the ultimate life of the ring up to good luck or fate on someone else's part someday.

That's when I told Lynn about the Viking funeral ritual that finalizes and puts to bed all kinds of unpleasant memories. Since the ring was a symbol of the relationship she had once had, the relationship that was now long dead, she could say a final goodbye with no chance of retrieval, Viking style. I knew we could create a ritual for getting rid of it that would allow her the same kind of closure that a funeral does for the death of a loved one, with complete finality. She was adamant that this was the way she wanted to go, so we put the ring on a paper plate decorated with paper flowers, set it on fire and put it to float in the river. It was hard for her and we both cried, then we started laughing fearing we'd be arrested for arson. But after the ceremony, she was able to begin moving forward. The ring was no longer a presence in her life, physically or emotionally. The ties to the past had been completely cut and she could move on.

For Sarah, it seemed as if practically everything she had reminded her of one old relationship or another. The diamond and ruby ring was only one of a number of things holding her down and keeping her back in one way or another. Even if the relationship had been friendly, the object—a photograph, dress, piece of jewelry—locked her into the person she had been. As long as she was that person, she would not be able to change the way she dealt with romance, and she would not be able to find the love she wanted. She agreed to the three day wait.

Sarah and I spent some time discussing how she might go about decorating her bedroom. As we did, I shared with her how I had decorated my own. Because my life's difficulties have taught me how to be a "strong" woman, I decorated my room to be a "girly-girl" room.

Sarah looked at me and laughed. "Girly-girl?" she asked as she raised an eyebrow.

"Well sure," I told her. "Look at me. I go out on appointments, and I move furniture! I don't mind getting my hands dirty. I'm a worker and always have been. But when it comes to romance, well, I want to be treated like a lady. In order to bring that balance into my life, I had to decorate my room in a very feminine way so that I would absorb that energy into my life as well."

"And?"

I smiled. "And what?"

"Did it work?"

Now it was my turn to laugh. "I wouldn't be here advising you about something that doesn't work in my own life," I laughed. "I never tell anyone to do something I haven't done."

Sarah decided that one by one she'd address the items she'd kept from her old relationships. She'd hold them and release them like a butterfly into the sky, either giving them away, selling them on consignment or disposing of them. The diamond ring that had peeked my curiosity, she told me later, had been sold and the money used for new bedroom linens and curtains.

When we create our environments, we're "setting the stage" for the drama of our lives. Didn't Shakespeare proclaim that "All the world is a stage ..."? How we set our personal stage is very important. It is not an accident that, when most men want to propose to the women they love, they choose a candlelit, intimate restaurant—or some similarly romantic setting—rather than a rock concert or a football game. Bright lights and loud music don't work for an intimate evening.

So set the stage for your love life!

There was a time in my life when I was perceived as "tough," and I was tough. I ran a business, and I knew that to run it right, I had to be tough. But I don't want to be tough anymore. Oh, I can go there if I need to because that energy is still part of me, but I am more interested in cultivating other energies now. I don't want to live in the past. I want to live here, in the present. So, in my own bedroom, I bought a different kind of bedspread. One with ruffles. Red. And a different set of sheets. New rugs as well. And now, when I walk through my room, when I walk across "my stage," I feel softer and more attractive. I feel ready for romance. Then, I'm not only the owner of a business; I'm a woman. And that's good. I love that.

I also explained to Sarah that no detail is too insignificant for scrutiny.

"Even the size of the bed," I told her.

"I love big beds," she confessed. "I don't know what I would do without my king-size bed."

"That's fine. A king-size bed is a wonderful thing, but you have to be careful of king-size beds. Many big beds—king-size, queen-size, even full-size—are deceptive. For example, a king-size bed might be nothing more than two single beds put together with a double mattress on top. Now, think about that for a moment. What does that suggest?"

Sarah shrugged.

"On the surface, it appears to be whole, but underneath the surface, there's separation. What does that say about relationships and intimacy?"

"Oh my gosh," she said.

I recommend beds with a solid box spring and mattress. There are some remarkably comfortable state of the art beds on the market now that provide no division between the partners. With a regular king size or extra large bed at the very least you can put a solid red sheet between the mattress and box springs to clarify your intention for a good love life, more sex and communication. Whatever size bed you have, if you want to enjoy real intimacy—at those deeper emotional levels—you need or have to create the illusion of one bed.

Another thing to consider is the material of the mattress. Because everything has energy, everything has life force, you have to think about the kind of bed you want, a feather mattress, a water bed, an air mattress. Each has a different energy. Each has its own life. Each will speak to you in a different way. As I told Sarah, one is not necessarily better than the other, they simply differ within personal experience.

What was really important for her to understand was if she was going to have a bed for two and wanted a relationship, the bedroom itself must also be balanced. She would need to have two bedside lamps, two nightstands. Otherwise, if there is only a lamp on your side of the bed, or one night stand, it says you're not even remotely ready to think about sharing the bed—or your emotional life—with someone else.

One of the most telling things about anyone's home is also the most individualistic: the photographs and art on the wall. They tell a story in their own right. Very often, when I go into a single woman's home, I look at the photographs and see picture after picture of single women. Pictures of the woman herself, alone on vacation. Pictures of her with friends. Her friends. All single. What these pictures do is reaffirm her status as, the energy of, a single woman.

Choose things for your wall that reflect who you want to be, not necessarily who you are, and certainly not who you were. Choose art that says something about the person you want to be, strong, sensual, loving, and happy. If you're interested in attracting a serious romantic relationship, then you should hang a "love picture" over your bed. Or certainly in the bedroom somewhere. Thankfully, Sarah didn't have exercise equipment in her bedroom.

The main thing is to be conscious of what you really want in a loving relationship. Go about creating your environment to generate the kind of energy you need to attract that particular relationship into your life. Tenacity and hope have a great deal to do with finding the right match. Finding love doesn't always have to do with the other person; often it has more to do with us.

Now About You–The Next Step in the Dance

Controlling your energy is a fluid process that is created by intentionally modifying your perceptions of the world.

You take new energy with you as you become more practiced at having embedded your desires through intention into your immediate personal environment. Your body translates this energy into how you react in the world, through its bodily structure, mental images and spiritual attitudes. This energy then attracts its compliment energy based on your intentions and receptivity.

Absorption

CHAPTER **25**

The Energy Travels With You

*E*LAINE IS A VERY successful business woman. When she first came to see me, she had encountered some sort of blockage in her life, and she was struggling to regain the balance, and the flow of energy, that she had once felt.

"Even at work, I have banged my head against the glass ceiling more times than I can stand," she complained. "I have a constant headache from it!"

We went through her workspace and her home, making all the appropriate adjustments. Three months after we finished, she returned to my studio.

"How are you?" I asked.

She smiled. "Much better than I was a few months ago," she said. "I've had two promotions, and I'm in a very loving relationship for the first time in a long time."

"That's wonderful," I said.

"It is . . ."

"But?" I asked, hearing the tone in her voice.

"But, there's a problem." Elaine explained that the changes that we had made in her work and living space had clearly allowed her to find greater balance in her life and, with that balance, greater success in both her career and her personal life. The only problem was that her promotions meant that she also found herself traveling more on work-related business.

"And that's where I'm finding a problem," she confessed. "I'm at a loss about what to do with the environments I find myself in when I travel."

The more we talked, the more I realized that she was feeling the same frustrations on the road that she once had felt at home and in her office, the same restrictions on her ability to succeed. Now she felt the restrictions even more acutely that she had an appreciation for what she was able to do by working with her environment.

"I can't march into a meeting and tell them they have to rearrange the furniture," she complained.

I was silent for a moment. Her frustration was palpable. Then I had something of a revelation. "Why not?" I asked.

"What?"

"Why can't you control your work environment even when you're away from home?" I wondered.

She looked at me. "I guess it never occurred to me that I could."

"Tell me again how most of your travel meetings are structured."

Elaine then described how she usually traveled alone to a city where one of her firm's partners was located, and she would conduct meetings and sessions in their offices.

"So you are in charge of the meeting, but it is on their turf?"

She nodded. "Exactly."

"Hmm. Is there any reason that you can't set up these meetings on neutral turf? Say a hotel meeting room or a restaurant?"

"I don't think there's a compelling reason," she said. "Not most of the time anyway."

Once we realized that it was possible to schedule the meetings where she wanted them to take place, it was not difficult to envision a way to set up the room to her specifications.

"But what about meetings that have to take place in other people's offices?" she asked.

"Well, then we're going to have to take advantage of your strengths," I said simply.

"What do you mean?"

"Your environment isn't a passive place. It is alive, and it is affected by the people in it because people also are part of the environment. So, even if you can't move the furniture around, you can certainly control yourself."

The first element she could control, I told her, was the way she dressed. "You cannot change the color of the walls, but you can sure control the color of your outfit."

I went on to explain that dark colors and the reds tended to be more authoritative; however, dressing in a specific color was less important than it was for her to dress appropriately, like a woman.

"Most women subconsciously give away their power in the boardroom," I explained. "They dress like men with pants and tailored suits, or they are so casual it's hard to tell their sex at all."

I reminded her that it is impossible to compete with a man on his terms, after all he is a man and we are not. But it is possible to compete with him on your terms, as a powerful woman, who is confident in her womanhood and claims her talents. So dress like one, with heels and skirts.

We also came up with additional subtle methods of establishing clear lines of energy in spaces. My favorite was to open her portfolio and have a small mirror attached to the interior corner. That mirror would function in exactly the same way as a mirror functions in any other space, to create unobstructed and directed energy flow.

"Won't they think I have the mirror because I'm vain?" Elaine worried.

I shrugged. "Maybe. Maybe not. The point is, if they are consciously or unconsciously subverting the balance you need for success—through controlling the energy in the room—then you need to reestablish that balance and energy control."

Elaine decided that she would incorporate two other strategies into her travel meetings. One would be to always take her laptop computer and place it on the table before a meeting. Then, she would turn it on, and it would play the sound of running water, albeit at a very soft, almost imperceptible level.

"I know it isn't real running water, but I find it soothing," she said.

The other thing she decided she would do was to always carry her own tea mug, one that was covered with colors and warm shapes, and her own tea bags—herbal teas that, when brewed, gave off a fresh, clean scent.

"I may not be able to control the environment when I'm away, but I can sure do a lot to influence it, and the effect it has on me and others in the room," she said with determination. Then she smiled. "You're great," she announced.

I looked at her curiously. "Why do you say that?"

"Well, look at me. I'm a very successful executive, and it had never occurred to me simply to take charge in such small but important ways. I don't have to be heavy-handed. Sometimes, little things are all that are necessary."

Before she left, we talked about the things she could do in her hotel room as well, from moving furniture around to placing small mirrors.

She laughed. "Three months ago, I would have thought you were crazy saying these things," she admitted. Then she leaned closer to me. "You know why?"

I shook my head.

"I always wanted to be successful, but I thought the only way to be successful was to overwhelm the object of my desire. I was infected with that male sensibility of domination. But now, I don't want to dominate. I want to be successful, but I want to be in balance as well. And you know what the irony is? The more I've surrendered to the balance, the more successful I've become!"

"I guess you don't have as many headaches as you used to," I observed lightly.

She looked at me curiously, not catching my reference at first. But then she remembered her comment and laughed. "No, not nearly so many. In fact, once I am able to use Feng Shui more on the road, I think the sky will be the limit."

A month later, I received a phone call from Elaine. She was traveling on business down South. "Annie," she said excitedly into the phone.

"Elaine? How are you?"

"I'm great! I just closed the biggest deal my company's had in years!"

"Really?"

"You know what makes this even sweeter? The deal is with men who never wanted to have to deal with a woman. To them, women belong in the kitchen, not the boardroom." She chuckled. "Well, I think these cowboys have learned a thing or two about little women this week. And I have you to thank for all of it."

"I think that might be giving me a little more credit than I deserve," I said.

"I don't think so," Elaine said. "All the things we talked about have worked beautifully. I feel so much in control—in the best possible way—and in balance." She was silent for a moment. "The word at work is that I'm being considered for another promotion. To vice president. Annie, I would be the first female vice-president in our company's history!"

I couldn't help but smile. I was so glad for Elaine. She deserved her success.

Travel, whether for business or on vacation, should be a positive experience. Going away can open up interests and opportunities that are trapped when you're at home, but only if you create the physical environment that allows for the balanced and unimpeded flow of energy.

A couple came to visit me not long ago for some Feng Shui advice. Mike and Lori seemed, at first glance, to be a perfect couple: Young, attractive, successful. They have two young children and no reason for anything but optimism about the future. And yet they were in my studio, Mike quiet and sullen, Lori near tears.

"We don't know what to do anymore," Lori said, her voice catching with emotion.

"I've done everything you've wanted," Mike said under his breath, glancing over at Lori.

She nodded her head. Pushing her thick, brown hair to the side, she looked directly at me. "It's true. We've both tried so hard."

"Well, what seems to be the problem?" I asked, feeling that the direct approach was the best.

Lori dabbed her eyes with a tissue. "Mike and I have been sweethearts since high school," she said. "We're each other's best friend, but something's been missing lately."

"It hasn't just been lately," Mike said, not unkindly. "It's been a while."

Once again, she nodded. It was clear that there was no anger between the two of them. There was an easy rapport, a strange sadness, and a kind of pained confusion.

"Maybe it was after Luke was born," she said, referring to their older son. "I don't know. I thought that all couples went through tough times."

"We both did," Mike agreed, looking at me. "And I was focused on work. Hey, I had a kid now. I had to get serious about making money. We'd just bought a new house, too."

I understood what they were saying. It seems almost unfair that young couples tend to have to confront such challenging financial and emotional situations at the same time. Still, these two seemed emotionally mature enough to survive and to thrive.

"We seem to have grown apart," Lori said. "We talk less and less. I was always exhausted from taking care of Luke."

"We were both always exhausted from Luke," Mike chimed in. He turned to me. "Luke was a colicky baby."

"I don't think he slept for more than twenty minutes at a time those first couple of months," Lori said, rolling her eyes. They both also smiled a bit, remembering.

"Anyway, we seemed to get through that all right. Then Brett was born, and we fell into a weird routine. Mike was working longer hours."

"Two kids to support," he piped in, shrugging his shoulders.

"I was focused on all those quote-unquote mom things. Activities for Luke and me, and play dates to arrange. Brett was a better sleeper, but he was still a baby and needed lots of time and attention."

They went on to paint a picture of a loving couple slowly drifting apart from the realities of life and not realizing that remaining a couple took a lot of work.

"By the time we realized that something was really wrong, we didn't know how to fix it." Lori looked nervously at Mike and then at me. "It was like we didn't even know how to be intimate with one another anymore."

"Every time we were together it was like a first date, with the awkwardness but not the excitement."

"We fell back on our friendship, but we both missed the passion." Lori shook her head. "We love each other very much."

Mike nodded. "That's true," he said.

"It's not like we were interested in anyone else."

Mike shook his head. "No, nothing like that."

"We knew that something was wrong and that we weren't happy. When the boys were old enough to stay with babysitters, we tried going out and stuff, but it was weird. Awkward. We ended up feeling even weirder than we had before. I don't mind telling you that it scared me."

"Me too," Mike admitted.

Lori looked at Mike sympathetically. "We were both feeling a little lost. We've always had each other to rely on, but it was as if we didn't even know one another. It was horrible."

"What did you do?"

"We did what every couple does. We went for marriage counseling," Lori said. "That was weird, too."

"I'll say," Mike said. "But I think it was helpful. At least it made sense. The counselor told us not to worry, that we were hardly abnormal. That was a relief anyway. I mean, we knew couples—friends—who were already getting divorced. That was the last thing we wanted for ourselves or the boys."

"The counselor suggested that we find more time to be with one another," Lori said, "more than just a couple of hours at the movies or dinner. He said that it would take longer than that just to get the stress of the day out of our systems. He suggested that we go away. Finding the time was going to be hard for Mike, but we knew how important this was. My parents flew in to watch the kids, and we were all set to rediscover our passion."

Mike lowered his eyes. "Unfortunately, it didn't work out that way."

It seemed that very little had gone right on the vacation. According to both of them, nothing seemed to come naturally. Everything, even their most intimate moments, seemed forced and unfulfilling. As I listened to them, not only did I recognize that the marriage counselor had been right, they were experiencing what many young couples experience, but they were also experiencing what I have come to call "Vacation Blahs."

The very premise of taking a vacation is to vacate, to "get away." The question is, from what? When we take vacations, we tend to want to get away from work, from home, from the daily grind, from the stress of our everyday lives, perhaps even from ourselves. The trouble is, too often, the very things that make our lives out of balance at home do the same on vacation. That is what happened to Mike and Lori.

Vacations create a couple of potential problems for us. One is that we get into a "vacation energy" while we're away that we'd like to maintain when we return home. That kind of "problem" suggests that, on at least one level, the vacation was a success. The other problem is that we take whatever we're trying to get away from with us when we go on vacation. As a result, our vacation is no different from being at home, with the added irritant that we know we're supposed to be having a good time.

After listening to Lori and Mike, I asked them about their hotel. What they told me made me shudder. It sounded like an overbearing honeymoon suite, right down to the round bed and heart-shaped bathtub.

"That's not what you are anymore," I explained, "if you ever were." Then I laughed. "If any of us ever were. It's amazing the pressure that is put on us to be the people someone else thinks we should be."

Vacation places are often constructed on the premise of what someone on vacation is supposed to do. The successful ones are constructed to allow people to do what they want to do, even if they didn't know they wanted to do that before they arrived. Instead, Lori and Mike's vacation sounded more like an attempt to reenact spring break than the romantic getaway of a young, married couple. They water skied and parasailed. They swam with dolphins and went to late night dances by the fire pit.

"Sounds exhausting," I observed.

"It was," Lori admitted. "But everyone else seemed to be having such a good time."

"We wondered what was wrong with us," Mike added. "And then, after drinking who knows how many of those concoctions they were serving at the dance, we'd go back to the room, where we thought we were supposed to have a wild, uninhibited time."

"Well, I have to tell you two," I said, "I think you really need a vacation from your vacation."

They both groaned.

I smiled. "Don't lose heart," I said to reassure them.

"But I can't get any more time off work," Mike moaned.

Answering his concern I said, "I think we can make this a long weekend thing, and make it a lot more successful than that week-long vacation fiasco."

Lori's expression changed. "Do you really think so?"

"I'd pretty much guarantee it," I told them.

Vacations should be Feng Shui's "best friend." After all, we go on vacation to change the energy of our surroundings so we can change the energy of our souls. Isn't that exactly the same reason that we do Feng Shui?

I gave Lori and Mike a crash course in Feng Shui. As I was explaining everything, I told them that, when they returned from their vacation, we would have to employ these same lessons and concepts in their home and at Mike's work.

"Hey, if what you're telling us works, I'll rip out walls," Mike said, sounding hopeful for the first time since coming into my studio.

I laughed. "I doubt that will be necessary," I told him.

I explained how I changed the energy of hotel rooms when I went away, whether on vacation or on business.

"You actually move the furniture in the hotel room?" Mike asked.

"Sure do," I said.

"You're allowed to do that?" Lori wanted to know.

I shrugged. "No one's said anything yet. Sometimes the maids move the furniture back in place, but then I move it around again. No big deal."

No matter whether I'm working in the hotel room or not, I always move the desk around to face the door. This is as important on vacation as when you're away on business. In fact, it was one of the first things I'd advised Elaine to do when she arrived in a hotel room.

"Order room service," I suggested to Lori and Mike.

"It's so expensive . . ." Mike began.

"Well, yes, it is," I agreed. "And you're worth it. Besides, don't do it so much for the food as for the vase of flowers they always bring up with the meal. You want flowers in your room. If room service doesn't bring them, ask for them or bring in your own. Keep those flowers throughout your stay. Move them around the room."

Next, I told them, they should keep the bathroom door closed and the shower curtain drawn.

"I don't get that one," Mike said, amused because he thought I did that out of modesty.

"It's so your energy won't go down the drain," I said.

"You're kidding," he said, doubting me.

"Do I look like I'm kidding?"

"No."

"And I keep the doors to that huge piece of furniture they put the television in closed," I told them. "You don't want that giant eye ruining your slumber."

I told them to keep the room and closet neat and orderly, so their attention could be focused on each other and not on disarray around them.

"That's it?" they asked.

"That's it," I told them. "Do it and see if it works."

They looked at each other and shrugged. I could see that they were silently communicating to one another, "Why not? It's worth a shot."

Two weeks later, Lori and Mike were back in my studio. This time, they were beaming and holding hands. It was clear from the moment they walked in that the weekend had been a glorious success.

"I don't know how you did it." Mike began.

Lori giggled.

"I didn't do anything," I reminded them. "I only made a few suggestions to allow your energy to flow more smoothly."

"Well, I'll tell you one thing," Lori said, the color rising in her cheeks, "the energy was definitely flowing smoothly."

Mike laughed and squeezed her hand. "And you say you can help us be like that at home?"

I nodded.

"Sign me up," he said.

"Me too," Lori agreed.

Some of the simplest changes can create the greatest shifts in personal energy that ultimately rewards us with a return priceless in value. This was one of those times for this couple.

Now About You—The Next Step in the Dance

Taking back control of your environment means that it won't hold you back, and creating the next level is the proactive state that pulls you into the future.

Deciding who you are and what you want to be is the foundational personal aspect that makes transformation possible. These choices need be made with a discerning heart and mind, using your own intuition, not advice from family or friends. Moving to the next level in life is based on your ability to take back control and develop a vision of the new you.

Once you have decided change is in order, you will be assisted by "unseen hands" and divine power. Imagine the kind of life this person—the person you'd like to become—would have. Then recreate the physical structure, metaphorical associations, and spiritual walk to be the same. You will soon discover new physical, mental, and spiritual levels are being manifest in your life, and you will change into the future you.

Healing

CHAPTER 26

Beginning Again Differently

*I*HAVE HAD CLIENTS WHO stared misfortune in the face and come back. Tess got ill nearly ten years ago. She is an example of how you can use the principles of Feng Shui to transform your world from what it is into what you'd now like it to be. Not only when you want to, but when you have to in order to survive.

I will never forget the day Pat called for Tess. Pat was a friend of both Tess and me. She had talked Tess into using my services. It was a setup, for both of us, we were to figure out later. Pat was clever, she knew my work, and she knew Tess needed the kind of help I could offer in order to get her life back in balance.

On the phone Tess and I talked about clutter. Boxes and bags of clutter. She said both she and her husband were, shall I say, "savers." And he ran his own business from the home, which required saving lots of stuff, not only papers.

The day I arrived at Tess's home, I was surprised to see Pat there. Actually I think she just wanted to make sure I'd stay because of the condition of the house. Tess was nervous about meeting me and a little anxious about Feng Shui in general.

After the formalities, Tess said to me, "Are you sure you want to do this? It may be beyond hope."

Smiling I said, "I guarantee you will be thrilled at the end of today, tired maybe, but thrilled, nonetheless."

So a smiling Tess looked at Pat, saying goodbye as she shooed her out the door. "Okay, what do we do next?" asked Tess.

"Let's put some tea on the stove and we can talk while you show me your home," I said as I picked my way through the clutter towards the kitchen. It was incredible. There wasn't a clear spot on the floor. Everything was covered with papers or half filled suitcases or unidentifiable stuff, only a pathway remained.

Tess was obviously embarrassed at the condition of her home but I assured her that was why I was there and not to worry. All that will change by the afternoon. We walked through the living area, then kitchen, then upstairs to her bedroom, and finally back down to their respective offices.

The living and dining room had become a depository for everything that came through the door. Personal stuff like toiletries, weeks worth of newspapers, bills and mail, things to be fixed, half unpacked suitcases, pet toys and most anything else you can imagine.

Certainly these were people who needed fewer horizontal surfaces near the door. I told Tess that our goal for the day was to reclaim her living room and dining room. She would then have at least one space in the entire home where she could retreat and recover the ills of the day. It's important to have such a sanctuary. New energy would come from this retreat for her to face the next phase.

In talking with Tess over tea, I discovered she had been under considerable stress over the last few months. A very close and dear friend from work had died. She'd had a couple of stressful job related trips, and she hadn't totally recovered from her losses in Hurricane Andrew as she had lived in South Florida before coming to this area. Plus, she and her husband were feeling the strains of life both emotionally and financially.

"Okay, here's the plan, Tess," I said.

I sent her on a mission to find a container for trash, and a box to house the unopened and yet important mail. I emptied the suitcases and put the remnants in a box on the stairs. We took what appeared to be a haphazard route in clearing the surface in the living room and dining room, but in reality I was working with a purpose.

"You see Tess, we need to get things off the tables and floors so we can move the furniture. When we break this old pattern of where the furniture sits now with a new layout, it will be easier for you to keep it up, and you'll be less likely to pile things up," I explained.

She was receptive though extremely nervous. She was worrying about what her husband was going to say, as he was due home anytime, and worrying if I would leave her in the middle of things.

When Jack arrived home for lunch he was very quiet in front of Tess, but as soon as he could he pulled me aside and expressed his concern for her.

"I want for this to help her get back on her feet," he said, "she's had a rough time of things and now it seems as if she's got a new interest in the house, and me."

"I understand," I said, "I'll help her get, at minimum, the main living areas done today. The positive energy you'll get from that will help both of you to continue with the de-cluttering process in the rest of the house. Not only will the junk be gone, but you'll have a system to know where the important stuff is located. And you'll have staging areas for things entering and leaving the house, like bills, mail and returns."

By the end of the day we'd reclaimed the living and dining room and her bedroom. The bedroom was a bonus, and all the rooms looked beautiful. I could tell how grateful she was by her gentle smile and the tears in her eyes. I know how much difference this process can make in peoples lives. I've actually seen them begin to change before I leave them. Tess was going to get back on her feet. She was going to make it.

"Can you come back for another appointment for the rest of the house next week?" Tess asked. "Please. My husband will be so surprised at what we've done so far, but I want to finish."

"Sure Tess, I'll come. Let's take a closer look at what's left to do," I answered.

Tess led me to his office, which was jammed with files, papers, supplier catalogues, and Vietnam War memorabilia, with a path into the room to the computer. This was his sanctuary.

It was easy to see that Jack's office was not in the proper area of the house, befitting the major breadwinner. His office would serve them both better being in the Wealth & Prosperity corner, and her office and exercise room should be moved to the Creativity area. But that was going to be a big job. The first step would be to clear her office to make space for him to move his. Whew! We'd need Jack's cooperation, too.

"Well here it is, my so-called office," she remarked sounding sad.

"Don't worry, by next week this will look as great as the living and dining room do today. It will be empty and ready for him to move in!" I smiled.

Her acknowledgement included a few tears, and she said quietly, "I think this room will be hard for me, and I'm scared. These bags are full of all the stuff I didn't want to address over the last few years."

I hugged her and said not to worry, that whatever it was we could get through it. It was then that I noticed the Breast Cancer Survivor button and all the medical records and calendars from nearly ten years ago. It dawned on me then, that she had waited this long because now she really believed she was going to live. On my way home there were tears in my eyes also.

The next week we started the process with the goal of getting rid of anything that reminded her in any way of the negativity of the events she had lived through. By the end of the third week, Jack had moved his office, Tess had the start of new way of living in her home, and they were planning a party to have friends over. She'd gotten her life back.

Most often it is a combination of factors that pull us down. Stress, death, illness, shock, betrayal, etc. When our physical environment becomes contaminated with nothing but negativity and sorrow, it is hard for us to break out of that pattern. That is why the ergonomic principles of Feng Shui are so valuable to us.

Everything in our environment affects us, including clutter, color and personal symbols. Our surroundings in total make up who we are, what we are like, what we think of ourselves, the energy we project into the world, how we handle ourselves, and how we handle others.

When clutter runs rampant in a space, all energy becomes stuck. A lack of color in people's lives inevitably leads to a lack of the life energy itself.

But symbols don't have to be missing to affect a person's life. Sometimes they are the things that set it askew. The wrong symbols. The wrong art. A dress that's two sizes too small. Pictures of a lost love. The golf clubs we never have time to use. Not realizing the subconscious impact of these items makes us totally vulnerable to the things that surround us whether defined as positive or negative.

In total, it's the content of our surroundings that define us. Since the beginning of time philosophers have said, "You become what you think about." What we think about are our surroundings. Our home. Our car. Our work. Our kids. Our partner. Our body. Our looks. We think about everything that surrounds us, literally, and our lives are created and shaped by those intimate and not so intimate thoughts. If our thoughts are positive and affirming, so is the energy that is created in our lives. If not, the negative but affirming thoughts create a force not for our good that is equally as powerful in our lives.

By consciously, and with intent, changing our surroundings to have positive impact on our thoughts, we ultimately "set up" our environment for success. We then subconsciously absorb those positive meanings into our bodies in the form of positive energy. It is that positive energy we take out into the world.

This is what I mean when I say, "You become your surroundings. Make sure they represent who you want to become."

The world always mirrors our own energy in its response. See it in this circular equation: Surroundings = thoughts = personal energy = response = identity = surroundings = thoughts, etc. Simple thinking but profound. We do it all to ourselves. We are responsible. We "set up" our own personal world in either a positive or negative fashion, but we often blame someone else.

Once we realize we have the capability to "set it up" for the way we want to be, we will then "set it up" to become the way we want to be. It almost seems that this was the part missing from life 101 we should have been allowed to take as kids. By choosing to create a positive intention in our surroundings, we assure ourselves of carrying a positive energy into the world, which responds in kind.

Sometimes the answers don't come easy. They didn't for a client I'll call Mora. She appeared to be in her late 40's or early 50's, fit and attractive, and very obviously not happy.

"I don't know what to do next," she lamented. "I've tried everything, for 20 years. I've tried affirmations, visualization, all that stuff. I was hoping Feng Shui would work."

I wasn't surprised her life hadn't worked by the looks of things. She lived in a very small studio apartment cluttered with years worth of stuff. Dust was so thick I could write in it in the out of sight areas. Things that belonged to an old flame were boxed under the bed and in the corner, although she didn't even have room for her own things. Everything was very unorganized.

"Well Mora," I said, "Feng Shui is a tool for balancing your life. But it requires active participation in the process. The first thing we have to do is clean up and rearrange the furniture to let the energy break free in this space."

We dutifully went to work and made great progress not only by putting the sofa and the bed in more powerful positions, but by clearing out junk and things that were not hers. Cleaning everything made a huge difference. I was pleased with the progress. And I could see she was feeling the energy shift.

"Make sure you drink lots of water tonight and tomorrow," I explained. "What you've done to your environment is very much like getting a massage for your body."

I encouraged her to drink water to enable the detoxification process within her body. When the energy shifts in a space, it has a physical affect on your body. Some people feel a slightly disoriented for a little while. Some get queasy. Some get a headache. All of these are normal symptoms that usually disappear by the next day. She seemed excited about the prospect of getting more out of life, and agreed to follow my instructions and call me in a week.

Our discussions early on had revealed her desire to "live the good life." Wanting to meet the perfect man, travel, not have to work, have no worries about money, go where she wanted when she wanted. This all sounded good to me, too. But something was not quite right here, I sensed. Soon I found out what.

"Annie, we need to talk," Mora said forcefully into the phone, "It's not working, all this Feng Shui stuff. It's been a week and nothing has happened."

"How so Mora?" I asked.

"I've done everything you suggested. I even bought flowers for the Helpful People and Travel area, as well has a symbolic heart shaped candy dish for my Love area."

Mora went on to explain, again, how she'd always wanted to be "rich" and do all the things the very wealthy had the money to do. Never once did she mention being happy.

She talked insistently about all the methods she'd attempted to get what she wanted. Now she was including everything from love potion spells to prayer, almost like a shot in the dark, covering all the bases. She was bouncing from one thing to another, all the while insisting she was quite spiritual. I was beginning to see the problem, and a pattern.

"Mora, you realize that Feng Shui is only a tool in the process. It's not the reason something good happens, it's the process. You actually change your energy, and that in turn changes circumstances and people's response to you," I tried to convey.

But I'm not sure she heard. I went on to explain that even though we have specific results in mind that we'd like to see materialize from our Feng Shui efforts, sometimes "we get what we need, not what we want."

It's an empirical law of nature. Cause and effect. God's choice.

And then I asked a big question, I realize now. "Do you pray?"

"Oh yes!" she eagerly replied. "I pray all the time for what I want."

This was a sensitive area I knew. I could see the tip of the problem, like an iceberg. She rattled off a laundry list of "God please give me . . . ," as if the Creator were a big vending machine in the sky. If I could only get her to pray, "God, help me to let you help me."

"Have you ever considered praying differently?" I questioned lovingly.

"What do you mean? How?" she quizzed.

"I mean, have you ever considered praying for God to enable you to do and have what He wants for you to do, and have, and be what He wants?" I said.

"Well no. I know what I want," she replied.

"That's the point Mora. Perhaps what He wants for you is not what you want for yourself," I replied. "Maybe you should tell him you'd be happy doing whatever He wants you to do."

Mora was obviously in new territory. Never before had she ever considered that it might be best to "let go and let God." I knew she was going to have to think about this. "That means giving up control," she said.

I concurred, thinking to myself, we never really have anything more than the choice to accept or decline His open invitation. Maybe this conversation was the real reason she called for an appointment after all.

"I don't know if I can do that," she replied. "I'll think about it."

"You know Mora, balance in Feng Shui represents letting go, on all levels," I reminded her.

Then we continued by talking about how, in order to be balanced, you have to be involved in all the areas of life. Not a workaholic, not a narcissist, not a love addict, not a goof off, not simply a Mom or Dad. You need all the pieces. You must let go of what is dragging you off balance. Let go of too much work and take better care of yourself and your family. Let go of desire to be with someone and learn to be with yourself. Let go of the kids and ask for help when you need it. Let go of holding on too tight and watch the butterfly return to your hand. Let go of all the methods of trying to get what you want. Be still and quiet, and let God balance you in your letting go.

But for now, Mora's thinking about it was good enough for me. God often works in mysterious ways.

Like Mora, I too question why things happen the way they do. I'm forever looking for clues on how to do things better as I examine how I feel and how I react in and around my home. I know just how important my surroundings are in feeding my personal energy in desirable ways. Here are a few things I've discovered.

Recently I hadn't been able to reconcile the fact that after some appointments I felt more drained than others. Sometimes all I seemed to want was to hunker down in my own home alone. Other times it wasn't even appointments that bothered me, it was just being around a lot of people.

One weekend I felt expended, as if there was nothing left. I was completely wasted, physically, mentally, and spiritually. I had nothing else left to give to anyone and I needed to rejuvenate, like I help my clients do. I needed to stay home and fill myself back up with energy, that is how we recover and heal.

It was during this planned quiet time that I also realized a few points about the type of living spaces we choose for ourselves, energy-wise. My home is comfortable but has, perhaps, more personal symbols than I usually recommend to clients. This has always made me wonder. Now I understood why.

When we go out into the world we carry a storehouse of personal energy. That energy is physical, mental, and spiritual. When we interact with others, we usually give a little away here and there. So we must have a place, a sanctuary, to return to and rejuvenate. My sanctuary is my home. All the many personal symbols in my home are emboldened with my intent. Specific intent. Strong intent. And when I'm run down and have been with people too much or given away too much energy, I need to return home and be filled with my own intentions again.

But I've discovered something interesting. When my environment becomes too full of personal symbols, it drains me. There is a thin line of balance. Too many symbols can drain you the way not enough symbols can leave you empty.

What's even more interesting is the fact that when I'm running on empty, I eat more and I shop more. It's interesting that negative energy = consuming. It makes me wonder about this consumption crazy culture we've created. When we balance our environment, we become more balanced physically, mentally, and spiritually, which affects our actions and energy out in the world. After applying Feng Shui principles we automatically consume less and what we do buy or eat is a conscious decision.

I have worked very hard at getting a stable home balance on each of the three levels. I notice when my energy is filled up physically, I feel better and I don't eat for no reason. When my mental energy is filled up, I don't shop as much or spend unnecessarily. And when my spiritual energy is filled up, I am more self-confident and feel better about myself. The difference in my being has been miraculous as I learn to read my energy levels and adjust my home to my particular energy needs.

Recognizing how space affects you is a very personal matter. It takes being quiet and feeling. Every culture in the world has some form of Feng Shui, even if it has a different name. But everywhere it is recognized on some level that your personal environment counts. Maybe that's what is so important after all.

Now About You—The Next Step in the Dance

When you raise the quality of your own life you automatically raise the quality of life of those around you.

The saying, "Do unto others as you would have them do unto you," can be broadened to include, "Do unto yourself as you would have them do unto you."

By setting higher standards for yourself you also set higher standards for others in your sphere of influence. These higher standards automatically set more appropriate boundaries for you and begin to teach other people how to treat you even better.

It is only when you reach for this next level that you can open the door to becoming even more of who you were really meant to become.

Ascent

CHAPTER **27**

No Easy Answers Since Everything Counts

*T*HE BODY NEVER LIES," I say in my classes.

It doesn't. That unmistakable tap on the shoulder where you think to yourself, "You know, this doesn't feel quite right," as you walk out of the grocery store with too much change. Or it could be the time your intuition says, "Go down this street," and that's when you find your child has fallen off his bike on the side of the road.

Paying attention to what is going on in your life is a big part of the Feng Shui principles, as is living in the present. By paying attention I don't mean getting all muddled up in the everyday drama of life. That's okay on a limited basis, on the third Thursday of every month under a blue moon. I'm talking about really living. I mean developing yourself to your potential, into the person that you dreamed you'd be years ago, before life took so many strikes at you and you lost some of your pizzazz.

That's who I wanted to be again. Interestingly enough, the more I studied and adopted the principles and applied the knowledge I was learning, the more I felt like I did in 1978. I was 26 years old then, and the world was my oyster. It was through the use of these principles that I began to permanently hold onto the discovery and personal growth work that I did after my divorce. I wanted to be able to lock in all the good things I'd learned, and the only method I could find that really worked for me was living life by following the process Feng Shui promoted. I could set up my physical environment to support me on my not-so-good days as well as my days of enlightenment. This was a critical step. For a long time I had no one to lean on and the Feng Shui work went from being a crutch to being a cane to being just invisibly there.

There are so many circumstances in life where we ignore the signs of what is really happening. It could be as simple as spending too much on credit cards, or over involving ourselves with the kids at the expense of the relationship with our mate, or even ignoring that the last cigarette or drink wasn't really in our best interest.

One night, when I awoke with the following saying flowing out of my pen onto the paper, I cried at its simplicity: "A present not fully lived is a past seen in sadness in the future," I wrote. I didn't want that to be me. So I made a commitment to understand and work this knowledge to the next level and then the next. Each time I thought I'd gotten it all, a whole new dimension opened before me, validating even more that everything is connected, and everything counts to a degree that still amazes me.

You can enhance all your self-growth work by putting Feng Shui to work for you in three ways. The practical, physical wisdom Feng Shui conveys is born of both form and function of the space. One of the very first things you do in Feng Shui is look for physical deficiencies and correct them. This is the practical wisdom of physically accomplishing things and heading in the right direction while staying out of trouble. Not a bad foundation.

On a more psychological or mental level, Feng Shui's emotional wisdom is about your self-talk, thought and intention. Being able to understand yourself and others metaphorically—by understanding what the space around you says to you and about you—is the key component in living well with yourself in the company of others. And your emotional states relate directly to your ability to enjoy the kind of life you would like to experience. It is during the less good states that you usually mess up and say or do things in the heat of anger or disappointment or hurt that erode the foundations of your own integrity and self worth.

Finally spiritual wisdom comes from finding the eternal values that are exemplified by living in grace and forgiveness. You often hear kids say, "When I grow up I want to be . . . " As we all get older, the search for meaning and spiritual wisdom becomes vital to our image of how we fit into the world. For many of us, that search takes on the form of finding a mature sense of purpose knowing the right track, treating others and our self the way we want to be treated, and letting our divine nature come through for the benefit of all.

The hardest part of this transformation is the starting. The letting go of things, of people, of judgment, of hurt. Once I started the process it got easier and easier to clear away the debris, not only in my physical space but in my mind, to allow for new metaphors symbolizing who I wanted to become. Then forgiving myself for all the time I'd spent on the wrong things, with the wrong people, was equaling as taxing but not as daunting as beginning the process. Once I forgave myself it was a lot easier to forgive others, and that was freeing.

When I finally admitted that there was a divine order to things, I began to see how it all connected. I saw how my tapestry was being woven, how that red thread of the ancient Asian concept had encircled me even when I was far off course how it had sewn me back into the fabric and purpose for my life.

It's not so bad being a late bloomer. I know more now and I'm wise enough to flow with the twists and turns my choices and circumstances have brought back to me. I now understand the responsibility that I take for the way my life turns out, nobody brought me to this place but me. That's why I say everything counts.

Everything counts for you also. The space. The condition of the space. Others. Their attitudes. You. Your attachments. Your emotional states. And most importantly your intentions. It is critical to make your space reflect your highest and best vision of yourself, because once you do, you've always got a friend to take your hand, even on a bad day.

As you've read these words, you have gained an appreciation for the basic truths of this wonderful process. You can see how Feng Shui is a process, and once you start to follow it, Feng Shui becomes a lifestyle. It is only one of many processes to attain balance and a life that works better, but it is a good process that is easily understood and followed.

In summary, Feng Shui uses metaphorical symbols as well as energy flow to become an external catalyst in your environment which causes an internal change in you. Every single object in your environment, their placements, colors, textures, all are subconscious symbols of the life you wish to lead. It's your choice. The quality of your life depends on the decisions you make about what surrounds you. You must intentionally make your environment representative of exactly what you want out of life and who you want to become. To choose not to do this, is to leave yourself at someone else's mercy. Someone always chooses. It's your life, and you should be making the choices.

In my own life, I frequently use jewelry to symbolize my personal vision of myself. The three necklaces I often wear are: a cross, a charm depicting all the religious symbols of the unseen God, and a dove. These are reminders of who I am, where I came from, and where I am going in the world. The cross represents my relationship with God, from the time I found him, through losing him, and finding him again. The charm of symbols reminds me that we are all connected as one. And the dove which I wear constantly confirms there is always hope and transformation in the face of great sacrifice.

How powerful this world would be if we all reminded ourselves of what was important instead of what was petty and trivial! Our world is full of the chi energy of the life force and light. Here, everything is connected, alive and changing. It's a place where the symbols are what we make of them, where the smallest change in our outer world can change our inner world on all three levels of existence—body, mind, and spirit. Feng Shui teaches us our world is defined by what we choose as we treat each other with honor and dignity.

I wish you success and peace in re-creating your world. Accomplish the task wisely and with intent. Live and love with intention, blessings, and grace.

A.M.D.G. ("To the Greater Glory of God")

297

Now About You—The Final Steps in the Dance

Summary Exercise 1—The Me I Want To Be

You can define who you would like to become by determining what kind of values you wish to develop, and enhancing the character qualities that support those values.

Make a list of 20–25 different people of your same gender that you admire. Beside each person's name write what it is about that person you admire. It could be a specific quality, characteristic or talent. You can choose anyone you like and you may like them as a complete package, or you may only like this specific quality about them.

The purpose of this exercise is to get you viscerally in your body to experience the quality that supports that value you admire. When you can visualize what that quality looks like in another person, you will know what it would look like in yourself.

Put your list somewhere obvious. After a short time reviewing these characteristics daily, you will begin to embody these qualities through this future vision of yourself. Guaranteed.

Example:
The Me I Want to Be has ...
    The smile of Laura Bush;
    The conviction of Katherine Graham;
    The courage and determination of Jackie Kennedy
       Onassis;
    The resilience of Katie Couric and Jane Pauley;
    The compassion and love of Princess Diana;
    The countenance of Ivanna Trump;
    The business savvy and public pulse of Oprah;
    The voice of Patsy Kline, Ann Murray and Lori Morgan;
    The quest for knowledge and truth as Diane Sawyer;
    The energetic daring of Madonna;

The patriotism and speech delivery of Ann Richards;
The audience connection of Joyce Meyer;
The fearlessness of Hillary Clinton;
The sensuality and sexiness of Sophia Loren;
The tenacity and perseverance of HRH Fergie;
The wisdom of Eleanor Roosevelt;
The understanding of life of Louise Hay;
The leadership of Margaret Thatcher;
The authorship of Marrianne Williamson;
The passion for self realization and acceptance of
    Martha Stewart;
The insight of Shirley MacLaine;
The brilliance of Arianna Huffington;
The love for God and the search for spirit of St. Teresa of
    Avila;
The faith of Mary Magdalene;
The patience of knowing myself as Annie through
    decision, attitude, and surrender to divine will.
I am Annie and this is my vision of her.

Summary Exercise 2—My Map of Life

Experience your goals, desires and dreams viscerally in order to create the personal energy necessary to draw them into your life.

Using the bagua map as a guide, draw the nine life areas on a 2' x 3' black poster board.

Cut out magazine pictures and words that represent what you want to achieve in those same areas of your life. Paste them with glue in the appropriate areas.

Add any words that inspire or clarify your intentions.

Use small pictures and overlap them image over image. This allows many more of your dreams and desires to surface. Let your imagination go free.

Keep cutting out pictures until you have what feels like a satisfactory amount covering all the black area of the poster board.

Know that your life will energetically move toward the desires you have dreamed.

I have done this exercise for the past five years and it is amazing how many things have been accomplished or attained in my life that were originally pictured on my five Maps of Life!

Example
Pictures you might consider.

Wealth and Prosperity
a family, beach vacation, Rolex watch, house/car/plane, promotion, more money, whatever increases your quality of life.

Fame and Reputation
employee of the month, an award, finish your book, lose 5 lbs., buy new dress, whatever gives you more self esteem.

Love and Relationship
picture of two at dinner, walking, on a beach, kissing, whatever picture evokes the feeling of your ideal relationship.

Health and Family
pets, people having fun, spa day, family gatherings, what to do to get motivated, nutritious food, exercise program whatever nurtures you.

Creativity and Children
bowling league, artist painting, horseback riding, crafts, sports, doing whatever makes you feel younger.

Knowledge and Self Cultivation
people reading books, praying, classes, yoga, listening to music, doing Feng Shui, whatever gives you serenity.

Career

tennis, club work, hobbies, the best part of work at your job, singing, the work you'd like to do, doing whatever turns you on.

Helpful People and Travel

places to visit on short local trips, vacation spots, Disneyland, Florida, Rio, London, Bermuda, Jamaica, people you'd like to meet.

Donkey

Critical Steps In The Dance

This is a summary of all the Now About You—Steps in the Dance by Chapter.

Introduction. The Healing Place

1. Let your body begin to acknowledge how it feels in different environments.
2. Assure the energy flows through your space freely.
3. Allowing your passion to show through to others will change your personal energy and you will begin to reveal the real you.
4. Take care of yourself first, before trying to help someone else.

5. Merging households means combining energies as well as things.
6. Appreciate that, right now, everything is the way it should be and things will work out all right.
7. Comprehend the results you achieve with Feng Shui are an expression of your intent.
8. Wake up and notice the unobvious energy that you are allowing to be absorbed into your body from your surroundings.
9. Determine your quality of living in all the major areas of your life.
10. Understand all the areas of life are interconnected in cause and effect, and too much of one thing often means too little of another, causing imbalance.
11. Make room for the new by clearing out the old.
12. Identify what must leave your life in order for you to move on.
13. Recognize and embody the emotional state associated with an area to achieve what is missing in that area of your life.
14. Imagine how you will change yourself and your environment to match the kind of home and work life of a transformed future you.
15. Understand that letting go of things, people, behaviors, ideas, attitudes and judgments makes room for you to move to the next level of life where you can begin to attract what you desire.
16. You do not have to throw anything away, or give it away or sell it, but you must have a defendable reason to keep it, a place for it, and understand the ramifications of holding on to it.
17. Making the space reflect the energy you want to feel is the first step in a remodeling or decorating project.

18. The things, people, attitudes, beliefs, or ideas you consciously choose to allow into your environment influence who you are now and who you will become.

19. Understand that buying a home is less about the house than it is how you want to live, and who you want to become.

20. Remember that you do not have to reinvent the wheel, because what has worked for someone else may very well work for you.

21. Seeing yourself where you are, simply as a starting point in the change process, removes the stigma of failing.

22. Creating your ideal environment is a crutch to give you physical, psychological and spiritual support on the days you are less than your peak self.

23. Structurally breaking old patterns in your environment will intentionally change your circumstances and situations to more desirable positive experiences.

24. Controlling your energy is a fluid process that is created by intentionally modifying your perceptions of the world.

25. Taking back control of your environment means that it won't hold you back, and creating the next level is the proactive state that pulls you into the future.

26. When you raise the quality of your own life you automatically raise the quality of life of those around you.

27. You can define who you would like to become by determining what kind of values you wish to develop, and enhancing the character qualities that support those values. And, as you experience your goals, desires and dreams viscerally you will create the personal energy necessary to draw them into your life.

sound

Everyday Prayers

Often I find many similarities between my own difficulties and those of my clients, and many have asked me for guidance in how to pray. I offer my prayers to you in the spirit of grace. They are powerful words when prayed aloud as you become comfortable in your relationship with God. May they bless you and comfort you in times of thanks, concern and trial.

I Am Not Alone

Lord, take my hand.
Help me walk with you.
If I should trip, steady me.
If I should stumble, catch me.
If I should fall, pick me up and

Carry me until I can again
Walk on my own at your side,
Holding your hand.

I Surrender Unto You

Dear Lord,
I will go where you want me to go.
I will do whatever you want me to do.
I will be with whoever you want me to be with.
Surround me with those you'd have in my life,
And take from me anyone not in your plan for me.
Ask any I have offended or hurt to forgive me,
And restore me in their eyes.
All I desire is clarity,
So I do not misunderstand your will.

Use Me As You Will

Lord, clothe me in a robe of white light,
Not only for the protection of myself, but that
All of those who hear me, see me,
        touch me, feel me, or are
Influenced by me in any way,
Shall be drawn to you and healed, as the
Light is composed of your wisdom, power, and love.

The Prayer of Jabez

Oh Lord, that you would bless me indeed, and
Enlarge my territory,
That your hand would be with me, and
That you would keep me from evil,
That I may not cause pain.
        (1 Chronicles 4:10)

Everyday Prayer

Thank you for all you have given me.

Guide me in how best to use these gifts for your purpose.

Direct me where to go and what to do so I do not misunderstand.

Please take my business, financial, and relationship worries from me so I can prosper to do your work.

Protect me from my own wrong thoughts and bring me to a new place of walking with you in your light.

Help me to let you help me.

Heal me of any hidden and formerly forgotten memories that do not serve you or me.

Let your joy show through me if ever I have a hard time smiling.

Protect me from all manner of evil and provide for me like your favored child.

Thank you for only opening doors for me to the places and people you'd have me be with, in the form of invitation.

Please close the doors that no longer serve your purposes for me.

I am yours to command.

Thank you for the knowledge and wisdom, compassion and love to walk with you in grace and truth.

Bless those close to me and open doors for them also.

Close off that which is not their path.

Thank you Lord for the invitation to live with you in your light.

Let my light shine so brightly that others are drawn to you through me.

And Lord guide me, protect me, and provide for me.

As it is in your name I pray.

Quick Blessings

God guide me.
God protect me.
God provide for me, and help me to let you help me.

Armor of God

Today, I put on the armor of God.
    the helmet of salvation,
    the breastplate of righteousness,
    the belt of truth,
    the shield of faith,
    and the sword of the spirit.
I claim dominion over any evil or negative force
    I may encounter today
    through the strength of the Lord,
    and deposit it at the foot of the cross.
In the name of Jesus the Christ.

Personal Intercession

Get behind me Satan.
Get behind me Satan.
Get behind me Satan.
I claim back my body and mind
    from any strongholds of pain and hurt.
Today I wash my body, mind and spirit
    in the blood of Jesus the Christ.
I lay any negativity or infirmaries
    at the foot of the cross
    or him to deal with as he will.
Be gone from me.
You can not have any part of me.
I am my Lord's own.
Amen

The Lord's Prayer

"Our Father in heaven,
   hallowed be your name,
   your kingdom come,
   your will be done
   on earth as it is in heaven.
Give us today our daily bread.
Forgive us our debts,
   as we also have forgiven our debtors.
And lead us not into temptation,
   but deliver us from evil."
For yours is the kingdom and the power
   and the glory forever. Amen.
   (Matthew 6:9–13)

Farewell

Acknowledgements

Thanks must go to those past and present students, clients, close friends and associates who daily encouraged me, suffering through the challenges only the birthing of a book can bring: Susie Gardner (desktop publishing), Shawn Sharkey (technology and counsel), Boyd Stazewski (video production), Linda Kovac (booking agent), Barbara Seymour (administrative), Brenda English and Michael Mort (editing), Karen Mason (assistant), Tony Ostian (direct response web copywriter) and Barry Kerrigan's team at Desktop Miracles (book design).

Thanks also to my family, especially my sister, Onda Gooding, for the grace and uplifting only prayers can bring.

I am forever grateful to all of you for your support, and loving kindnesses.

Ubiquity

Suggested Resources

The discernment that comes with maturity is often acquired from unlikely sources, not always formal in identity. It is this mature insight that grows into wisdom only because of the depth of perception and the ability to see from many viewpoints.

I am an eclectic culmination of information from a myriad of sources. Wisdom I recount in this book I know, viscerally, intuitively, and empirically. It has become part of my being from practical experience and insight.

Aside from the Holy books and the great philosophers, there are many scholars that unknowingly contributed to my development through the years in various forms of delivery. You may find them of value in your journey now.

The following are the bodies of work, specific authors' books, and some of the people whose brief words profoundly influenced and touched me. There is some sequence in this 30-year culmination of knowledge, yet it is more than a chronological search for truth. It is the foundation for how I became who I am.

After reading thousands of books and listening to hundreds of tapes and CD's if I have neglected to mention someone it is purely unintentional.

Bodies of Work

The Association of Research and Enlightenment. As a young woman I was intrigued by the sleeping prophet that gave healing instructions while in trance because it was a confirmation regarding one man's supernatural Christian life. Over the years the Edgar Cayce Foundation's research library and bookstore provided a wealth of resources that gave me the ability to see from a diversity of perspectives. www.edgarcayce.org.

Anthony Robbins' body of work resonated with my soul as I attended the following nine seminars. *Mastery University's Date with Destiny, Wealth and Life Mastery, Leadership and Trainer Academy, Competitive Edge, Results 2000,* and two *Unleash the Power Within* events. His CD program *Get The Edge* is one his best works yet. I identify with his message and style of delivery. His three newest DVD products with Cloe Madanes on *Reclaiming Your True Identity: The Power of Vulnerability* ISBN 1-932578-03-X, *Conquering Overwhelming Loss: Rediscovering a Compelling Future* ISBN 1-932578-10-2, and *Negotiating Conflict: Leadership in Times of Crisis (Live 9/11/01)* ISBN 1-932578-01-3 show his true gifts to empower personal transformation. As I remember that name from years ago a heartfelt expression of thanks is extended. www.anthonyrobbins.com.

Brian Tracy's work was a foundational aspect in my life and real estate career for nearly 20 years. I have owned nearly every tape or CD he produced and within the last couple of years greatly benefited from his year long coaching program offered through Nightingale Conant with coach Lynn Murray. His audio programs *The Psychology of Self Confidence and Advanced Learning Techniques, Million Dollar Habits,* and *The Luck Factor* are a few of my favorites. www.briantracy.com.

Wayne Dyer has been one of my favorite authors and producer of audio programs since the beginning of my career. His audios *There is a Spiritual Solution for Every Problem, You'll See it When You Believe It,* and *It's Never Crowded Along the Extra Mile* are invaluable. I find him very down to earth and easy to listen to while still gentle on the heart lessons. His recent video program *The Power of Intention* on www.pbs.org is an excellent work and also in print (ISBN 1-4019-0215-4). www.waynedyer.com.

Deepak Chopra was a favorite of my late mother's long before he achieved notoriety. I have read all his books. One of my favorites is *The Spontaneous Fulfillment of Desire* (ISBN 0-609-60042-7) and two of my favorite CD's are *SynchroDestiny* and *The Higher Self.* He exalts the healing capacity of the mind-body concept in a scientifically spiritual way. His books and videos are timeless and even in his novels he weaves the threads of ancient wisdom. www.Chopra.com.

Jay Abraham taught me that marketing was more like spiritual selling because it was truly relational in nature. The knowledge I gained at his marketing seminar and through his products are to this day beneficial to me. My favorite audio *Your Secret Wealth* and his book *Get Everything You Can—Out of All You've Got* (ISBN 0-312-28454-3) are basic business staples regardless of industry. www.abraham.com.

Louise Hay's teachings on health have affected me for over 20 years. Her book *Heal Your Body* (ISBN 0-937611-35-2) was a life affirming companion for many reasons and even though I have numerous copies, it is the original dog eared copy I cherish most. The original information is in a special edition *You Can Heal Your Life* (ISBN 1-5617-0628-0). Her *Wisdom Cards* and *Power Thought Cards* have been of great value to me in my own life and in my workshops. www.hayhouse.com, www.louisehay.com.

EST Training came into my life in 1979. I remember the $300 tuition I didn't have when I signed up, came to me just as the registrar said it would. I found the original seminar event, as it was structured, sufficient to give me what I needed at the time. Today the associated organization is called Landmark. When asked by one of my recent students how I liked the original EST training I said those 2 weekends and the 3 additional nights long ago changed my life and the way I thought forever. I got it. www.rickross.com/reference/est.

Feng Shui Training

Terah Kathryn Collins' audio program *The Western Guide to Feng Shui* impacted me so greatly, it got me to sign up for her *Western School of Feng Shui (WSFS)* in San Diego, CA in the middle of the night with non-refundable airline tickets not knowing if the class was full! What she was teaching I recognized in myself as an instinctive ability that I had been using in the real estate field for my entire career. It felt right and it was. Her book of the same title (ISBN 1-56170-324-9) is the cornerstone of westernized Feng Shui, along with its many other literary siblings under her pen. www.wsfs.com.

Karen Kingston profoundly affected me when I attended one of her workshops. I could feel her integrity and reverence to these ancient teaching principles. It could have been her teaching style or the indigenous links to Bali or the UK, but I was highly impressed with her realistic approach and reverent appreciation for the sacred in daily life. Her books *Clearing Your Clutter with Feng Shui* (ISBN 0-769-0359-5) and *Creating Sacred Space with Feng Shui—Learn the Art of Space Clearing and Bring New Energy into Your Life* (ISBN 0-553-06916-0) will affect you the same. www.karenkingston.com.

Daniel Santos, DOM (Doctor of Oriental Medicine) is the Feng Shui master mentioned in this book. He agreed to tutor me privately for a week in Santa Fe, NM to expand on and clarify the teachings in his book *Feng Shui for the Body*. The first thing he taught me was how to walk and be connected to the earth. Then I watched his skill as an acupuncturist make the swelling in my knee (post 2 ACL surgeries) reduce by 50%. He is truly a shamanic healer of mind, body and spirit. *Feng Shui for the Body* (SBN 0-8356-0762-3), 1998; *Luminous Essence* (ISBN 0-8356-0755-0), 1997.

Serge Polakoff and I met at the first *International Feng Shui Conference*. We discussed the new work in psychological Feng Shui that he was presenting in Europe and Asia. I asked for private study and he agreed, going out of his way to share his knowledge with me, and I found yet another aspect of Feng Shui to integrate into my understanding. www.sergepolakoff.com.

Denise Linn was recently one of the guest instructors at the advanced trainings for *WSFS* in San Diego. She has numerous books and videos, but my favorites are *Space Clearing* (ISBN 0-8092-9739-6) and *Feng Shui for the Soul* (ISBN 1-56170-731-7). She is one of the most gifted, guided meditation voices in the field. Denise's supernatural experience of death is testimony to her understanding of the spiritual realm and its relationship to our worldly life. www.deniselinn.com.

Sean Xenja's two video programs on Feng Shui techniques were very helpful to me in learning how to teach Feng Shui principles. More importantly he was the first to give me assistance in perfecting the release of negative energies encountered in my healing practice out of my body. I appreciate the help and knowledge he gave with dignity and concern for a fellow consultant. www.hayhouse.com.

There are very many notable authors writing and recording audios about Feng Shui. Special thanks should also go to the following Feng Shui authors **Angie Ma Wong, Nancy San Peidro, Nancilee Wydra, Daniel David Kennedy, Anthony Lawlor, Sharon Stasney, Evanna Maggiorie, Gill Hale, Sarah Rossbach, Lillian Too, and Master Lin Yung** for their contributions to the field.

Specific Authors' Books/CD's

Ordering Sources:
 www.nightengaleconant.com, www.soundstrue.com,
 and www.hayhouse.com

Richard Bach, of the mid 70's *Jonathan Livingston Seagull* (ISBN 0-380-01286-3) and *The Bridge Across Forever* (ISBN 0-688-03917-0) fame, went on to write many more books with a gentle way of looking at life from yet another perspective which still grace my shelves. www.richardbach.com.

Isabel Hickey, *It's All Right,* Library of Congress #A787210, is out of print, but might be found in this day of the internet. This book was my first insight into divine rightness and psychic-spiritual protection. I found the parable "Allegory-Why" in the back of the book profound. www.alibris.com (source for out of print books).

Shakti Gawain's book *Creative Visualization* from the late 70's (ISBN 0-553-24147-8) was one of the first expressions I encountered using positive mental energy to transform lives. Fifteen years later I was fortunate to hear her speak and was still impressed with her knowledge and insight. www.shaktigawain.com.

Stuart Wilde's work was introduced to me in the mid 80's through his many books such as *Weight Loss for the Mind and Miracles* (ISBN 1-56170-163-7). His audio work, *Infinite Self—33 Steps to Reclaiming Your Inner Power* is his best yet, enlightening one step by step to self discovery. www.stuartwilde.com.

Shirley MacLaine's book *Out On A Limb* (ISBN 0-553-05035-4), 1983, was the book that confirmed in me a committed direction of self discovery and growth, finally knowing that there were others who had experienced the same search for self I was attempting at the time. www.shirleymaclaine.com

Bill Moyers work on Public Television with **Joseph Campbell** and *The Power of Myth,* 1988 (ISBN 0-385-24774-5), in book, video or audio format, is a foundational must for serious students of philosophy or religion. Also investigate his work at PBS on *Healing and the Mind* (ISBN 0-385-46870-9) interviews physicians, scientists, therapists and patients who examine the mind-body relationship from many viewpoints. www.pbs.org.

Gregg Braden's work in video form, *Walking Between the World's,* I found to be an enlightening teaching but his most recent books

The Isaiah Effect (ISBN 0-609-80796-X) and *The God Code* (ISBN 1-4019-0299-5) are even a measure above in relating to prayer, quantum science and prophecy. His new audios *Speaking the Lost Language of God* and *Unlocking the Secret of the Lost Mode of Prayer: Discover an Ancient Spiritual Technology for Generating Compassion and Peace in the World* are well worth the listening. www.greggbraden.com.

Marianne Williamson's *A Return to Love–Reflections on the Principles of a Course in Miracles* endeared her to many. I was impressed with her reflections having been exposed to *A Course in Miracles* in the late 70's. I knew she was a gifted teacher when I heard her minister at the Renaissance Church in Grand Rapids, MI. www.mariannewilliamson.com.

Oriah Mountain Dreamer's *The Invitation* (ISBN 0-06-251584-5) and *The Dance* (ISBN 0-06-251693-0) will both tug at your heart to remember who you really are and who you'd like to become. This author speaks gentle truth that resonates with true grace. www.oriahmountaindreamer.com.

Don Miguel Ruiz's Toltec wisdom book, *The Four Agreements* (ISBN 0-965-046363), made me think. Every other page of my copy is dog-eared and its wise simplicity still fascinates me. These four agreements should be taught in schools in just this manner rather than waiting for the learning to come from life experience. www.donmiguelruiz.com.

Neal Donald Walsch's series of books *Conversations with God-An Uncommon Dialogue* (ISBN 0-399-14278-9), that started in the mid 90's, gave many people a new way of looking at their spiritual values and meaning in life. One of the very best points brought forward was that "all we need do is ask." www.infinitehealth.com.

Norman Vincent Peale's The *Power of Positive Thinking* from the Peale Center for Christian Living, and the monthly *Positive Thinking* booklet from *Guideposts* influence me to this day. This book, as old as I am, still resonates in the hearts of people worldwide and you will come to understand that our similarities are much more powerful than our differences. www.guideposts.org.

Caroline Myss's work in the energy field has interested me and given me much insight into the body-mind connection. Her video on *The Energetics of Healing*, her work with the chakra system and latest two audio tapes *Personal Healing and Essential Guide for Healers* are excellent resources for anyone and necessary for those in the healing fields. www.myss.com.

Caroline Casey is a brilliant woman whom I consider a friend. Long before we became seat mates in a chance meeting on an airplane in 1999, I had purchased the book *Cosmic Connections* from a *Time-Life* series in which she was a featured resource. Her book and audio program Inner and *Outer Space—The Astrological Language of the Psychie* (ISBN 0-609-60058-3) is fascinating and a totally different perspective on the subject of astrology. www.spiritualintrigue.com

David Deida is a gifted teacher and author. Two of my favorites are *The Way of the Superior Man—A Man's Guide to Mastering the Challenges of Women, Work, and Sex* (ISNB 1-889762-10-5) and It's a *Guy Thing—An Owner's Manual for Women* (ISBN 1-55874-464-9). In 1999 I attended one of his workshops and found his viewpoints worthy of note, very practical and ponderable. www.deida.com.

Dr. Wu Jing-Nuan. The late Dr. Wu was one of Washington, DC's most sought after acupuncturists. I found that his treatments helped me immensely, but it was his soul counsel that will never be forgotten. Once, upon asking him his opinion, he looked at me with a tad bit of wonder, and said I already knew the answer, because it was a principle that had been the subject of a piece of work I'd written. He built confidence in people by gently reflecting back to them their greatness, and he is missed. This book, which he translated from ancient Chinese, is a readable yet technical book on acupuncture. *Ling Shu* or *The Spiritual Pivot—Asian Spirituality and Taoist Studies* (ISBN 0-8248-1557-2), 1993.

Jim Rohn is one of America's foremost Business Philosophers. The live audio program of his *Weekend Seminar on Life Skills for the 21st Century* were the tapes I listened to while I was on the first marathon de-cluttering of my home Thanksgiving weekend in 1999. Hour after hour, letting go of things, and ultimately old unhealthy attachments, became like mental blows to my mind and direct hits to my body. His confident teaching style replaced those blows with renewed confidence and hope. www.jimrohn.com.

Iyanla Vanzant and I meet every morning during my devotional time when I use her book *Until Today—Daily Devotions for Spiritual Growth and Peace of Mind* (ISBN 0-684-84137-1) as one of the components to my daily prayers. I have two copies, the first of which has its spine broken from over use and pertinent words and phrases underlined on each page. Her other books are equally as moving. www.innervisionsworldwide.com.

Mark Victor Hansen from *Chicken Soup for the Soul* fame gave me the tools and confidence to take on the self publishing of this book. Many times during the process I referred to the materials he and others presented in his seminar on *Mega-Publishing*. Ironically, many years ago I purchased his great audio program entitled *The Aladdin Factor* but I did not make the connection that it was his until recently. www.markvictorhansen.com.

Ken Wilber is unique and one of the most influential and widely read American philosophers of our time. See *A Brief History of Everything* (ISBN 1-57062-855-6) and *Eye to Eye* (ISBN 1-57062-249-3) for his insights. I find his work fascinating in content, challenging in concept, and ripe for engaging conversation. As a primarily audio learner I love his latest 10 CD program *Kosmic Consciousness* which explores the evolution of self. www.soundstrue.com, www.integralinstitute.org.

Andrew Cohen's magazine *What is Enlightenment? Redefining Spirituality for an Evolving World* is one of my favorites and gets read cover to cover. Looking at the world through new eyes, these perspectives on contemporary subjects give much food for thought. www.WhatIsEnlightenment.org, www.andrewcohen.org.

Important Books to Read or CD's to Hear

Daniel Goleman, Ph.D., gives the reasons why *Emotional Intelligence* (ISBN 0-553-09503-X), 1995, can matter more than IQ, and the importance in realizing the power of emotional intelligence in *Primal Leadership* (ISBN 1-57851-486-X). www.eiconsortium.org.

Martin E.P. Seligman, Ph.D., uses the new positive psychology to realize your potential for lasting fulfillment, in *Authentic Happiness* (ISBN 0-743-2297-0), and has started a coaching program based on the same concept. www.authentichappiness.org.

Rupert Sheldrake, Ph.D., has done the clinical and scientific studies proving his theories that I believe back up how following the principles of Feng Shui works without calling it Feng Shui in his *The Sense of Being Stared At and Other Aspects of the Extended Mind* (ISBN 0-609-60807-X). www.sheldrake.org.

David Hawkins, MD., Ph.D., *Power vs. Force—The Hidden Determinants of Human Behavior* (ISBN 1-56170-933-6). This is a must read for all teachers, speakers, and those of influence. I have long maintained "the body doesn't lie" in it's intuitive responses and that if we raise the energy frequency of a space to match the highest vision of the individual themselves having already attained the desired outcome, that outcome comes. Dr. Hawkins takes this further and documents how it all happens. Serious students might also read his book *I—Reality and Subjectivity* (ISBN 0-9715007-0-3) and listen to his audio *The Highest Level of Enlightenment—The Data Base of Consciousness for Total Self Realization.* www.nightengaleconant.com, www.veritaspub.com.

Laurence D. Martel, Ph.D., the audio CD program *Real Intelligence—The Intelligence System for Becoming Smarter and More Effective* is another must for all teachers and speakers. It shows how we learn and how to broaden our abilities. I believe it is also backdrop research that enhances the workings of applying Feng Shui principles. www.nightengaleconant.com.

Gary De Rodriguez's audio program *Charismatic Presentation Skills* is another program for all speakers and presenters. I first met Gary at the *Western School for Feng Shui Advanced Training*. His program on neuro-linguistic training is by far the best of its kind and teaches graduate level techniques so speakers can fulfill their mission of delivering the message with clarity and intent. www.lifedesigninternational.com.

David Allen's audio program on *Getting Things Done Fast—The Ultimate Stress Free Productivity System* is one of the best on managing your personal and professional life in terms of things to do and time to do them. www.gyronix.com.

Paul Ray, Ph.D. and Sherry Ruth Anderson, Ph.D. wrote the *Cultural Creatives—How 50 Million People are Changing the World* (ISBN 0-609-604-67-8). This is a fascinating book about our culture, who we are, what we like, what we will do in given situations, all based on our values. www.culturalcreatives.org.

The Art of War, forward by James Clavell (ISBN 0-340-27604-5). Sun Tzu wrote his treatise on war in the 5th century BC. James Clavell has taken a 1910 translation of this philosophy of successful leadership and clarified it for the contemporary reader.

Additional Scientific Material Worth of Interest

Albert Einstein, *Out of My Later Years* (ISBN 0-517-09380-4), *The World As I See It* (ISBN 0-8065-0711-X), and *Ideas and Opinions* (ISBN 0-517-00393-7) are collections of this brilliant man's writings and words taken from his teachings and speeches.

Stephen Hawking, *The Universe in A Nutshell* (ISBN 0-553-80202-X) explains the intricacies of physics in comprehensible analogies from every day life.

Yatri, *Unknown Man: The Mysterious Birth of A New Species* (ISBN 0-671-66070-5). A beautifully written overview of the species of man, compiled just as a pseudo-scientist and pseudo-mystic would want.

Brian Greene, *The Elegant Universe* (ISBN 0-965-088806) is an understandable book of cutting edge physics dealing with superstring, hidden dimensions, and the quest for the ultimate theory.

Fritjof Capra, *The Tao of Physics* (ISBN 0-553-26379-X) is an stimulating exploration of the parallels between modern physics and eastern mysticism.

Additional Spiritual Material Worthy of Individual Study

Joel Beversluis, ed., *Sourcebook of the World's Religions* (ISBN 1-57731-121-3) is an interfaith guide to religion and spirituality.

C. S. Lewis's *Six By Lewis* (a series, ISBN 0-2-02-086770-0), my favorite being *The Screwtape Letters*. This conversation between demons and the sanctity of a soul is memorable. The series also includes *The Abolition of Man, The Great Divorce, Mere Christianity, Miracles*, and *The Problem of Pain*.

M. Scott Peck, MD, *The Road Less Traveled—A New Psychology of Love Traditional Values and Spiritual Growth* (ISBN 0-684-84724-8), *Further Along The Road Less Traveled-The Unending Journey toward Spiritual Growth* (ISBN 0-684-84723-X), and *People of the Lie—The Hope for Healing Human Evil* (ISBN 0-684-84859-7). An Anthology on mental healthiness. www.mscottpeck.com.

L. Ron Hubbard, *Dianetics—The Modern Science of Human Health* (ISBN 0-88404-632-X). A study on the reactive mind and how it affects your life. www.dianetics.org, www.scientology.com.

Rabbi Chaim Solomon's basic video teachings from *Kabbalist Rav Berg—The Wisdom of the Kaballah*. My summary: the premise is choice, both individual and collective, to eliminate chaos in order to experience God, who allows us to learn to love ourselves and others at the level of no conditions or unconditional love. I prefer to say intent of integrity vs. the bread of shame, and that the evil of Satan comes from the outside. My interpretation is that the bread of shame has been removed by the light of the cross for all, not only Christians. www.kabbalah.com.

Ruqaiyyah Maqsood, *ISLAM*, of the *Teach Yourself Series* (ISBN 0-8442-3746-9), and **Suzanne Haneef**, *What Everyone Should Know About Islam and Muslims* (ISBN 0-935782-00-1), are basic books of understanding, and *Guests of the Sheik* by **Elizabeth Warnock Fernea** (ISBN 0-385-01485-6) is a book about Muslim women by a western woman from her point of view from the inside.

Science of Mind's United Church of Religious Science. Change your thinking, change your life, a philosophy, a faith, and a spiritual way of life. www.religiousscience.org, www.scienceofmind.com.

Shambhala: The Sacred Path of the Warrior (ISBN 0-553-26172-X) and *Great Eastern Sun: The Wisdom of Shambhala* (ISBN 1-57062-293-0) are books that evoke the message that we are each genuine and powerful individuals who can help the world. www.Shambhala.com.

Deng Ming-Dao, *TAO: Daily Meditations* (ISBN 0-06-250223-9) is a book applying directly to one's contemporary life the simple yet accessible ideas derived of ancient principles on how to live. www.TAO.org.

Joy Lamb, *The Sword of the Spirit-The Word of God* (Library of Congress #TX3-619-279), 1993, is an invaluable Handbook for Scriptural Intercession and defense in psychic and spiritual warfare. www.aboundingjoy.com, www.christianhealingmin.org.

Magazines of Interest

Besides my never ending subscription to *Oprah*, I have a number of magazines that keep me abreast of new things and nuances in the world: *What's Enlightenment, Science and Spirit, Spirituality and Health, Scientific American, Psychology Networker, Psychology Today, Selling Power, AdvantEdge, Fast Company, Science of Mind*, and *Shift* from the Institute of Noetic Sciences founded by astronaut Edgar Mitchell. This group ranges from science and religion to business and self help, but in my mind the lines begin to cross over and blur on many of the topics mentioned in these resources.

**People who have influenced me but
not otherwise mentioned.**

Woodbridge Virginia's Christ Chapel Assembly of God
Church for encapsulating my vision of what church should
be like; Old Bridge United Methodist Church for its support and counsel; the Pahlavani family for "You are welcome
here;" Gen. (Ret.) Norman Schwarzkopf's "Do the right
thing;" Donald Trump's "It's the priceless things you cannot
buy;" Bill Gates's "You have to ask and risk to win big;" Zig
Ziglar's "Profess your faith;" Nido Qubein's "It never hurts
to say thanks;" and Becky Robbins' "Share how you did it."

In Closing

People say you refine who you become through education.
By growing through the mediums of reading, video/audio
learning programs, the people you meet, the places you go,
and your environment, you can transcend any challenge.

It is essential in this day and age to get this education
in order to be able to step first as transformed individuals, and then as a culture transformed into the next level of
evolution.

I hope you find *satori* here.

Unbound

About the Author

Annie Pane is nationally recognized as one of the country's leading Feng Shui experts and advisors. She began her company East Coast Feng Shui in 1998 having previously owned and operated a Real Estate and Property Management company for nearly 20 years.

As an entrepreneur all her life, Annie combines her broad background of business, real estate knowledge, and Feng Shui principles in a unique and memorable way that benefits her clients and audiences.

Her consultations are transformational in nature whether in a personal or professional setting. She specializes in ergonomically optimizing small business and departmental performance by altering physical space.

Annie speaks on Feng Shui at major events around the country including the International Builder's Show for the National Association of Home Builders. She is an advisor to professionals in the real estate industry including real estate agents, developers, builders and architects. She has taught Feng Shui principles for continuing education credits to real estate licensees.

She has worked with clients and executives from the World Bank, Foreign Service, National Institute of Health, Department of Labor, USA Today, and the US Chamber of Commerce. Her work range includes individual consultations, new home floor plan analysis & lot review, more profitable retail sales floor alignment, and personal & organizational layout efficiency.

Annie empowers businesses and individuals with ergonomic makeovers through de-cluttering. She helps her clients create and sustain the physical space that substitutes productive patterns in place of bad habits and emphasizes quality of life issues by addressing how to attain more balance between home and work.

She has studied with notable Feng Shui authors. She is a graduate of The Mastery University and The Leadership & Trainer Academy from Robbins Research International, as well as numerous other trainings related to Feng Shui, self-development, communication, and sales management.

Annie has been featured in the *Washingtonian* and *Washington Woman* Magazines, the *Washington Times* newspaper, Fox TV News' *At Home,* Voice of America's *Cultural Odyssey* broadcast in Taiwan, China on *Feng Shui in America,* and *The Diane Rehm Show* on National Public Radio.

Breakthrough

Contact Information

Annie Pane encourages you to continue your journey towards a more fulfilling and balanced life. If you are interested in how her Feng Shui services can make a real difference for you, please contact her either by phone or e-mail.

On Annie's website, you will find the most up-to-date information about personal consultations, classes, workshops, speaking engagements, and the East Coast Feng Shui products and classes currently available. There's a place to sign up for the mailing list, receive newsletters and workshop announcements. To find out when Annie will be in your area or to make arrangements for a consultation or speaking engagement please fill out the contact form on the website.

Annie Pane
Speaker, Consultant, Teacher
East Coast Feng Shui
1-888-638-9770
Website address: www.EastCoastFengShui.com or
www.DanceofBalance.com

Order Form

ONLINE ORDERS: www.DanceofBalance.com

FAX ORDERS: 703–897–8998

TELEPHONE ORDERS: Call toll-free 888-638-9770
(have your credit card ready.)

E-MAIL ORDERS: orders@DanceofBalance.com

POSTAL ORDERS: 4110 Churchman Way
Woodbridge, VA 22192

Products

TITLE	PRODUCT	PRICE	QUANTITY	SUBTOTAL
The Dance of Balance	softcover	$18	_____	_____
	hardcover	$27	_____	_____
		Sales Tax*		_____
		Shipping & Handling**		_____
		TOTAL		_____

*Sales Tax: Please add 5% tax for products shipped to Virginia addresses.
(Please add $0.90 for each softcover, and $1.35 for each hardcover)

**Shipping and Handling: (US) Add $9 for first product and $3 for each additional product.
(International) $18 for first product and $3 for each additional product.

Autographing ❑ I would like my copy autographed

Shipping

Name: _____

Address: _____

City, State Zip: _____

Telephone: _____

E-mail address: _____

Payment

❑ Check enclosed   ❑ VISA   ❑ MasterCard

Card Number _____

Exp. Date _____

Security Code _____
(3 or 4 digit number on reverse)

Signature _____

Name on card _____

Billing Address _____

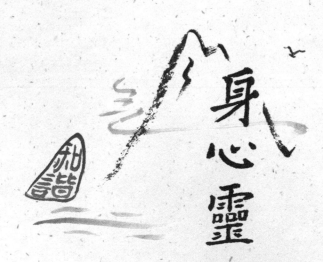